AFTER LIFE IMPRISONMENT

NEW PERSPECTIVES IN CRIME, DEVIANCE, AND LAW SERIES

Edited by John Hagan

After Life Imprisonment

Reentry in the Era of Mass Incarceration

Marieke Liem

Foreword by Robert J. Sampson

NEW YORK UNIVERSITY PRESS

New York

NEW YORK UNIVERSITY PRESS
New York
www.nyupress.org

References to Internet websites (URLs) were accurate at the time of writing. Neither the author nor New York University Press is responsible for URLs that may have expired or changed since the manuscript was prepared.

Library of Congress Cataloging-in-Publication Data
Names: Liem, Marieke, author. | Sampson, Robert J., 1956– writer of foreword.
Title: After life imprisonment : reentry in the era of mass incarceration / Marieke Liem ; foreword by Robert J. Sampson.
Other titles: New perspectives in crime, deviance, and law series.
Description: New York : New York University Press, [2016] | Series: New perspectives in crime, deviance, and law series | "Study of over sixty homicide offenders who served long sentences before being released"—Foreword. | Includes bibliographical references and index. | Also available as an e-book.
Identifiers: LCCN 2016014071| ISBN 978-1-4798-0692-8 (hbk ; alk. paper) | ISBN 1-4798-0692-7 (hbk ; alk. paper) | ISBN 978-1-4798-8282-3 (pbk ; alk. paper) | ISBN 1-4798-8282-8 (pbk ; alk. paper)
Subjects: LCSH: Prisoners—Deinstitutionalization—United States. | Murderers—United States. | Life imprisonment—Social aspects—United States. | Ex-convicts—United States—Social conditions. | Ex-convicts—United States—Economic conditions. | Recidivism—United States.
Classification: LCC HV9304 .L54 2016 | DDC 365/.6470973—dc23
LC record available at https://lccn.loc.gov/2016014071

New York University Press books are printed on acid-free paper, and their binding materials are chosen for strength and durability. We strive to use environmentally responsible suppliers and materials to the greatest extent possible in publishing our books.

Manufactured in the United States of America

10 9 8 7 6 5 4 3 2 1

Also available as an ebook

CONTENTS

FOREWORD

ROBERT J. SAMPSON

Life-course criminology has witnessed dramatic growth in recent decades, with concepts such as trajectories, turning points, and desistance commanding the attention of researchers. What are the developmental sources of persistent involvement in crime across the life course? Who desists from crime and why? What is the role of human agency in criminal decision-making or the choice to "go straight"?

Questions such as these gain currency in an era of mass incarceration. If there is one thing we know about prisoners, it is that most are released at some point—even, it turns out, those sentenced to life in prison. How to reintegrate ex-prisoners who have spent years and often decades behind bars is thus a central challenge for the field. How do we understand "lifers" once they hit the street? Do our life-course theories of criminal desistance, mostly based on younger men on the outside, apply to the increasing number of ex-lifers who will be trying to make a go of it after years of institutionalization? In short, what makes an ex-prisoner successful in remaining crime-free after being released from long-term imprisonment?

The discipline of criminology is fortunate that Marieke Liem chose to tackle these questions in her important new book, *After Life Imprisonment*. A fascinating work of original and creative research, Liem presents a rigorous, close-up study of over sixty homicide offenders who served long sentences before being released. Because of their long spells behind bars, many of the potential turning points we often read about passed these men by, such as marriage or jobs. For example, Liem uncovers a stream of hardships among lifers in finding pro-social intimate partners after release, and the sting of being officially marked as a criminal hinders attempts to find employment in an era where criminal record checks are ubiquitous and often online. But it is not just role transitions such as marriage and employment that come under scrutiny, as Liem finds that cognitive transformations (e.g., identity shifts) also do not distinguish those who recidivate from those who do not.

In trying to reconcile these findings Liem focuses on agency and self-efficacy, whereby hardened men try to exert control over their typically chaotic lives. Based on detailed interviews, she uncovers new insights on the processes by which some men were able to overcome profound adversities. The resulting book is an advance for theories of criminal desistance, and as more and more men are released from long prison terms, the policy stakes could not be higher. Of interest to both criminological researchers and policy-makers, *After Life Imprisonment* deserves careful reading.

Robert J. Sampson
Harvard University

Ruben is a tall, bald, forty-six-year-old black lifer. He wears brand-new sneakers, jeans, a wide sweatshirt, and a gold necklace. One Saturday, more than twenty years ago, together with a friend, he killed a man. He starts by talking about his childhood: He grew up in one of Boston's poor neighborhoods. When he was nine years old, his parents separated, his mother moved in with another man, and his brother joined the United States Marine Corps. Then, he recalls, "I started having problems in school, with the new makeup of the household. So, from there I started acting out a little bit. I kept getting a lot of beatings because I was staying outside a lot longer than I was supposed to, not obeying the rules." He continues, "It was about, I want to say, age fourteen, my father was killed and then that began the downward spiral. My grades in high school started slipping tremendously, my relationship with my mother was moving further apart. I got into a lot of fights at school and in the neighborhood, I guess that I was really angry."

When his brother came home from the marines, Ruben moved in with him. His brother had problems of his own and started to become physically abusive: "I was much younger and I was small; he was pretty big, pretty buff." He recalls how one night, "I said something smart back to him, and he smacked me so hard it left a print on my face for about four days." He takes his breath, and resumes: "The anger and the hatred that I built up for him, I reflected it to other people. And that was pretty much the cycle of my life for a lot of years: on drugs, violence, drugs, violence, work."

At age twenty-one he moved in with his girlfriend, who had become pregnant. Life was better; he had a job and enjoyed the domestic life. One night he joined a friend at a party, he remembers: "And there was another girl down there, and we became friends, quickly became friends [...] and her ex-boyfriend is very abusive, you know, he came over and beat her up. And one night me and a couple of friends were there, and he showed up, walking in the room, choking her, beating her, and we get into it. To make a long story short, he died from injuries. And then I went to prison."

At age twenty-three he was convicted of second-degree murder. In prison, he says, "the first few years was, you know, it was a serious transition, and no, it was more mental than physical. Physically it was easy because I had lived that way so long on the streets and prison was just another place." In the beginning, he says, he was still involved in the "street life": "The violence, hanging with certain people [. . .] putting myself in situations that I knew I should not be in. And then at some point I ended up changing." He started becoming involved in education and rehabilitative programs.

After fifteen and a half years Ruben was paroled. He describes how the first six months after his release were "mentally, up and down." He was able to get a job and find an apartment. He summarizes as follows: "So everything looked fine on the outside, but on the inside I was just an edgy shell. You know, inside it was just, if I was around people I felt uncomfortable, or for some reason they felt uncomfortable around me, so I stayed away from visiting my family." After being out for six months, he was re-incarcerated for a parole violation: "A drug case. Somebody had some pills and some cocaine in the car with them. And because I was a passenger, they charged all of us."

When he was released again after several years, he obtained a job at a local supermarket and started therapy at a reentry organization, which was where I interviewed him. Soon thereafter he became a counselor himself. When I talked to him, he had recently married a woman he met through church. Life was good. Still, he says, "I am almost afraid of becoming comfortable. I am a work in progress [. . .] I have my good days and I have my doubtful days where the paranoia, the uncertainty, the feeling that I don't deserve this, [prevails] and I look back at all the work that I put in. It's not that someone came in and gave this to me, I worked for this, this is what I did, you know, I put in a lot of hard work."

***

For two-plus years, I interviewed over sixty lifers like Ruben, who had committed a homicide and, as a result, had been incarcerated for decades. The term "lifer" can be somewhat deceptive. It is used in much of the literature to refer to those given a life sentence *without* or *with* the possibility of parole.[1] Those not eligible for parole, or those sentenced to a term of years that exceeds their natural life expectancy, will spend the rest of their lives behind bars. Those serving life sentences with the possibility of parole may be released at some point, but not after serving an average of twenty-nine years in prison.[2] Because one of the main focal points of my research is the reentry process, I will use the term "lifer" to refer to the interviewed lifers who were at one point paroled from their life sentence. After release, some were successful in staying outside the prison walls, while others found themselves back behind bars.

***

I have been studying homicide in various ways. In prior research, I have tried to characterize different types of offending, patterns of homicide, and trends over time. The study object in these research projects was usually the homicide itself. I became intrigued by the questions: What, then, happens after the homicide is solved and the individual arrested and put behind bars? And after decades of confinement, how do they fare after their release?

To answer these questions, I applied for funding and obtained a Marie Curie Fellowship.[3] The fact that this is a European grant highlights the relevance of what has been termed "penal expansionism," now also reaching the shores of Europe. The tendency to punish harsher and longer, coupled with a lack of insight into how best to respond to and manage those who commit the most violent offenses, has ramifications not just for those sentenced to life, but for the public in general.[4] The costs to the public for keeping lifers in prison for ever-increasing periods in these times of economic crises is now more significant than ever before.

Even though I published the main findings of this research in academic journals, I felt that there were simply too many aspects to the story—just talking about one aspect did not do justice to the complexities I encountered; and stories that were too wrenching to be kept from the public. I wanted to share this full story.

This book is an attempt to shed light on the perspectives of lifers regarding their experiences of a life sentence. Against the backdrop of tough-on-crime policies, this book talks about the lives of the men and women I interviewed, the events that led to their incarceration, and the struggles they faced upon release. Ultimately, this book tries to answer the following question: What makes lifers successful in remaining crime-free after their release from long-term imprisonment?

I first gained entrée to these men and women by contacting key figures in organizations that work with ex-offenders. One of the first to respond positively to my request was Lyn,[5] who ran Span, a Boston-based initiative that helped ex-prisoners getting on their feet following release. She had been working in the civil rights field since the 1960s and proved to be an invaluable source: she introduced me to numerous lifers on parole, all of whom she knew personally. Over time I came across many of these men and women, either at Span's office in downtown Boston or at various speaking engagements, so that after two and a half years they became familiar faces. Through the Massachusetts Department of Correction, I was able to talk to lifers who were recalled to prison.

Due to the nature of their crimes, lifers are in the public eye. In describing their lives and presenting their narratives, I have taken the precautions of not mentioning their real names, and disguising their cases in small ways, neither of which involve significant distortions.

***

My hope is that, by providing a deeper view into this forgotten population, this book will contribute to a critical debate on the use of long-term imprisonment. I am committed to the idea that in such a debate, the voices of these lifers need to be heard.

1

Introduction

Today, one out of every nine prisoners is serving a life sentence.[1] This adds up to roughly 160,000 people,[2] or an entire midsize U.S. city, such as Eugene, Oregon, or Fort Collins, Colorado. Even though a proportion is serving a sentence of life without parole,[3] the majority of life-sentenced individuals will at one point be paroled to society.

Life sentences are of great consequence to the individuals who receive them and the society that imposes them. Over the last decades, the number of lifers nationwide has been rising dramatically. Since 1984, the lifer population has more than quadrupled in size.[4] Trends in Massachusetts generally mirror this growth.[5] Not only are more people being admitted to prison with life sentences, but lifers are serving increasingly longer terms of incarceration before being paroled, now averaging thirty years compared to an average of twenty years in the early 1990s.[6] It has been well documented that this growth is linked to policy changes, not to increases in crime rates. Since the mid-1970s, the political climate in the United States has progressively embraced tougher policies as the primary focus of a crime-control strategy.[7] This shift was grounded in the belief that one of the best ways to confront what was perceived as a growing crime rate was to radically increase both the number of persons being sentenced to prison and to extend their period of incarceration.[8] This period of rising crime and rapid social change provided a context for a series of policy choices across all branches of government that significantly increased sentence length.[9] During this time policy-makers and the public grew comfortable with the idea of incarcerating people either for very long terms or simply for the rest of their lives. As fear of crime among the public and policy-makers was crystallized by sensationalized media accounts of formerly incarcerated persons reoffending, imprisonment came to be accepted as a retributive tool.[10] The growth in incarceration rates in the United States over the past forty years is historically unprecedented and internationally unique.[11] In recent years, however, there has been a significant shift in both public discussion and policy attention to the goal of imprisonment, public safety, the social and fiscal costs, and the implications of imprisonment for victims and offenders.[12] This conversation needs to be expanded to the application of life sentences.

We know, however, very little about what happens to those released after a life sentence. With the demise of the rehabilitation model and the increasing "get tough on criminals" public attitude,[13] the politically easy solution is to allow people to wither away behind bars. Over the years, instead of rehabilitation, punishment and incapacitation have become identified as the primary goals of imprisonment, and many have abandoned the idea of reforming offenders.[14] A more difficult course is to accept the possibility that even individuals who have committed serious crimes may so develop as to be able to live in society crime-free. What, then, makes these lifers successful in staying out once they are released? Given that they have been removed from society for decades, their reentry[15] process cannot simply be equated to that of prisoners who have served much shorter prison sentences.

Why Should We Care?

At the time of writing, the United States has the largest prisoner population and the highest per capita incarceration rate in the world: 2.3 million adult prisoners and a rate of about 750 per 100,000 of the general population.[16] Aside from the staggering size of the general prison population, there are at least four reasons why we should pay particular attention to the use of long-term incarceration for homicide offenders: the absence of crime reduction through incarceration, the financial aspects of applying prolonged imprisonment, the adverse social and psychological effects of long-term incarceration and, finally, recent developments in legislation that may result in more life-sentenced individuals being released.

First, contrary to public perception, older offenders who have committed homicides are the least likely of all offenders to recidivate and highly unlikely to repeat their violent crimes.[17] Specific recidivism (i.e., committing a second homicide) among homicide offenders is very rare, and ranges from 1% to 3%.[18] If we look at broader measures of recidivism, such as rearrest, homicide offenders also constitute a category that is least likely to be rearrested: a large-scale Bureau of Justice Statistics study based on over four hundred thousand released U.S. prisoners found that homicide offenders had the lowest five-year rearrest rates (47.9%) compared to all other groups of offenders, including violent offenders.[19] Studies further show that if homicide offenders reoffend, they mostly do so within two to three years of release from prison.[20] Studies assessing specific recidivism (i.e., committing another homicide) similarly report the time that elapsed between release and the second homicide to be three to nine years.[21] The still relatively high rate of reported general recidivism[22] seems to be largely attributable to parole violations, new drug charges, or offenses committed during imprisonment. The rates of violent recidivism are more moderate and range from 7%[23] to 16%.[24] It has been well established that being convicted of a violent crime may not necessarily be indicative of a high risk of sustained violence.[25] In short, research so far fails to demonstrate a strong causal link between long-term incarceration limiting the risk of recidivism.[26] Overall, findings from previous studies suggest that individuals serving long sentences do not seem to pose a distinctive threat to the community when compared with other former prisoners.[27]

data issues

Further, research shows that long sentences, including life sentences, have little to no effect on crime reduction through either deterrence (the threat of punishment may discourage criminal acts) or incapacitation (crimes averted by physically isolating the potential offender).[28] The deterrent value of long sentences appears to be minimal, as the decision to commit a crime is more likely influenced by the certainty and swiftness of punishment than by the severity of the criminal sanction.[29] There is little evidence that research findings like these have had any role in the adoption of long-term confinement, despite calls in recent years for more evidence-based policy.

The second reason why we should care about this specific group of prisoners could be summarized as the "money issue." Given the serious crimes of many long-term prisoners, public protection demands the provision of secure custody.[30] The costs associated with such custody are considerable: in Massachusetts, incarcerating an offender costs $43,000 per year. The costs for housing an inmate, including lifers, at maximum-security facilities accumulate to $48,000 per year.[31] These figures are based, however, on young prisoners. Inmates undergo a process of accelerated aging compared to their age-matched counterparts outside of prison.[32] This accelerated aging process is likely due to the high burden of disease common in people from poor backgrounds, coupled with unhealthy lifestyles prior to and during incarceration.[33] To illustrate, to account for accelerated aging, the National Institute of Corrections defines "older inmates" as those fifty years of age or older.[34] Many state correctional departments consider prisoners aged fifty-five and older as "geriatric."[35] As their health is further exacerbated by substandard medical care either before or during incarceration,[36] the increased burden of illness, disability, and special needs make them an expensive prison population.[37] Older prisoners cost approximately $70,000 per year[38]— two or three times that of younger prisoners. Currently, Massachusetts houses 1,975 lifers, of whom approximately half serves life without the possibility of parole.[39] In total, lifers make up almost 20% of the overall Massachusetts prison population. Aside from those who will spend the rest of their lives behind bars, considering that the average lifer spends thirty years in prison we may wish to evaluate to what extent we are willing to pay the price for their captivity.

Third, despite the well-worn maxim that, eventually, nearly all prisoners will be released to the community, there is virtually no literature on the community integration of long-term prisoners.[40] Long-term imprisonment constitutes an extreme on many fronts. On one hand, it entails considerable deprivations and requires substantial and long-term allocations of scarce correctional resources; on the other, it may cause harm to inmates, thereby becoming ineffective. This highlights the need to shed light on the unknown effects of long-term incarceration. The effects of incarceration on offenders who spend several months to several years in prison are well documented: ex-prisoners earn less money during their lifetimes, find it harder to stay employed, are less likely to marry, and suffer a range of medical and psychological problems.[41] Very little is known, however, on the effects of imprisonment among those spending decades behind bars. The lack of research in this area can be traced back to the 1960s, when the influential Radzinowicz Report,[42] reflecting the status quo of long-term prisoners in maximum security prisons in the United Kingdom, noted, "Practically nothing is known about the vital subject of the lasting effects on human personality of long-term imprisonment, yet pronouncements on the subject continue to be made and very long prison sentences continue to be imposed."[43] Little has changed since then: although more studies have been conducted on the effects of imprisonment, these have mainly based their conclusions on those serving much shorter sentences, rather than on long-term prisoners specifically. Lifers, however, constitute a unique population. The average age of male lifers leaving state prison is about thirty-five years.[44] By the time lifers face the possibility of parole they are much older, and hence they are likely to face different problems and to have different needs from those in their twenties or thirties.

Fortunately, the vacuum in research on lifers has not remained entirely void, as recent journalistic accounts,[45] books based on a small samples of long-term prisoners,[46] and thorough dissertational research[47] have shed light on the issue. One of the most well-known works on life in prison is John Irwin's book *Lifers*, in which he describes seventeen incarcerated men serving sentences of twenty years or more. He finds that most lifers changed drastically during the course of their prison sentence. These men experienced a process of awakening, a point at which they understood that their actions have led them to their current situation.[48] In their recent work *On the Outside*, the Canadian scholars Melissa Munn and Chris Bruckert give a unique insight to the lives of twenty former long-term prisoners, among whom were sixteen life-sentenced men released or paroled from Canadian prison at least five years ago who have remained charge-free ever since. Through interviews with these men, the authors unveil some of the effects of long-term incarceration, including what they term "fragile freedom": being out on parole but constantly fearful of returning to prison on a parole violation. These men, the authors found, "are left with a profound sense of being abnormal, of being outside, of not belonging."[49] With this book, I hope to add to the research literature by specifically focusing on the American context of lifer reentry: How are these men and women able to live a life beyond bars after having been incarcerated for decades?

Finally, recent developments in legislation make the study of lifer reentry even more warranted. Currently, approximately 2,500 juveniles are serving a sentence of life without the possibility of parole (LWOP). The United States is the only country in the world that imposes this sentence on youth. Juvenile LWOP sentences have recently garnered attention because of two major Supreme Court cases, *Graham v. Florida* and *Miller v. Alabama*. In *Graham*, the Court decided in 2010 that because of their cognitive, behavioral, and emotional differences from adults, youth under eighteen at the time of their crime who did not commit a homicide could not be sentenced to the harshest available sentence. In the *Miller* case two years later, the Court again relied on expert knowledge from the field of adolescent brain science to find an Eighth Amendment violation in sentencing youth to LWOP in a mandatory way without allowing for consideration of their age and other relevant factors. According to estimates, the *Miller* decision might affect the sentences of two thousand of these life-sentenced individuals, but cases are pending in as many as ten state supreme courts about whether *Miller* applies retroactively.[50] One of the outcome scenarios entails *Miller* being applied to already-sentenced juveniles, potentially leading to many life-sentenced individuals being eligible for parole. These developments highlight the need for studying this unique offender population.

This Book

The sample of lifers on which this book is based is different from previous work in many ways. First, all these lifers have committed a homicide. While homicide remains the offense for which most lifers are sentenced, life sentences are today authorized for robbery, assault, drug offenses, and even some property offenses.[51] While other work on lifers also includes these offenders,[52] this book focuses on homicide offenders alone. Second, previous work on lifers has been based predominantly in the United Kingdom, where lifers typically serve less than fifteen years in prison,[53] as opposed to the United States, where lifers spend on average twice as many years.[54] In this book, I hope to shed light on the status quo in the country with the largest lifer population worldwide. In doing so, I should reiterate that I was interested in what determined success versus failure post-release. Hence, I did not talk to people who served a life sentence without the possibility of parole. In six states—Illinois, Iowa, Louisiana, Maine, Pennsylvania, and South Dakota—and in the federal system, life means life.[55] Massachusetts, like forty-two other states, has laws that permit sentencing defendants to life with or without parole.

As a European citizen, I should emphasize that the United States is an outlier in many ways: With its mobile, heterogeneous, and urban population, it is low in what the American sociologist Francis Cullen termed "communitarianism" and high in "utilitarian individualism,"[56] or the dominance of individual self-interest in the pursuit of the desired, usually material ends. Accordingly, the structural basis for creating and sustaining supportive social relations is weak. In addition, the current penal climate in the United States is distinctive from its European counterparts in the length of its punishments and the sheer numbers of people it involves.[57] In contrast to European countries, where social assistance is viewed as a right, irrespective of the causes of poverty,[58] Americans arguably hold dear the creed of individualism, which admonishes people to "pick themselves up by their bootstraps" and fend for themselves.[59] Given these large differences, there is a strong need for comparative research in other parts of the world. I hope that, by starting in the United States with a lifer population of over one hundred thousand individuals, this research provides a first step to explore such barren terrain.

***

In this book, I explore the experiences of men and women before, during, and after serving a life sentence. In doing so, I aim to offer insight into the lives of long-term incarcerated individuals and come to an understanding on how to explain their successes and failures post-release. In order to answer this question, I recruited lifers who were "successful," in that they were on parole at the time I interviewed them, as well as those who were "unsuccessful," in that they were recalled to prison.

The data necessary to investigate this question are inevitably different from those used in empirical models estimating the impact of the length of sentence on post-release "success" versus "failure." Not only are the methodological issues associated with these regression-based approaches substantial,[60] but this type of research "fail[s] to recognize the fundamental humanity of the individual offender."[61] Similarly, it has been argued that public and academic discussions surrounding prisoner reentry usually leave out the voices of those studied, relying instead on crude statistics.[62] Much of the criminal career research proceeds as if the meaning of social relationships can be simply established by their presence or absence.[63] To address the gap between statistical reality and real-life experiences, throughout this book I will focus on giving voice to those having experienced this process firsthand.

Hence, this book primarily reflects the perspectives of lifers regarding their experiences of a life sentence. Following others in the field,[64] I leave questions related to the degree of sentencing to criminal justice experts, questions on legality and constitutionality to legal scholars, and economic considerations to economists. This book reflects on the lives of the lifers I talked to, the years they spent behind bars, and the ways in which they lived their lives after release.

***

The structure of this book is as follows. In the next chapter, I draw from two predominant criminological theories that have been used to explain desistance from crime: life-course theories and theories of cognitive transformation. This chapter also addresses the nature of homicide and the influence of imprisonment to help us understand how the homicide offenders on which this study was based fare post-release. Did prison act as a school of crime, as a deterrent, or simply as a "deep freeze," which implies that offenders came out the exact way they came in? Finally, the chapter discusses potential harmful effects of imprisonment, including institutionalization.

In chapter 3 I describe how I encountered these lifers, and the context in which I conducted the interviews. Here, I also briefly touch on the characteristics of the interviewees, and the geographical and cultural background that shaped their lives.

In the chapters that follow, I take a chronological approach, following the life of the interviewees before incarceration, throughout incarceration, and after release. Chapter 4 talks about the lives of the interviewees before they committed the homicide: their childhoods, family relations, neighborhoods they lived in, previous criminal behaviors, and lifestyles, how these factors lead up to them becoming involved in a homicide and how, consequently, they were sentenced to life in prison.

Chapter 5 portrays in depth the factors peculiar to long-term imprisonment, how the interviewees coped with these conditions, and how they managed to adapt to confinement over the years. In this chapter I will also go deeper into what differentiates the lifers' prison experience from those who are "passing through" the prison system.

In chapter 6 we will take a closer look at the notion of prison as a turning point. We will see that the majority of interviewees described having experienced a "personal change." I will examine the process underlying this change, and the associated narrative. I will show that this narrative is not necessarily fake, in the sense that interviewees pretend to be someone they are not, but rather a reflection of how they wish to present themselves.

Chapter 7 continues with a chronological timeline, exploring the initial effects of reentering a world they left so many years ago. The chapter highlights specific roadblocks to reentry: finding a place to live and obtaining a job. Deriving indicators from life-course theories, I further explore how relationships with family members, intimate partners, and children developed and influenced the interviewees over the years. Chapter 8, then, extends beyond the impact on social relations by focusing on the effects of incarceration on mental health.

In chapters 9 and 10 I arrive at the question who was able to stay out of prison and who was not. I will first discuss the nature of being on parole and the strategies these lifers employed to navigate such conditions. In chapter 9 the interviewees mentioned several themes in terms of "failing" to stay out of prison: being recalled for political reasons, making up for lost time too quickly, falling back into old habits, and returning to prison as a safe place. Conversely, in chapter 10 I delve deeper into the factors the participants mentioned as key to staying out. These included aging out of crime, a healthy fear of the conditions of parole, and, most important, self-efficacy, or having a sense of choice and control over one's life.

Chapter 11 concludes by exploring the boundaries of two main theoretical models—life-course theories and theories of cognitive transformation—in explaining success and failure among these lifers. It highlights that conventional pillars of social control as suggested by life-course theorists, such as family relations, parenthood, and intimate partner relations, are unable to explain desistance among this group. Similarly, theories of cognitive transformation fall short, since virtually all interviewees describe themselves as "transformed" individuals. In this final chapter, I discuss ways we can put the findings of this research into practical and policy recommendations to better prepare this unique group of offenders for release to the community: by reclaiming self-efficacy in prison and through employment, by evidence-based programming, and by acknowledging the psychological aftermath of long-term incarceration. The chapter concludes with a discussion of reform in both prison and parole systems for lifers. Providing lifers a fair chance on the job market, adequate programming taking into account the prolonged period of confinement, and a sense of certainty in terms of reasons for recall will enable them to start a life beyond bars.

2

Understanding Desistance

In recent years increased attention has been paid to the reasons why people stop, or desist from, offending.[1] Despite its relative youth, this field of study has produced much research, which can roughly be divided into two groups. The first group includes studies that are mainly based on quantitative analyses and generate "strong social" models that stress the importance of life-course turning points in desistance, such as marriage or employment.[2] The second group of scholarly work consists of empirical qualitative research. Models of desistance based on these studies emphasize the motivation and will-power of the individual concerned, or, as the criminal justice scholar Thomas LeBel and colleagues summarized, "One need only decide to change and envision a new identity for oneself in order to go straight."[3] I will discuss these two main theoretical streams, as well as a third perspective focusing on the nature of the crime, and a fourth perspective that specifically assesses the influence of imprisonment on desistance.

The Life-Course Approach

Life-course theorists view criminality as a dynamic process that changes over one's lifetime. In what follows, I will elaborate on life-course theories to provide an answer to the question of why some homicide offenders do well after release while others return to prison. This approach is different from previous studies on homicide offenders using a developmental approach, which attempt to predict future homicide offenders from an at-risk sample population.[4] In other words, these studies consider homicide as an *outcome* of specific developmental trajectories, while my focus is on homicide as a *starting point* to long-term incarceration and the life that follows.

Aging Out

Arguably, "no fact about crime is more widely accepted"[5] than the association between younger age and increased criminal activity. The founding fathers of what became to be known as "the age-crime curve" were the sociologist Travis Hirschi and his colleague Michael Gottfredson. Their research, and many studies since, showed that across historical time and cultures, involvement in criminal behavior shows a rapid increase at puberty age, followed by a slow decline after reaching its peak between sixteen and eighteen years old (with the peak somewhat earlier for property than for violent crime). The same is true, Hirschi and Gottfredson argued, for the inverse age-crime curve. As postadolescent age increases, crime decreases. The authors, in short, assert that the relationship cannot be explained by sociological or psychological variables, but rather is simply due to "the inexorable aging of the organism."[6] This theoretical perspective has been coined "the inexplicability hypothesis,"[7] and since then, several scholars have attempted to explain the age-crime curve by assessing factors associated with age.

Some of these scholars have pointed to biological and psychological factors such as bodily strength, physical energy, and psychological drive to explain the cessation of criminal behavior. The peak and decline in these factors coincide with the peak and decline in overall deviant behavior.[8] Others have similarly pointed to the relationship between advancing age and conformity—namely, the psychological evidence showing that rebellious and antisocial tendencies decline with age.[9]

Others, such as the sociologist Darrell Steffensmeier and his colleagues[10] also challenged Gottfredson and Hirschi's notion of invariance by allowing for differences across offense types in the age distribution. In line with routine activities theory, they suggested that older individuals do not engage in "low-yield, high-risk" crimes, as their day-to-day activities are not associated with these crimes in the way young people's daily activities are.[11]

Terrie Moffitt, an American clinical psychologist, in turn proposed that the aggregated age-crime curve can be disaggregated into separate groups.[12] She holds that there are two main types of antisocial offenders: a small group of subjects that engage in antisocial behavior at every stage of life who are relatively immune to changes in life circumstances, and a larger group of offenders who commit crime somewhat later in life and generally have much shorter criminal careers. Later studies that have assessed criminal careers of a range of offenders (including homicide offenders)[13] seem to corroborate Moffitt's findings. These studies found that a prior criminal record, most notably for previous violent offenses, was one of the main factors predicting recidivism.[14]

***

In short, based on perspectives focusing on age—including early age of onset—as an explanatory variable, it would be expected that offenders who are older at the time of homicide, and hence at the time of release, are less likely to reoffend. Conversely, the change in crime associated with age can be explained by co-occurring changes in psychological and sociological factors, including changes in biological, neural, cognitive, emotional, and interpersonal functioning. Additionally, significant changes occur in every life domain as age increases. Formal education is completed, new jobs obtained, living situations change often, romantic relationships form and dissolve, marriages, families and careers are launched.[15] Without examining the underlying dynamics of age-related factors, the age-crime curve as such has been supported by several studies examining recidivism of homicide offenders, finding that young age at the time of the homicide,[16] and therefore younger age at release,[17] increases the likelihood to recidivate.[18]

This theoretical approach does not seem to sufficiently explain, however, who among those at an older age desist and who do not. More recent life-course theories, therefore, point to the change in criminal engagement as important life events change and new social roles are adopted.

New Roles

From previous research on the development of crime, particularly the virtuous work by Robert J. Sampson and John H. Laub, desistance from crime in adulthood can be meaningfully understood by changes in social roles and, in turn, changes in informal social control.[19] They based these findings on the original data of Sheldon and Eleanor Glueck, who collected information on five hundred delinquent boys born in Boston during the Great Depression. All these men had spent time in a state reformatory. Sampson and Laub followed these men to age seventy, allowing for a life-course view on the development of crime.[20] Their age-graded theory of social control derived from this research predicts that criminal behavior changes as important life events change—the stronger the ties to family and work, the less the criminal behavior. In this view, the positive influence of a spouse or an employer creates a social dynamic that produces informal social control. Prior research has shown that assuming traditional roles within a family, such as a new role as a parent or a spouse, can be a benefit in the reentry transition process as it aids in the development of pro-social identities.[21] Living with a spouse may give one "more to lose" or "increase shame" in committing crime.[22] In addition, living with an intimate partner may significantly influence the nature of daily activities, suggesting that these lifestyle changes may also work to limit involvement in criminal behavior.[23] It is important to note that employment "by itself" and marriage "by itself" does not support desistance; rather, it is the strength and quality of employment (job stability, commitment to work, mutual ties binding employees and employers) and marriage (cohesive relationship) that predict desistance.[24]

In the age-graded theory of social control, Sampson and Laub further emphasize that they mainly focus on social roles that are acquired in adulthood: "If we begin with children and follow their paths to adulthood, we find considerable heterogeneity in adult outcomes. It follows that the adult life course matters and that childhood causation models are woefully inadequate."[25] Further, it is important to note that in their new roles as husbands and fathers, the desisting men in Sampson and Laub's study did not only desist because they *received* social support. Equally important was that they desisted from crime when they assumed a role as *providers* of support.[26]

The assumption of such a new role is described as a "turning point." The sociologist Andrew Abbott pointed out that "what makes a turning point a turning point rather than a minor ripple is the passage of sufficient time 'on the new course' such that it becomes clear that direction has indeed been changed."[27] Turning points are thus best envisioned as short, consequential shifts that redirect a process. Not all sudden changes are turning points, but rather only those that "are preceded evincing a new regime."[28]

Recently, the Spanish researchers José Cid and Joel Martí focused on the role of preexisting family relations—opposed to newly assumed social roles as a parent or intimate partner—and emphasized that family support should be considered not as a "turning point," but as a "returning point" in the desistance process. They found that preexisting social bonds, such as family ties, were fundamental in moving away from criminal behavior. In this dynamic, the offender ceases criminal behavior in order to compensate for the supportive role of the preexisting relationship.[29]

Further, informal social control is not limited to the nuclear family, but also includes larger social networks and institutions, such as religious and volunteer groups.[30] Social support can thus stem from a variety of sources that have been shown to reduce recidivism. Together, these "webs of conformity" provide not only constraints but also supports.

Employment, marriage, parenthood, and family ties are thus thought to constitute "(re)turning points": mechanisms of informal social control that facilitate the alteration of criminal trajectories, putting ex-offenders on a path toward desistance.[31] Successful participation in a personal relationship, a job, or some other conventional area of life thus provides personal rewards and reinforces a noncriminal identity.[32] This notion is supported in a recent study on prisoner recidivism in Massachusetts. When prisoners returning to prison were asked what could have prevented them from committing the act that caused their return, most answered "work" and "children."[33] In short, crime is thought to be less likely when social support (in its broadest sense) for conformity exceeds social support for crime.[34]

A potential limitation of Sampson and Laub's important body of work is that the sample on which the analyses were based was composed entirely of white male offenders who matured into adulthood during the 1950s[35] and mostly served relatively brief periods in prison. So far, we do not know whether this theoretical approach effectively captures the experiences of those who have been incarcerated for lengthy periods and, more generally, offenders coming of age in a more contemporary social and economic landscape. In this book, I hope to contribute to the literature on desistance processes by focusing on those who have been locked up for prolonged periods. Before doing so, let us now turn to a second cluster of studies aimed at explaining desistance from crime.

Transforming into a Better Self

The second group of desistance studies consists of empirical qualitative research which suggests that people who abandon criminal activity make identifiable changes to their personal identity and self-narrative, and produce a new, "improved" self that no longer cognitively or emotionally coheres with offending.[36] In his groundbreaking study on sixty-five convicted offenders, the criminologist Shadd Maruna found that the people who were desisting from crime had established a coherent and forgiving narrative,[37] which made sense of their offending past and presented a believable "prototypical reform story."[38] In contrast, individuals in his study who continued their life of crime presented a "condemnation script," in which they made sense of their lives in terms of blocked opportunities and insurmountable obstacles.[39] Their explanatory style was consistent with "learned helplessness,"[40] feeling doomed to a life of criminality, addiction, and incarceration. Those who were desisting from crime portrayed their offending as something their "old self" had done, someone who was never the "real me." A process of "identity deconstruction" was necessary to begin a long-term process of desistance. Maruna showed that the desisters in his study started their "road to redemption" when they hit rock bottom. The ex-offenders told him that, successively, with the aid of some outside force, someone who believed in them, they became able to do what they were "always meant to do."[41]

The American sociologist Peggy Giordano and her colleagues also conducted in-depth interviews with numerous (ex-)offenders and found that personal transformation resulted from a succession of cognitive shifts that started with a "hook for change."[42] In their now-classic theory of cognitive transformation, they outlined four consecutive changes. The first step consists of discernment: the desisters' "openness to change," followed by a "hook for change," such as being offered a job, being admitted to a reentry program, or getting involved with an inspirational other. Drawing from life-course research, these "hooks for change" can be understood as the previously discussed "turning points." Giordano and her colleagues emphasize, though, that a hook for change alone is not sufficient for long-lasting change: both exposure to a hook and one's attitude toward it are necessary for successful change. For a hook to be useful, it has to provide the individual with new definitions and replacement behavior. Then, once the individual has considered different options as alternatives for a life hitherto dominated by crime, a stage of deliberation follows. In this stage, the individual reviews the possible pros and cons of potential courses of action[43] and is able to envision an appealing and conventional "replacement self" that can supplant the marginal one that must be left behind. This concept of a "replacement self" shows many similarities to Maruna's concept of "the new self," or "the real me."[44] The final stage in this process is that of dedication. In this stage, individuals regard their new identity as incompatible with ongoing criminality. Their old behavior is regarded as negative, unsustainable, and personally irrelevant.

While life-course theory, as outlined above, thus views the individual's motivation or proclivity to deviate as a constant, theories of cognitive transformation emphasize the actor's own role. More recent qualitative work, however, has underscored the need to understand both social changes (e.g., in marital or employment status) as well as subjective changes (e.g., motivation or self-concept).[45] This poses, as the criminal justice scholar Thomas LeBel and his colleagues point out, a "chicken and an egg" dilemma as to what came first: internal changes or external changes. In other words, is it strong social ties that encourage a positive mind-set, or a hopeful mind-set that leads to finding employment and an intimate partner? The answer appears to be in favor of the mind-set; their analysis showed that belief in one's ability, or belief in self-efficacy, strongly contributes to desistance. Conversely, the belief of being doomed or stigmatized before release turned out to be a main predictor in coming back to prison.[46]

The work by Maruna,[47] Giordano and colleagues,[48] LeBel, and other scholars following their approach[49] made great progress in our understanding of success and failure post-release. However, these studies almost exclusively included individuals convicted of lesser types of crimes than homicide, serving relatively brief periods behind bars. It is therefore difficult to simply copy these findings and apply them to lifers who spent decades in confinement. A notable exception to this observation, however, is the recent work by Catherine Appleton, who focused her dissertation work on over one hundred released lifers in England and Wales.[50] She found that re-incarcerated lifers, in contrast to those who resettled in the community, were less able to overcome obstacles or rise above setbacks and disappointments following release from prison. While "successful" lifers in her sample presented a redemption script, in line with Maruna's earlier work,[51] the narratives by persistent offenders corresponded to the cognitive themes in Maruna's condemnation script. In chapter 6 I will go further into the degree to which these scripts could be found among my sample of interviewed American lifers.

Nature of the Crime

Aside from life-course factors and changes in personal identity, much empirical work on homicide offender recidivism has focused on the nature of the original homicide. I undertook one such study together with Margaret Zahn and Lisa Tichavsky, in which we looked at individuals who committed a homicide in Philadelphia in the 1970s and 1980s.[52] Of the ninety-two paroled homicide offenders, more than half were sentenced of a new crime and 15% committed a new violent offense. We found that those with a conviction for a felony homicide were most likely to recidivate, and to do so violently. Our results particularly showed that the financial motive underlying felony homicide was a strong predictor for future criminality: those who commit a felony homicide early in their career may have developed a belief in the legitimacy of their violent actions as means to an end and thus reoffend more frequently after release.

The results from our Philadelphia study showed that those who were involved in a domestic homicide recidivated to a lesser extent: 36% after five years, and 55% after several decades of follow-up. Similar recidivism rates among domestic homicide offenders, and spousal homicide offenders in particular, have been reported in other studies.[53]

In our study on ninety-two Philadelphia homicide offenders, certain groups were virtually absent, such as sexual homicide offenders. A previous study on 139 sexual homicide offenders found that three men committed another (attempted) homicide. Another, smaller study that included eleven sexual juvenile homicide offenders found that three committed another sexual homicide.[54] Similar to studies assessing other types of homicide, the likelihood for violent recidivism among these sexual homicide offenders was associated with age-related factors, such as young age at first sexual offense, young age at the time of the homicide, young age at time of release, and shorter duration of detention.[55]

Another group of homicide offenders that we did not include in our Pennsylvania study were women. In a study on criminal recidivism of eighty-four female homicide offenders in Finland, the forensic psychiatrist Hanna Putkonen and her colleagues found that two committed a second homicide. Prior criminal activity was the best predictor for repeat offending.[56]

A final cluster of studies that specifically assesses the type of homicide in relation to recidivism focuses on psychotic homicide offenders. A recent Russian study relying on data from 133 schizophrenic homicide offenders showed that 11% committed a repeat homicide within the thirty-year study—this included homicides committed before the index homicide.[57] At the time of the second homicide, eight offenders were thought to have had an acute exacerbation of schizophrenia. The authors pointed out that all recidivist offenders lived in rural areas, which suggested that reduced access to care and interrupted treatment were contributing factors in many cases. Other studies taking into account offenders' mental status found alcoholism,[58] schizophrenia,[59] and prior suicidality[60] to be significant predictors for future criminality.

The Influence of Imprisonment

A School of Crime or a Deterrent?

From a theoretical perspective, incarceration is associated with desistance in at least three ways: as a deterrent for future criminal behavior, as a breeding ground for future crime, or simply as a "deep freeze," which implies that offenders come out the exact way they came in.[61]

First, from a deterrence point of view, those who have direct experience with the discomfort of prison life should be particularly loath to repeated punishment. Thus, individuals who have been released from prison may be deterred because they are certain of receiving a prison sentence. Along this line of reasoning, the costs of imprisonment are higher than the benefits of committing new crimes.[62]

Others argue that prisons may actually have a criminogenic (crime-enhancing) effect. From a social learning perspective, theorists have referred to prisons as "schools of crime."[63] According to this perspective, association with criminals and imitation of these criminals make prisoners more likely to develop norms that favor crime and, consequently, more likely to engage in criminal activities after release. Further, the hardening required to survive in a prison environment that is often violent and unpredictable can make inmates less social, more violent, and more likely to internalize the stigma associated with being a criminal.[64] Rather than pointing to prison as a source of stigma and social learning, life-course scholars suggest that imprisonment may reduce the incarcerated offender's legal prospects by eliminating pathways for conventional development.[65] When these areas of social control—found in employment, marital, and parental attachment—are reduced, offenders have a smaller incentive to abstain from reoffending. This mechanism has been supported in a Canadian study on eighty-six homicide recidivists, which found that reduction of family and community support after prison release explained why some homicide offenders recidivated and others did not.[66]

Third, from a minimalist perspective, imprisonment has no impact on future offending. From this point of view, prisoners go into a "psychological deep freeze" where their preexisting behavior is stored away, only to be reactivated upon release.[67]

Arguably, there is also a fourth perspective to the influence of imprisonment on criminal behavior: namely, that prison itself creates a unique set of mental and social problems that inhibits the offender upon his or her return. These theories of "insitutionalization" or "prisonization"[68] posit that the prison environment socializes inmates toward heightened criminality. Prison, from this point of view, closes many doors and increases the likelihood of further involvement in crime, which, in turn, forecloses opportunities and makes persistence more likely.[69] Social segregation from society implies decreased exposure to pro-social influences, as well as increased exposure to crime-producing influences.[70] Several empirical studies have corroborated this theory, finding that longer incarceration times reduce prisoners' optimism about life after incarceration and hence the actual likelihood of succeeding.[71] Also, the longer the time in custody, the less likely it is for prisoners to maintain external ties to family and children that can provide a positive outlook on their return to the community, their ability to find a job, and their likelihood to stay out of trouble.

The idea that a prison can create negative effects has remained absent from public debate.[72] In the first place, studies have tended to take undifferentiated samples and look for general patterns. These general studies neglect the experience of particular groups and individuals, such as lifers, but also women, the old, segregated prisoners, and so on.[73] Second, the prison researcher John Irwin held that this absence is related to the way society views the ex-prisoner. He may know better than any other scholar, as he served a five-year sentence for armed robbery himself.[74] While in prison, he realized that education and going straight was a better alternative. After leaving prison, he transitioned to a career as a tenured sociology professor. As he writes in his classic work *The Felon*:

> From one perspective the ex-convict is regarded as an erratic person—he is "emotionally disturbed," "sociopathic," or "potentially dangerous." Therefore, any unusual behavior or any "symptoms," such as the actions that have been reported by "normal" returnees in other instances, would be attributed to the personality propensities of the ex-convict and not to the transitional experiences. From another perspective the ex-convict is seen as a person of low moral worth who is being granted the special privilege of early release provided he agrees to live up to certain minimum standards of behavior—the special parole regulations. [. . .] He should be thankful for this privilege and should find no difficulty, if he has regained some worthiness, in responding by conducting himself properly. Failure to do so is interpreted as stemming from his thanklessness and/or unworthiness.[75]

Again, by paying attention to this special population, and by assessing the influence of imprisonment on their lives post-release, I hope to rectify some of this lack of attention.

Length of Imprisonment

Similar to other studies on desistance, the vast majority of studies on the effect of imprisonment have focused on short-term prisoners. The findings of these studies are not conclusive. Some point to a lack of a relationship between recidivism and how long persons are incarcerated, while controlling for age and other related factors.[76] Opposed to the influence of imprisonment on nonviolent delinquents, who can be sanctioned by imprisonment, community sanctions, or monetary sanctions, it is difficult to empirically examine the exact influence of length of imprisonment among homicide offenders. By their very nature, homicides carry long sentences with not much variability, let alone alternative sanctioning. In a recent study, Pieter Baaij, Paul Nieuwbeerta, and I took a first step to see to what extent the length of imprisonment affected the likelihood to reoffend. Based on more than six hundred homicide offenders, we found that length of imprisonment was inversely U-shaped: overall, longer imprisonment appeared to increase recidivism, but when the length of imprisonment exceeded eight to ten years, it decreased recidivism. These and other findings specifically assessing homicide offenders are thus not straightforward. Evidence proves to be inconclusive as to whether there is a preventive effect of imprisonment on recidivism for homicide offenders. Two other studies focusing on adult homicide offenders[77] and one study on juvenile homicide offenders,[78] for example, indicated that longer imprisonment increased recidivism, while three other studies observed that longer imprisonment reduced recidivism.[79] The findings of this body of scholarly work, however, should be interpreted with caution. First, some studies only provide descriptive—rather than statistical—evidence of the relationship between imprisonment and recidivism.[80] Second, most studies are based on considerably small samples, limiting the generalizability and not allowing for controlling of selection effects or testing the effect of imprisonment on different types of homicide offenders.

In presenting the life narratives of the interviewed lifers, I intend to address these theoretical approaches in coming to understand their ability to build a life for themselves before, during, and, most important, after release. Before doing so, however, I will first give a short overview on how I came in contact with these individuals, and how their narratives took shape.

3

The Context

I first encountered the lifers interviewed for this study with the help of Lyn. Lyn started her career as a passionate civil rights activist in the 1960s, advocating for prisoner's rights. In the 1970s she established Span, a Boston-based organization that helped ex-prisoners get on their feet. I approached Lyn in the fall of 2011. She believed in the project's necessity and importance and was willing to help, by introducing me to released lifers she knew. My inclusion criteria were pretty straightforward. Individuals were eligible if they were convicted of a homicide, and received a life sentence with the possibility of parole in the Boston metropolitan area; had served and completed their sentence for this offense over the past fifteen years; were released or paroled following their sentence; and were either currently re-incarcerated or out on parole. Note that I use the term "lifers" throughout this book to refer to individuals who have received and served a life sentence *with the possibility of parole* (with the exception of four interviewees who were exonerated and two who "wrapped up" their sentence and lived in the community without being on parole). Because I was interested in the factors that determined success or failure post-release, I did not speak to lifers who were serving life sentences without the possibility of parole.

On my behalf, Lyn gave them a letter that explained the background of the study. Once they decided to opt in, I contacted them to set up an appointment. In the course of this study, I met people working in other organizations, including lawyers advocating for prisoner's rights and volunteers at religious organizations. All of them were willing to help me and introduce me to lifers who were living in the community.

The recruitment of lifers who returned to prison went through one primary source, the Massachusetts Department of Correction, which selected individuals who had been convicted of a homicide, had served and completed a life sentence for this offense, and were currently re-incarcerated. Even though my original request stipulated that I was particularly interested in talking to lifers who had been re-incarcerated for a criminal violation of their parole (i.e., committed a new crime), virtually all re-incarcerated lifers seemed to have returned to prison due to technical violations in varying degrees. I should note that throughout this book, I will use the terms "technical violations" to refer to violations such as missing parole office meetings, positive drug screens, irresponsible conduct, and so on. I will use the term "criminal violations" to refer to new criminal offenses while on parole.[1]

Once the Department of Correction identified a potential interviewee, corrections program officers at each facility presented a letter to the interviewee on my behalf, inviting him or her to participate in the study. If he or she opted in, the program officers referred back to a central coordinator, who in turn scheduled an interview.

Sitting Down to Talk

I would typically start the interview by introducing myself and the purpose of the study. I ensured the interviewees that everything they shared would be made anonymous and unidentifiable, and that their participation or their refusal to participate did not influence their parole conditions or, in the case of re-incarcerated individuals, their parole eligibility or prison privileges. They were not offered incentives. I then gave them a copy of the informed consent statement. Most reacted with something along the lines of "You can write down anything you like, my name and everything, I want my story to be told!" After the interview, I debriefed the participants by reiterating the purpose of the study, and thanked them again for their participation. With some of them, I kept in touch over time by letter or e-mail. Some of them wrote me in the hopes that I could contribute to their re-parole or make a change in the criminal justice system to help others like them. Through Lyn and others working in the field, I heard that most of the re-incarcerated interviewees were denied re-parole, and that others who were paroled at the time of the interview obtained a job, got married, or passed away.

In the literature, the type of interview I conducted is referred to as "the narrative interview"[2]—a technique used to identify how interviewees construct their narratives and evaluate their lives. I was interested in obtaining a thorough description of factors that characterized these individuals and their lives. To keep the interview open yet semi-structured, I would ask the interviewees to share with me their lives before, during, and after incarceration. At times, I would ask open-ended questions, such as "Could you describe some of the challenges you initially faced after being released?" Second, I used a life-history calendar to determine the context in which important life events took place.[3] This dual approach—using a combination of the narrative interview and the life-history calendar—allowed me to better structure the sequence and timing of potential traditional "turning points," which in turn allowed me to analyze both objective and subjective factors related to the formation of the narratives.

⁎

The interviews with paroled individuals typically took place at one of the legal or religious organizations, during a period of almost two years (November 2011–August 2013). The interviews were one to six hours long, depending on the participants' responses and their willingness to share. With most interviewees I sat for hours straight. Tonya was an exception. She talked to me only because she wanted to do a favor for people like Lyn, who introduced me to her, and therefore wanted to keep our interaction as short as possible. Tonya viewed me as an outsider who would never understand what it was like to live the life of a "third-class citizen." Also, since I could not change anything about her predicament, why should she waste her time by talking to me? With the exception of Tonya, all interviewees were eager to share their stories. With some, I conducted multiple follow-up appointments in person and by phone to get their full narrative. I audio-recorded the interviews with paroled lifers (i.e., those who were not incarcerated at the time of the interview) and transcribed them verbatim. As audio-recording was prohibited inside the prisons, Jen or Kristen, who were graduate students at the time, took detailed notes of interviews with re-incarcerated lifers that we transcribed immediately after the interview.

I interviewed re-incarcerated individuals over the course of ten months, from November 2012 through August 2013. The interviews were approximately two hours long, which was mostly dependent on the time allowed by the prison schedule. The interviews that I conducted in prison were of a different nature than those conducted with released lifers. Holding interviews in prison brings along a whole set of dynamics very different from those of the outside world. Gresham Sykes first identified these dynamics in his 1958 classic work *The Society of Captives*, in which he described the issues faced by guards and the deprivations experienced by inmates in the New Jersey State Prison. In this work he pointed to the signs of a prisoner's degradation: the anonymity of a prison uniform, having a number instead of a name, the insistence on gestures of respect and subordination when addressing officials, and so on. In this respect, not much has changed since the time of Sykes's observations. In one prison, the correctional program officer warned me about the "weirdos" I was about to encounter. "They belong here," another correctional officer told me. "They are supposed to be in here, they are real predators."

The prison interviews were also clearly different from the non-prison interviews in terms of time and place. We sat in an enclosed area of the visitor room or in a separate classroom in the prison education building. Guards were close by, and there was a very strict schedule we had to follow: I could not enter the prison during "count time" or during "moving time," which sometimes implied waiting for hours before being allowed in, and then having that much less time for the interview. Interviewees in prison often expressed that they liked having "a visitor," or someone other than their fellow inmates which whom to talk. Some reported at the end of the interview or later on, in a letter, that the interview had a therapeutic effect. Joel, a thin, white fifty-two-year-old man with his hair tied together in a ponytail, was one of them. He spoke with tears in his eyes, and said, "Thank you for letting me vent and stuff."

Another aspect that stood out in the prison interviews was the difficulty for some interviewees to recognize that their participation did not influence their parole eligibility or prison privileges—even though I made sure to emphasize this in recruitment letters and in the informed consent procedure. In some interviews, the participants spoke as if they were presenting their case to the parole board. Such interviewees often presented their story in a vocabulary typical of counseling and 12-step meetings. Jay was such a man. When I met him in prison, he was fifty-eight years old. He came to the interview with a file, two inches thick, full of certificates of completed programs, letters of support, and legal documentation. Showing me each document, he said, "I have done everything humanly possible to prove that I am rehabilitated [. . .] I have done all the programs. I even started a program here in prison, for youth. I try to avoid them from going down the same road as I have." These interviews were sometimes painful. While the interviewees felt powerless and helpless in their current situation, I was simply there to hear their story yet unable to change their predicament.

Worlds Apart

The differences between the interviewees and me went further than the presence or absence of a life sentence. I am a white woman from Europe in her early thirties. The majority of the interviewees were men in their fifties and sixties. When I asked them if they could share their life histories with me, some interviewees would remark, "You don't know what it's like to be black in America," or "You don't know what it was like to grow up in the 1960s, being poor." In my mind, there was only one answer: "No, I do not know. Please tell me so I can try to understand." This is in line with Sudhir Venkatesh's observation that the researcher and the research subject are never on equal footing. Venkatesh describes his study on the life of urban poor in Chicago in his book *Gang Leader for a Day*.[4] Even though he became friendly with gang members and residents of local housing projects, he was never "one of them." There may have been mutual respect between the two, but they never became equals. Further, one may argue that if the researcher controls the question and decides in the final instance how the subject's world is represented in text, how could the subject ever really have voice and be recognized in this process? These interviews therefore do not simply constitute "collected data," as the sociologist Lois Presser has critically pointed out, but rather form a *co*production of data. In other words, these narratives did not exist independently, but were created through the exchange between these lifers and myself.[5] In addition, in conducting these interviews it was virtually impossible to avoid my "moral self" in framing the stories of the interviewees. This is partially the reason why, throughout the book, I write in the first person. My hope is that this type of narrative, combined with the first-person narratives of the participants themselves, not only brings their voices to light but also serves as a means of understanding limitations in the data.

The differences between the interviewees as research participants and me as a researcher were also reflected in the use of language. Over four decades ago, in their study on narratives, the American sociologists Marvin Scott and Stanford Lyman already pointed out that "the every-day language of lower-class teenage gangs differs sharply from that of social workers who interview them."[6] Hence, they argued, "the usage of particular speech norms in giving an account has consequences for the speaker depending upon the relationship between the form used and the speech community into which it is introduced."[7] In other words, it is not unlikely that the lifers I talked to presented a different type of account to me—a member of an "out-group," compared to the one they might present to their "in-group." This perhaps also provides an explanation for why a handful of the interviewees seemed to press their "play" button as soon as we started talking. To them, I was not unique, but rather a part of that very "out-group," including parole officers, social workers, and academics, to whom the lifers presented the narrative in the form and content they deemed appropriate.

***

Studies that rely on qualitative data mostly take for granted what respondents say about their desistance from future crime as being an accurate representation of what has happened. This is not to say that, as the British criminologists Stephen Farrall and Benjamin Bowling[8] point out, interviewees are actively lying, but rather that they may attempt to make sense of their lives with rationality and intent during the interview. I therefore cross-referenced the interviewees' statements with background information consisting of newspaper accounts of the homicide, court files, and written parole board decisions. I attended several lifer hearings to get a better understanding of the parole board decision-making process.

Analyzing the Data

Even before analyzing the transcribed interviews, I tried to make sense of the wealth of information by listening, taking notes, and testing hypotheses that arose from the material. While the first interviews I conducted for this study were exploratory in nature, subsequent ones increased in depth along the way—going deeper into certain aspects of the life course and delving into lifers' perspectives on what constituted successful and unsuccessful reentry. After about forty interviews with both non-incarcerated and re-incarcerated lifers, I reached a "state of saturation," in which the interviewees did not add new themes or new topics to the already-collected information.

In analyzing the transcribed interviews, I applied content analysis techniques used in previous work.[9] Initial data analyses consisted of reading the interview transcripts several times and noting connections, associations, and preliminary interpretations. Analytic conclusions were formulated by coding. Then I categorized similar statements of experiences from data. With the aid of qualitative software,[10] I grouped these statements into categories and compared them across all transcripts to identify connections, patterns, or contradictions.

When reporting the findings, I gave all interviewees pseudonyms. Some interviewees indicated a preference for a certain name to be used; I respected this wish if it did not resemble their legal name too closely.

The Lifers

The majority of the interviewees were male (see table 3.1). Most participants were white (47%), two-fifths were black, and approximately one-tenth was Hispanic or identified with another race. Their racial distribution reflected the overall Massachusetts lifer population, which is mostly white (56%). Interviewees' ages at the time of the interview ranged from thirty-seven to seventy-five. Interviewees in both the re-incarcerated and the non-incarcerated group committed the homicide in their teens or twenties, between the late 1960s and early 1990s. The time spent in prison for the homicide was on average twenty years, with 95% confidence intervals ranging from nineteen to twenty-two years, which was somewhat lower than the national average in the range of twenty-five years.[11] For those who served two sentences for two separate homicides, such as Hakim, who served six years for one homicide and thirty-two for another homicide, I coded the time served for the first homicide. Several individuals had served time—usually a couple of months to several years—before committing the homicide. At the time of the interviews, the large majority of interviewees (N=62; 91%) were

TABLE 3.1. Demographic characteristics of interviewed lifers (N=68)

	Non-incarcerated interviewees (N=30)		Re-incarcerated interviewees (N=38)		Total (N=68)	
	N	%	N	%	N	%
Demographic characteristics						
Gender						
Male	28	93	36	95	64	94
Female	2	7	2	5	4	6
Age at offense	25.6 ± 8.8		19.9 ± 3.5		22.3 ± 6.9	
Age at time of interview	55.7 ± 9.8		53.3 ± 8.7		54.4 ± 9.2	
Race						
White	13	43	19	50	32	47
Black	13	43	15	40	28	41
Latino	3	10	3	8	6	9
Other	1	3	1	3	2	3 [a]
Life sentence characteristics						
Total years incarcerated for homicide						
≤ 15 years	11	37	5	13	16	24
16–25 years	14	47	22	58	36	53
≥ 26 years	5	17	11	29	16	24
Average sentence length	18.6 ± 7.7		21.8 ± 6.2		20.4 ± 7.1	
Age at time of first parole[1]						
≤ 35	4	14	8	21	12	18
36–45	14	48	19	50	33	49
≥ 51	11	38	11	29	22	33
Average age at parole	44.4 ± 11.6		41.7 ± 6.7		42.9 ± 9.2	

1. For one person, the age at first parole was unknown.

on lifetime parole. It should be noted that of the non-incarcerated interviewees, four had their cases overturned and two "wrapped up" their sentence and lived in the community without being on parole.

Even though it has been argued that lifers constitute a legal group rather than a sociological group,[12] the commonalities between individuals were striking. At the outset, these similarities include sociodemographic characteristics and life sentence characteristics. They are a heterogeneous, though collective, group of individuals, whose histories leading up to the homicide were remarkably similar. Their demographic characteristics (see table 3.1) also suggest that this selected group of interviewees have much in common with first-degree lifers[13] who, because of the nature of their sentence, are not eligible for parole.

The interviewed lifers differ drastically, however, from the overall released adult prisoner population in Massachusetts in terms of their age at parole.[14] While on average, statewide, inmates serve about six years, the lifers in this study served an average of thirty years and hence were much older at time of first parole.

The Nature of Parole

The origins of parole date back to the nineteenth century, when prisoners were granted release from incarceration if they accumulated a designated number of "marks" by following institutional rules and working toward self-improvement.[15] Parole is often misunderstood, and the general public confuses it with probation. Parole is similar to probation in that both refer to the supervision of an offender who lives and works in the community. Parole is different from probation, however, in that the latter is an alternative to imposing a jail sentence. Probation is ordered when the circumstances and seriousness of the crime suggest that the probationer is not a threat to society and that incarceration is not an appropriate punishment. Parole, on the other hand, is granted after an offender has served a portion of his or her prison sentence. Thus, parole differs from probation in that it is not an alternative sentence, but rather a privilege granted to some prisoners after a percentage of their sentence has been served.

In its early stages, parole was mainly viewed as a mechanism to allow inmates the opportunity to be released if they showed promise that they could rehabilitate and demonstrated a willingness to conform to society's rules.[16] Further, parole supervision was thought to provide parolees with the opportunity to receive rehabilitative services in the community. The design of the system is geared toward ensuring that parolees do not recidivate after completing their court-imposed sentence.[17]

Over time, however, parole release came under attack because critics began to see it as too lenient. These views initiated a change in the nature of parole, shifting away from providing services toward control-oriented activities.[18] To put the matter more starkly, nationwide, about one-third of all admissions to prison consist of individuals who return for technical violations such as missing appointments with a parole officer, not maintaining employment, or failing a drug test.[19] Parole figures in Massachusetts mirror these nationwide findings. The most common technical violations include a positive test for drugs or alcohol, and failing to report to a parole officer.[20] The lifers I interviewed felt that parole conditions in Massachusetts were strongly tightened following the Cinelli case in 2010 (more on that below). According to Derrick, who has been on parole for twenty-three years following his life sentence, "But now, the parole stuff has got harder. Each time a cop has got killed out there, they come down on ya. I used to see them once a year, now I'm seeing them like twice a month."

Parole officers are responsible for ensuring that parolees fulfill the terms of their contract. Most agents have the legal authority to carry and use firearms and to search places, persons, and property without a warrant and without probable cause. The search power applies to the household where a parolee is living and the place of business where a parolee is working. The ability to arrest, confine, and in some cases re-imprison a parolee for violating the conditions of the parole agreement gives parole agents a great deal of discretionary authority.[21] Historically, parole agents have played an important role in providing job assistance and family counseling, mixing authority with help. This mixture is now sometimes seen as a conflict—service versus surveillance. It has been argued that parole officers can be thought of as gun-carrying social workers. Today, parole agents seldom provide direct counseling services, but many do still orchestrate referrals to community agencies. Of course, it should be noted that the help parolees receive differs vastly, depending on the state and jurisdiction in which they are being supervised.[22]

The major responsibility of the parolee is to follow a number of conditions. Individuals on parole can violate their parole agreement by committing a new offense or by not following a technical condition. Before a parolee faces the parole board, the parole officer must make the decision to file a complaint.[23] One of the reasons for high re-incarceration rates among parolees is that most parole officers believe that technical violations, such as failure to report or attend treatment and other necessary meetings, are a precursor to criminal activity, especially as it relates to substance abuse.[24] At the same time, parole officers are tied by the supervision conditions set by the parole board, as they do not have the discretion in modifying or reducing these conditions. The process for petitioning the parole board for a change is cumbersome, lengthy, and often goes unanswered. Research shows that in the view of many Massachusetts parole officers, the recidivism rate would be lower if parolees did not pile up numerous technical violations that result from the unreasonable number of conditions tacked on to their supervision.[25] Ultimately, the parole board determines when or whether to revoke parole after a parole violation. The board maintains the responsibility for granting parole to lifers, and in the case of parole revocation hearings, deciding whether the offender should be re-institutionalized for violating the court-prescribed conditions for release.[26]

For the interviewees, parole conditions included meetings with parole officers, participating in community-based programming, reporting changes of address, not leaving the jurisdiction, submitting to drug testing, obtaining and retaining gainful employment, and of course remaining crime-free in the community.[27] If the crimes they were incarcerated for involved alcohol or drugs, they are required to attend AA or NA meetings. Parole officers typically monitor the activities of parolees in the community, perform home and work visits, schedule parolees to attend office visits, and refer those they supervise to social services.[28] Parolees are not allowed to associate with fellow ex-convicts or enter drinking establishments.[29] Some criminal justice experts argue that few parolees can meet all of the more stringent conditions and that imposing and enforcing them almost guarantees failure.[30] Since many of the specific parole conditions are nearly impossible to enforce, critics often view them as evidence that the entire parole process is a joke.[31] Joel was re-incarcerated after a friend brought a bottle of alcohol to his birthday party. When I talk to him in prison, he expresses in dismay, "Parole wants us to be too perfect. We make mistakes. Everybody makes mistakes. We should be allowed to make mistakes. [They should] help us, instead of sending us back." He has been re-incarcerated for almost three years. At his first parole board hearing, he received a five-year setback.

Several nationally representative studies,[32] as well as international studies on lifers specifically,[33] have indicated that parole is not overly effective at reducing recidivism relative to those who are not supervised upon their release from prison. But many state legislatures have become more "anticrime" in the last few decades, which has translated into both stricter requirements for granting parole and closer supervision for parolees.[34] Instead of producing conformity, coercive contact with parole officers may create greater defiance of authority.[35] Cedric expresses this defiance as follows: "After being incarcerated so long, [parolees] need someone to talk to, not to have someone talk down on them. The dialogue needs to be more open. Like 'See what we can do,' instead of talking down on them." As we will see, abiding by conditions of parole heavily influenced the day-to-day lives of these men and women after release.

The Context of Time and Place

When I set out to perform this research on the influence of long-term imprisonment, I did not think I would spend so much time talking about the politics and events of the time period in which the interviewees grew up, committed their crimes, were incarcerated, and ultimately released. But telling the stories of these men and women without considering the crucial element of time and place would have twisted their narratives and orientations to the world. In order to understand their experiences, we need to understand the broader historical and social forces shaping their lives.

In the 1970s, most interviewees were in their teens and twenties. This period was characterized by the appearance of the lower middle class that ran alongside the economic prosperity of postwar America. The Vietnam War ended in 1975 and with that, veterans returned home. In Boston, like many urban areas, LSD thrived to such an extent that interviewees referred to downtown Boston as "the combat zone": an area that organized crime, prostitutes, drug addicts, and motorcycle gangs called their work and living area. The civil rights movement of the 1960s began to fracture in the 1970s, and groups such as the Nation of Islam and the Black Panthers bloomed both inside and outside prison. Racial tensions were an everyday part of these individuals' childhood and adolescence. Hakim, an African American lifer in his sixties, grew up in this period. I talk to him in an attorney's office, where he started working as a paralegal after his release. He comes across as gentle and quiet. He is very articulate, and one conversation is simply not enough to capture his entire narrative. In one of our first talks, he sits back in his desk chair and gives an insight into his childhood years in Boston:

> Boston has a history, going back [. . .] the climate in Boston was always very racist. The playmates, the neighborhood that I lived in was multicultural: there were African Americans, there were Asians, there were Jewish, Irish, Italian, Cape Verdean, really kind of a mixed neighborhood. But one of my playmates in the third grade [was] a white female, Anne was her name. Her mother did not like me playing with her, at that time black people were called "darkies" or bad names. But her mother didn't like the idea that she was playing with the "darkies" in the neighborhood and she would reprimand her daughter when she became aware that her daughter was playing with any of us. And one day at eight years old the police came to my house, to my parents, they owned their own home. And a complaint was taken out by the mother that I had allegedly assaulted her daughter.

The police came to his house to question him, and together with his father he had to go to court. He states that as this point he lost faith in not only the police and the criminal justice system but also his father, who did not speak up against the white judge. "It was a traumatic event," he recalls, "as my father not once stood up for me." As a result of the alleged assault, he was sent to a disciplinary summer camp. When he came back, he turned away from his family and started hustling in the streets; he says, "Shoe-shining became my hustle."

Tyrone, a fifty-two-year-old African American man, is the eighth out of nine children, and the youngest boy in his family. Like many other interviewees, he describes being subjected to busing: "I was victimized by the busing[36] era. We were bused to white areas to go to a white school [. . .] [where] I had to fend for myself rather than being educated." He describes how at the white school, young black women were beaten up because of their color. He became very much aware of the role of race, and the implications of race in the larger society at that time: "When I was in seventh, eighth grade, I got attacked because I was black."

Fifty-nine-year-old Clarence is also of African American descent and has been running a nonprofit for troubled youth since his release more than twenty years ago. He spent fifteen years behind bars for his involvement in a robbery homicide. We sit on the couch in one of the rooms of his organization commonly used for family therapy. He summarizes the status quo at the time as follows: "It's a racist city, Boston, much better now than it used to be in 1975."

The racial tensions described by Hakim, Tyrone, and Clarence were not limited to the environment outside prison. Fifty-nine-year-old Brandon is an African American man, dressed in an orange shirt and wearing golden bracelets around his wrists. He has short-cut, gray hair. He has been out on parole for almost five years. I meet him in one of Span's counseling rooms, which are furnished with couches and chairs of various kinds. He leans forward from the couch and says how in prison, "You know it was a predatory environment. And you can throw the racism in there, too, because, you know, during the time of busing, and things of that nature, right. The whites ran the prison. The guards were connected with the whites, right . . . There was the racism in the prison. There was a constant fight for power. And the white dudes ran everything with the support of the white cops [guards]. There were something like, maybe two black cops at the time." Brandon was not the only one emphasizing the role of race in his experiences with the criminal justice system before, during, and after imprisonment. Forty-four-year-old Cedric, for example, grew up in South Chicago and was first arrested for "gang recruitment," about which he says, "There were basically two different groups of kids fighting." When his mother sent him to live with his grandfather in Roxbury, a poor Boston neighborhood, he became involved in what he terms "smokin', drinkin', stealing cars, robbing people, and selling drugs." At age eighteen, together with a black girl and a white man, he stabbed someone in an altercation that followed a crack deal. When he was charged with first-degree murder, he pleaded guilty to second-degree murder. He served fifteen years before being paroled and is now back in prison for violating the conditions of his parole. He says, "Something I have to cope with every day, and what I do not understand, is that there was another person involved in the crime, a white guy. He ended up doing ten years probation. But me and the girl did time. And the girl, she wrapped up, and I'm like, 'Why can't I get the same type of sentencing?'"

Places of Incarceration

Cory, who was sixty-six years old at the time of our interview, was first sent to prison in 1962, at age seventeen. We sit down to talk at a medium-security prison where he has spent a large part of his life. The worn-down sweater he wears on top of his prison jumpsuit has his first name embroidered on the chest, each letter a different color. He comes across as cognitively impaired. With his gray, uncombed hair and big eyes, he gives the impression of being a child trapped in an adult male's body. Other than being one of the oldest interviewees, he is also one of the most institutionalized. He files appeal after appeal but will probably never see the outside of prison again. This does not diminish his naïve outlook on the future. In some way, he takes pride in being one of the inmates with the lowest inmate number, indicating the long time he has spent in the Massachusetts prison system. In our conversation, he looks back on the growing prison population over time. Back in the early 1960s, he says, "The state only had two prisons to put the men at the time—Walpole and Norfolk prison with about two hundred men and each had his own room to himself. Not like today with fifteen hundred men in one place doing nothing to get out." Most interviewees were incarcerated in the 1970s and 1980s and cycled through the system, moving from maximum-security facilities such as Walpole State Prison to medium-security prisons, and eventually to minimum-security prisons such as Bay State Prison before being transferred to prerelease housing.

It is important to note that the "supermax" prison is different from prisons designed as maximum security. Inmates in supermax prisons are incarcerated by themselves, in single-cell confinement for twenty-three hours per day with few or no privileges, services, or opportunities for participating in programming.[37] Maximum-security prisons, however, have generally allowed movement, inmate interaction, and work opportunities.

Virtually all interviewed men started their prison "career" in Walpole State Prison. Some were moved to a medium-security setting shortly thereafter, such as Thanh, a fifty-year-old immigrant from Cambodia, who recalls, "I went to Walpole for a year for classification, and they classified me to Norfolk. Now, when I went to Norfolk, they had a big community there. [. . .] I saw the volunteers, and I met them and they helped me a lot how to change my life." Others, such as Frank, a sixty-one-year-old native Bostonian, spent their entire incarceration in a maximum-security facility: "When I was in Concord, I was involved in so many fights with guards and riots that I ended up going to Bridgewater. When I was in Bridgewater, it was the same thing, I did the same thing and then [they sent me] back to Walpole. They would just always move me around. I was a handful back then." Since there is only one prison in Massachusetts for women, all female interviewees spent their entire prison career in Massachusetts Correctional Institution–Framingham. Women's facilities such as Framingham are different from men's in that they are more likely to offer parenting programs and groups that discuss surviving child abuse and domestic violence. Also, there is generally a lower rate of serious violence within women's prisons compared to men's.[38]

In line with international developments, two notable changes occurred in prison culture over time, including in the Massachusetts prisons where the lifers served their sentences.[39] The first concerned the importation of a more overt and violent "street life" and culture, as well as a sharper sense of the injustices of social exclusion and penal politics. A second development, as prison researchers Alison Liebling and Helen Arnold point out, included political aversion to "pampering long-term prisoners." In practice, this meant that some of the activities and sense-making opportunities for prisoners facing long sentences gradually disappeared.[40]

WALPOLE STATE PRISON

Soon after its opening in 1956, Walpole State Prison was quickly filled with young men who had spent their adolescence in the state's juvenile detention centers.[41] Walpole was geographically remote and phone calls were not allowed. Walpole State Prison was hidden behind twenty-foot walls topped with eight guard towers, and it housed ten cell blocks with forty cells each. Every cell block had an observation deck and was separated from the rest of the prison. Two blocks, known as "Nine Block" and "Ten Block," were designed as segregation units. Within them there were four isolation cells aptly called "blue rooms," as the floor was covered with blue tiles; the cells had no windows to the outdoors and only a hole in the floor as a toilet. These blue rooms, interviewees described, largely functioned as disciplining rooms. The effects of solitary confinement on prisoners residing in these units, such as hallucinations, amnesia, and paranoia, have been well documented by the psychiatrist Stuart Grassian.[42] After the first couple of interviews, the word "Walpole" soon became synonymous with "extreme violence." One of the first lifers I talked to was Derrick, a sixty-five-year-old lifer who came to Walpole at age eighteen and describes how in Walpole his friend died in front of him: "He got stabbed right in the heart. [. . .] When I'm shaving and getting ready for a visit, and I'm looking in and I see him killed right outside of my cell, and I knew as soon as I got up there, I could hear the gurgle, I knew he was dying. I knew there was no way he was going to live." His friend was killed in retribution over drugs, Derrick describes, "prison stuff: that one little pill is what your life is worth."

In addition to Walpole being an exceptionally violent prison, according to research describing this period in penal history it was common practice in Walpole and other state prisons to keep prisoners heavily sedated.[43] Interviewees related that their access to necessary medical treatment was virtually nonexistent. There were no written rules; guards acted with impunity, deciding policy and punishment arbitrarily. It should be noted that—as both human rights organizations and social scientists point out—such guard brutality is not unique, and continues to occur in today's prisons.[44] Men who spent part of their sentence in Walpole described that beatings were a regular part of prison life. Frank is one of them. He describes Walpole in the late 1960s as "a place, that started out as a room where they keep the broken toys and the broken toys cannot mend themselves, they cannot mend each other, they just get discarded." Randall, a fifty-three-year-old African American lifer, also spent a considerable portion of his thirty-two-year sentence in Walpole. He is tall and has a muscular build. He comes across as respectable, intelligent, and well spoken. His first encounter with Walpole occurred at age nineteen after committing a homicide together with a friend. At that time, he was deeply involved in the street life, using drugs and stealing. "If I had not been arrested for the homicide, it could have been something else," he summarizes. When entering Walpole, it was, he says, "a traumatizing experience. [. . .] There were a lot of racial tensions [. . .] and also, the conditions that you are forced to live in there were just awful: trash, feces everywhere. [. . .] There was a fear of dying at any time. [You had to] be strong or you die." Victor, a sixty-four-year-old Italian American who started a sober house after his release, has a similar recollection of Walpole State Prison. He was twenty-nine years old when he committed a homicide at the height of his addiction and was sent to Walpole in the mid-1970s. "There was literally just shit flowing. And piss. There's nothing to block it out. You gotta sleep like that, live like that. It's gross."

What further characterized the atmosphere at Walpole State Prison at this time was the antagonistic relationship between prisoners and guards. Victor further describes how in Walpole, the prisoners had "shit fights with the guards, getting pissed on, throw it at the walls. [Then they would] flood it out. Floodin' the flats. The water would be this high [points to his knee]. Flooded with garbage [. . .] and they kept leavin' it. Heh. They had it so high one time, one of my friends lit up a tray and [. . .] on fire. And it was—you know—looking [. . .] ah it was terrible. And that went off a lot of times." As a result, the guards put on rain gear, Victor continues: "And they come in with rain gear to feed us, 'cause they didn't know what they'd get hit with. And they had rain hats, rain jackets, rain pants [laughs]. Rain boots." For many prisoners, the existence of "us" (prisoners) and "them" (correctional officers, or "screws") was a starting point in their conception of prison life. There were exceptions to this rule, however. Victor recalled how one of the correctional officers at Walpole made his life easier on the inside. One day, he says:

> I'm layin' down half asleep and I hear, "Victor! Victor!" and I look up and I said, "Well, who's that?" and he says, "It's me—Chucky!" It was a screw but I used to play Little League with him! He was from East Boston where I came from. And I said, "Chucky!" I said, "What are you doin' here?" and he says, "I work here," and he says, "I'm so sorry! What happened?" and he says, "You know, you need anything I can help you with?" and well you know I said, "OK," I said, "I'm all right." And uh that was nice.

Some other prisoners may have recognized the existence of good correctional officers, but in the end the officers were considered all bad, for they were simply on the wrong side of the bars—a finding also reported in other studies on the experience of incarceration.[45] Donald, a white-haired, heavy-set seventy-year-old Italian American, illustrates the prisoner-guard dynamic with one of his many jokes: "Did you hear about this great [correctional officer], a real good guy? He died." Despite being on the street for seven consecutive years, he still expressed a deep-rooted hatred for correctional officers. This could be traced to his time in solitary confinement:

> Every time you leave the cell they come in your cell and turn it over. I mean, they wreck your cell. [. . .] They're mixing up my legal papers. So when I get in there, all my legal papers are all mixed up. I mean, you talkin' a couple of weeks to unravel the whole thing. Footprints on my sheets, on the floor. Also, the food comes in a container with a cover. They put it in a microwave oven. They take the cover off, they give you the container. Sugar, salt, pepper are soakin' wet 'cause of the microwave. You have to put it on your desk and dry it out. The next day, you take the wet stuff, put it up there, you take the dry stuff, and you use it. They come in, they take that. Contraband. There's all these micro-aggressions that are attacking you, aight. And it's getting you in here. I had fantasized cutting guards' heads off. And throwing it down the corridor. [. . .] There was one guard, a big, big guy. A devout coward. Had the door ever opened, with him and me, with no chains and shackles on, I most definitely would have, within my physical power, killed this man with my bare hands. The hate and anger was that intense.

Since his release, Donald has been doing public speaking engagements on the conditions of confinement. Because of his involvement in the prison political system, for me he proved to be a major source concerning the events that took place in Walpole State Prison.

In 1971, in the wake of the Attica uprisings and with recent examples of the civil rights and Black Power movements, prisoner groups had organized in several Massachusetts prisons to fight back against the brutal conditions. This formed part of a larger movement of opposition to cruelties of the prison system. In Walpole State Prison, inmates formed the National Prisoners Reform Association (NPRA).[46] In March 1973, after months of negotiations between the institution's administration and the NPRA, the situation came to a standstill in which the guards went on strike against the planned reform. The NPRA sought to prove that prisoners were state employees and, as such, were entitled to form a union and collectively bargain.

Figures 3.1, 3.2, and 3.3. Aftermath of the Walpole prison riot. Photos © Spencer Grant; courtesy of the Boston Public Library.

On March 15, 1973, two hundred guards walked out of Walpole prison and a state of emergency was declared. The NPRA ran the prison in the absence of the guards. The strike left prisoners and citizen observers in charge of Walpole. Under their leadership, interviewees such as Donald report, there was almost no violence. Donald hastens to add that the NPRA, of which he was a part, invited in outside observers and the media to monitor their actions. However, the governor and the public were putting pressure on the prison authorities to regain control, put guards completely back at posts, and shut down the NPRA. A task force was established that decided on a lockup and shakedown of the prison.[47]

In May 1973 the strike ended when the state police entered Walpole and removed the prisoners; they emptied the cells by throwing prisoner's belongings out onto the flats, the area in front of the tiers (see figures 3.1, 3.2, and 3.3). Those in charge of the organization, including Donald, were put in the segregation unit. Correctional officers were in charge of the prison again. The NPRA put forth a "Prisoner Bill of Rights" that laid out the minimum living standards with which Walpole prisoners could live.[48] Even though following these ill-reputed events, town residents successfully lobbied for changing the name of Massachusetts Correctional Institution–Walpole to MCI Cedar Junction, the interviewees still commonly referred to the prison and this time in history as "Walpole."

BRIDGEWATER STATE HOSPITAL

Another institution that many interviewees mentioned as characterizing the penal climate in the 1970s was Bridgewater State Hospital. They described how, at that time, prisoners who were struggling with mental health issues or were known as "troublemakers" were sent to Bridgewater for further evaluation. One of them was Kenneth, an amiable, sixty-five-year-old African American man. He was incarcerated for twenty-four years for a robbery homicide. Since he has been paroled, he has been working as a paralegal in the same office as Hakim, in downtown Boston, where I interviewed him. Articulately, with a soft voice, he describes his experience at Bridgewater:

> They were, like, beating people down. [. . .] It was, it was just a mess, we had to go to the bathroom in buckets and when you went to breakfast in the morning you had to stand in line with a bucket of waste, and you

dumped it down these slots there where you would have breakfast. The place was filthy, it was nasty, it was brutal, archaic, it was just a mess. And so [...] I got more and more outspoken against it, they put me in a hole, and I went back to court, and they asked me if I wanted to go back, and I told them, that if I had to go, I [would rather] go to the electric chair, than go back to Bridgewater. You know, I said, "I'm not going back there. I don't care what we have to do, [but] I'm not going back there."

Bridgewater State Hospital originally served as a place of confinement for "defective delinquents":[49] men who were diagnosed with mental illness and had been convicted of crime through civil court. In 1967 the grisly documentary *Titicut Follies* was released, exposing the horror of life at Bridgewater.[50] The film contains images of naked inmates being tortured by guards, being confined to bare, unlit cells that were periodically hosed down, and being force-fed.[51] The Department of Corrections responded to the public pressure that followed the movie release by closing the "defective delinquent" section, and opening a segregation unit to collect what interviewees referred to as the "worst of the worst" across the Massachusetts prison system. This included inmates such as Donald, who were involved in political organizing. They were held in cells in which a pot served as a toilet. As Donald told me, the "defective delinquents" who had been the previous residents had often smeared feces and urine on the walls of the rooms. When the unit was prepared as a punitive segregation unit, rather than disinfected, the walls were simply washed and painted. He says that many of the people who lived in the wards above the segregation unit were so highly medicated they were incontinent. The building was in such despair that when it rained, feces and urine would run down the walls. Many of the prisoners, including the interviewees, became infected with hepatitis. It was not until years later that the conditions at Bridgewater State Hospital improved.

Prison Programming

Another aspect key to the context of these lifers' incarceration was the availability of prison programs. Due to increased rates of incarceration and overcrowding, inmate programming has changed significantly over the past four decades.[52] In the 1970s, programming was largely the responsibility of each institution superintendent. Due to increasingly limited resources, programming came to be largely run by inmates. Substance abuse programming was primarily volunteer-run AA and NA. Interviewees stipulated that they mostly formed their own clubs along ethnic lines. Other programs included religious organizations, veteran affairs groups, and programs geared for at-risk youth. In the 1970s, the Department of Correction operated a variety of programs that were popular with inmates, including avocations: inmates were allowed to operate their own private businesses and sell their products to staff and outside visitors. Other programs included the manufacturing of leather goods, ceramics, cabinet making, jewelry, and a variety of other products.

These programs, as elsewhere in the United States, have ceased to exist.[53] Currently, most prisons have a very limited range of program opportunities.[54] The prison researcher Hans Toch points out that most prisons have very few opportunities for involvement that can plausibly transfer or apply to post-release life in the community.[55] An exception to this observation is a recently established treatment-oriented program, the Correctional Recovery Academy, a six-month intensive residential program aimed at working towards relapse prevention and "developing the skills necessary to be a productive member in a community setting."[56] In this program, inmates participate in class five days a week. The curriculum and methodologies are based on the principles of cognitive behavioral treatment. While participating in the program, all participants are drug-tested within twenty-four hours of program admission and on a monthly basis thereafter.[57]

Throughout the 1970s and 1990s in Massachusetts, college degrees were offered to prisoners through Boston University and various community colleges. Over the years, college programming has been reduced significantly. Boston University still provides free college education for approved inmates. Other programs that have remained fairly constant over time throughout the United States include lifers' clubs and similar organizations within prisons. Many lifers' clubs are support groups in which persons with mutual interests come together to pursue common aims, such as legislative reform and the communication of members' needs to organizational hierarchies. Some long-term prisoner organizations evolved as prevention-by-outreach groups, with the principal objective of educating youth. Others have taken on a service role and serve the needs of the prison population or the surrounding community.[58] In general, however, among the lifers I interviewed, the development of correctional programs oriented around their problems, needs, or preferences has been minimal. This may be explained by the fact that criminal justice policy-makers have largely overlooked the distinctive profiles of long-termers, who are often at the bottom of the list of priorities.[59] First, because of the serious offenses that have led to their long sentences, these men and women are often regarded as less-than-ideal candidates for intervention programs. The public is not particularly optimistic about the potential for change among these prisoners. Second, because correctional resources are often scarce, priority tends to be granted to prisoners who are approaching release.[60]

Perhaps the most well-known exception of the general lack of programming for long-termers is the furlough program, which had its heyday in the 1970s. Furloughs are authorized, unescorted leaves from prison granted for specific purposes and for designated periods, usually twenty-four or seventy-two hours, although they can be as long as several weeks or as short as a few hours. Throughout the 1970s and 1980s, inmates serving life sentences were eligible for furloughs in the community. Once approved, an inmate could receive up to fourteen furlough days a year and could participate in furloughs that were several days in length. Furlough was designed to give the inmate a chance to acclimate to the free world and develop work and social relationships that would aid the release process.

In my interview with Jeffrey, we extensively talk about the furlough program. Jeffrey is a Vietnam veteran in his sixties who wears a leather motorcycle waistcoat. He is well connected with other lifers involved in motorcycle clubs around Massachusetts. Jeffrey has been paroled and re-paroled several times. His parole violations were mostly due to his drinking habits, including drinking and driving. He committed a homicide in the late 1960s, when he was in his early twenties. He did time in Walpole, Bridgewater, and several medium-security facilities around Massachusetts when the furlough program was used throughout the prison system. We sit down to talk in one of Span's counseling rooms, where he talks at length about the nature of the program: "And so we started doing things, and you go out on a furlough or you have seven days a year, but you can go out three times in a six-day period, and on the second day and the second time you can go out on a four-day if you had that fourth day left over. Provided you had no disciplinary reports or you know you did the right thing. And it gave you some incentive to do the right thing." For Aaron, a sixty-six-year-old African American man, the furlough program was a life-changing experience. Aaron stands apart from the other interviewees in that he had his case overturned after having been confined for thirty-seven years. Unlike other men and women I talked to, he had never been on parole. After his release two years ago, he started working as a paralegal, just as others such as Hakim and Kenneth. Sitting down in a local coffee shop, together with his wife, he describes how his furlough program entailed taking care of severely disabled individuals who needed constant physical care. "It was a job," he said. "For the first time, it became a job. [. . .] I loved it! And I never really held a job or worked like that. It was good." He adds, "It changed my whole life. [. . .] Because when I went in, I didn't really have any values. I was just doing time. I didn't realize that life didn't really hit me until I was in minimum [security], until I started working with people that weren't able to eat, and just . . ." He pauses, and takes a deep breath. He became very attached to the people for whom he cared. They did not know he was in prison, nor did many of his coworkers. For Aaron, the furlough program had a positive influence in many ways. He and his wife first met at his workplace. Asking him what he thinks about the effect of the furlough program, he tells me, "The guys who went through the program stayed out. I think every one should've went through that program. Every lifer that was [. . .] phased out of the system should've went through that program." Furloughs were used extensively throughout the United States between 1950 and 1975, but were hit hard by an increasingly punitive penal climate[61] and the Horton and Cinelli cases, which will be discussed below.[62]

Horton and Cinelli

In the time when these interviewees served their sentences or were on parole, two tragic events heavily affected their lives: the cases of Willie Horton and Dominic Cinelli.

Willie Horton was convicted of the murder of a gas station attendant and sentenced to life without the possibility of parole. In the late 1980s he was released from prison under a Massachusetts's weekend furlough program for prisoners. While on furlough, and outside the walls of Massachusetts Correctional Institution–Concord, Horton fled to Maryland, where nearly a year later he raped a woman and assaulted her fiancé.[63] The Willie Horton case became a political issue during the 1988 presidential campaign, in which George H. W. Bush used the infamous "Willie Horton ad," depicting his presidential opponent, Michael Dukakis (the governor of Massachusetts at the time of Horton's release), as "soft on crime."[64] Reacting to the adverse publicity given Horton's crime, the Bureau of Prisons reduced federal furloughs by half[65] and eliminated them completely in Massachusetts. This also meant that those who were already out on furlough were re-incarcerated. For those on parole, emphasis was put on punitiveness rather than rehabilitation, with stricter supervision as a result.[66] In my conversation with fifty-year-old Raymond, we discuss the Willie Horton case and what has been termed the "Hortonization" of the U.S. criminal justice system: namely, more draconian sentencing policies, particularly for people of color.[67] Raymond, an African American native Bostonian, has been incarcerated for sixteen years. He has been out on parole for seventeen years and intends to apply for termination of parole. Now he works as a counselor at a local nonprofit. We talk in his office, where pictures of his two grandchildren line the walls. He recalls how his furlough program terminated: "So after that [Willie Horton case] happened, that was a worse situation than Cinelli, lifers weren't allowed furloughs anymore. If you had a first-degree sentence you were brought back behind the walls [. . .] and for people like me doing second [degree], not only did we not get furloughs, it kinda hindered our progress throughout the system, including parole."

Almost two decades later, in 2009, Dominic Cinelli was released on parole. He had been serving three life sentences for a series of armed robberies and shooting a security guard during one of them. On December 26, 2010, while out on parole, Cinelli killed a police officer while committing a robbery at a department store. Cinelli died in the shoot-out. Subsequently, five of the seven Massachusetts Parole Board members resigned. This dynamic is not unique, as parole boards are heavily influenced by public opinion and the desire to avoid a political backlash from the release of someone convicted, for example, of a notorious violent crime.[68] Up until the time I conducted this study, the new parole board has been reluctant to grant parole to lifers, regardless of their individual circumstances. Because of the Cinelli case, interviewees in this study who were already transitioning out of the system through halfway houses and pre-release centers were brought back behind the wall.

The effects of the Horton and Cinelli cases were not limited to those in transition to the free world, but also extended to those already out on parole, as parole officers tightened their grip on their parolees. This is not unique to the state of Massachusetts, as in recent years nationwide the parole function has shifted from a service-oriented to a surveillance-oriented, control-based strategy centered on monitoring behavior, detecting violations, and enforcing the rules.[69]

Sergio, a fifty-year-old Hispanic lifer, feels that this process has affected him as well. We talk in a medium-security prison. He says he was arrested for a crime he did not commit. Even though the criminal charges were dropped, he is still incarcerated for violating his parole. During the interview he is hopeful that he will be re-paroled in his upcoming parole board hearing, but later I find out that he received a five-year setback. He summarizes the situation as follows: "They made every lifer in the state Cinelli's codefendant." Interviewees frequently referred to the Dominic Cinelli case, such as sixty-one-year-old Frank, who was hired by a plumbing company after being paroled from his twenty-two-year prison sentence. He recounts that one day:

> My parole officer says, "You have to leave the job today. You have to quit, you cannot go back." Are you kidding me? Because I am getting a career here, I am working with sober people, but he is like, "This guy has a history with the Dominic Cinelli case. He had hired Cinelli, and Cinelli quit, and six months later he shot that cop. But this was the last job that he worked at." And I tell my boss, "I cannot work here anymore." And he is like, "Are you kidding me?" And he is like, "I've never done anything wrong. I just try to help inmates." And my parole officer is like, "You are the last guy he worked with. And a lot of parole officers lost their jobs."

In the days that followed, he sent out dozens of applications and eventually found work at a large DIY store, where he still worked when we talked.

In short, the context of these interviews was shaped by unique circumstances in time and place that, in turn, were reflected in the individuals' lives. These circumstances ranged from long-term societal tendencies, including the role of racism and religion, to violent incidences having far-reaching implications such as the Horton and Cinelli cases. In the chapters that follow, my aim is to provide a closer look at these individuals' lives in the context of these events—before, during, and after their life sentence.

4

Lives Spiraling out of Control

With few exceptions, all these men and women made a false start in life. Most interviewees grew up in relatively poor neighborhoods in urban areas, mostly in or around the cities of Boston, Worchester, or Springfield (see map 4.1). They came from urban neighborhoods such as Charlestown, Roxbury, and Dorchester, characterized by a low median income per household (see map 4.1) and a high violent crime rate (see map 4.2). Interviewees from these areas served a life sentence because of their involvement in a robbery homicide, a drug-related homicide, or an alcohol-induced homicide. Interviewees who were raised in more affluent suburban areas had become involved in domestic or other argument-related homicides.

The Street Life

Perhaps not surprisingly, the vast majority showed a uniform pattern typifying their childhood: uncaring parents, poverty, bad neighborhoods, poor schools, and, for African American interviewees, racism. Many had been involved in delinquent behavior, ranging from substance abuse to drug dealing and shoplifting. For some, these behaviors evolved to robberies and car theft. A common thread among these childhood narratives was emotional or physical neglect by their parents that pushed them to the streets.

Glenn is no exception. He is a fifty-three-year-old lifer I interview in a classroom in one of the medium-security facilities. He comes across as a hardened biker and wears his graying hair in a ponytail. He was incarcerated at age eighteen for killing his sister's ex-boyfriend, joined by his brother. He served twenty-two years behind bars before being paroled. With an extended vocabulary, he tells me about his upbringing in a family of nine children: "I come from a broken family. My mother had a lot of boyfriends, I didn't really have a father figure." He describes his mother

Map 4.1. Median income in home locations for desisters and non-desisters.

as "a very sick human being. She was a monster. I mean, my sister was molested by my mother's boyfriends. She even prepped my sister when her boyfriends were coming, making her ready." At age eleven he was caught stealing: "I was in with the older kids. It went from breaking a window and being rebellious to breaking into cars and stores." Not long after, "my mother put me in foster care, she wanted to get rid of me, and then she took me back." In the years that followed, he hung out on the streets, developed a passion for motorcycles, and rarely went to school.

Miguel is a forty-year-old Hispanic lifer. We sit down to talk in the interview room in a medium-security prison. He has served eighteen years on a murder charge. Nine months prior to our interview, he received a three-year setback. When talking about his youth, he shares a narrative similar to other lifers. He talks about how "my upbringing wasn't too good. They [his mother and stepfather] used to struggle to make

Map 4.2. Violent crime rates in home locations where desisters and non-desisters reside.

ends meet. [. . .] We lived in an attic. [. . .] I didn't really have anybody to guide me or teach me how to be a man." He felt he "had to be my mother's protector" against his stepfather. When he was nine years old, he started hanging out on the streets "to escape stuff that was going on in the house. In the streets, I found love and respect, kids who cared about what I thought. [. . .] They were going through the same kinds of things I was." Some interviewees ran away from home and lived on the streets. Sixty-nine-year-old Mike cries when talking about his childhood. I interview him in a small, windowless office in prison, where he makes a depressed and hopeless impression. He hunches forward, his white hair showing bald patches. He recalls his adoptive father being away from home most of the time. His adoptive mother, he says with watery eyes, "She beat me up, a lot." About his childhood, he recalls, "I don't think I look at it too much anymore. I used to go to reform school [at age fourteen], for run-

ning away. There, the beatings continued, so that wasn't anything new."
The more people I talked to, the more familiar such a narrative of absent
fathers and abusive mothers became, irrespective of race or gender.

Russell is a forty-one-year-old lifer of Irish descent. With a small ring
beard he appears younger than his age indicates, and he looks healthy
despite the grim circumstances in the medium-security prison. He be-
gins our conversation by saying, "My mother is a severe alcoholic. My father lived in Maine and just lived his life his way." Russell finished school
in eighth grade and has been using drugs steadily from age thirteen on-
ward. In his neighborhood, he says, "the people I hung out with were
all petty criminals. Those were my role models, they taught me how to
dress, how to act. I was thirteen, fourteen, fifteen at the time. And that's
where I found acceptance. At home, my mom would be abusive with
her hands and stuff. These people, they taught me how to rob banks."
Russell was thirteen years old when he was arrested for receiving stolen
goods. Seven incidents involving the Department of Youth Services and
three psychological evaluations followed, but nothing in his behavior
changed. His criminal career progressed to car theft until, eventually, at
age sixteen, he was convicted of a robbery homicide. He describes himself at the time as "a selfish sixteen-year-old kid [. . .] all that mattered
to me in those days was hanging out with the wrong people."

Even though the reasons for becoming involved in the street life varied, none of the interviewees admitted to a deliberate choice of crime
as a career. These interviewees "slid into" their initial delinquent acts
for a variety of nonrational, often situational reasons. In hindsight, they
tried to make sense of these behaviors by presenting "failure events," in
which they attributed past criminal behavior to emotional and physical
neglect, resulting in drug and alcohol use, which in turn caused juvenile
delinquent behavior. Consider Ruben, whom I introduced in the preface
of this book. His father was killed when he was fourteen years old. After
that event, he says, "I noticed I became short-tempered, a lot of negative
energy, I was angry a lot, I started getting high a lot, you know, I had
been dibbling and dabbling in marijuana and a few other drugs, earlier,
you know, but, you know, it wasn't, you know, nothing that I could do
every day, it was nothing that I've looked at as doing something every
day. Once my father passed, you know, I started getting high on a regular
basis. Almost every day, I started getting high." For Ruben, the passing

of his father is a "failure event" that in his mind is the cause for his initial involvement in crime.

I talk to Keith, a forty-one-year-old white man in a job-preparation program. He was recently re-paroled. He talks about his involvement in a neighborhood fight that ended lethally, and attributes his lifestyle at the time to the following event:

> I guess like a significant event in my life was I was twelve, I was sitting in like the project courtyard with a couple of friends of mine, and five kids came in and beat the crap out of us. Like really bad, for no reason, and I went home crying to my mother, and she hugged me and nurtured me, and told me everything was going to be all right. Right, like any mother would do, but for me, when I went up in my room that night, somehow I equated the fact that you know, I was like a mumma's boy, somehow equated a sissy, and that was the reason why I got beat up. And I just made a determination that I would never get beat up again in my life. And I pushed away from my mother, stopped really obeying her curfews and rules, and my behavior changed.

Soon thereafter he was removed from school. He continues, "And I [. . .] met a couple of kids who all came from broken homes like myself. [. . .] So you know, we started hanging together, and you know, uh, uh, drinking more, smoking marijuana. Beating people up a lot of times for no reason, just to do it. We formed like, uh, what would be considered now like a gang in our neighborhood."

Ruben's and Keith's narratives constitute what is referred to as "sad tales"[1] or a "selected arrangements of facts that highlight an extremely dismal past, and thus "explain" the individual's present state."[2] In providing these accounts, men like Ruben and Keith employ socially approved vocabularies for mitigating and relieving responsibility. They put their lives, particularly unfavorable events such as the homicides for which they were incarcerated, in the context of a bad childhood, a bad neighborhood, and a weak social support system.[3]

Early Incarceration

For some interviewees—and those from the Boston area in particular—juvenile delinquency between the ages of thirteen and fifteen resulted in incarceration in the Lyman School for Boys or, for children over fifteen, the Shirley Industrial School.[4] In the 1950s and 1960s, the "crimes" these boys could be incarcerated for included juvenile delinquent behavior but also truancy and being a "stubborn child."

The Lyman School was a large custodial institution that could house up to 250 boys. The institutional structure was extremely regimented,[5] and interviewees stated that cruel physical punishments were a rule rather than an exception. Hakim, who is of African American descent, was first sent to Lyman, where he stayed until age fifteen and then was transferred to the Shirley Industrial School. He likened the Lyman School to a slave plantation because of its setup and the ways it made the boys "assimilate to apple pie, white, Anglo-Saxon America." He elaborates: "We were taught to walk and talk in a certain way, and it denied my own sense of self and the culture that I came from. That in itself again reinforces someone like me and the mind that I had to be rebellious. And oftentimes they would be physically abusive, assault you. There were a lot of abuses going on in these facilities. Sexual assault and abuse." Others emphasize that in reform school they acquired the tricks of the trade that they subsequently applied to the streets upon release. For seventy-year-old Donald, reform school provided him with the criminal know-how he could later apply on the outside. He was sent to reform school at age thirteen for breaking and entering into a department store, about which he says, "It was more of a kid thing; not really serious chronic behavior. In reform school, I learned how to steal a car [. . .] and to make a zip gun that would fire .22 rifle-long bullets." He summarizes: "All of the basic killers went through that [reformatory] school. And these were adults beating children. [. . .] It's unavoidable. Everybody gets beaten. You know, there's just no way out of there."

The Shirley Industrial School was meant as a reform school for boys age fifteen and over. Its goal was to steer troubled youths away from crime by giving them the skills to earn a decent living.[6] The Department of Youth Services closed down this and other reform schools in the 1970s. According to some accounts, boys at the school were punished for running away by having their ring fingers bent back and broken.[7] In one of the school's cottages, where teenagers with disciplinary problems were held, the staff made them scrub floors with toothbrushes. Other forms of punishment included being held naked in the "tombs," rooms without windows or toilets. Hakim, who went to both Lyman and Shirley, remembers the latter as follows:

> They would push you to work out in the field, to harvest in the field, and [they would] constantly use physical punishment meant to get you in line. I mean, in the morning, we would line up. [. . .] And, in this particular cottage, there was this elderly guy who was in charge of us. We had to get in line in a certain way and they had a ring of keys that they used on doors and this elderly guy would come by and would just whippin' it on us to regimentally line up the way he wanted [us] to. And I couldn't deal with him, so I assaulted them and they would call other officers and they would beat you down and put you in a solitary confinement cottage.

Hakim concludes that "Lyman School was more the ideal place to be, it was tolerable for the things that we could do. Shirley, nothing of that. You know, you just got beat down in a regiment that was not conducive for anybody."

Frank was sent to the Shirley Industrial School at age fifteen. He came from an abusive home in one of Boston's housing projects. About his time at Shirley he says, "I believe that it made life in prison less harsh, because the reform school was tough, especially for a fifteen-year-old kid. So I was very, very young at Shirley. And there were people there until they were eighteen years old. Now, if you think about people from fifteen to eighteen, that's a large discrepancy of maturity, age, size, everything else, and so I had to fight just about all the time. By the time I got to prison, prison was nothing compared to that." These early incarcerations provide the basis for what Robert Sampson and John Laub termed "cumulative continuity,"[8] or the idea that delinquency incrementally mortgages the future by generating negative consequences for the life chances of stigmatized and institutionalized youth. For example, arrest and incarceration may lead to failure in school, unemployment, and weak community bonds, in turn increasing the likelihood for adult crime.

Spiraling Marginality

"I messed around with the wrong kids. And that's what ended me up in prison," says sixty-three-year-old Carl. We start our conversation in an interview room in a medium-security prison by talking about his childhood, and how he grew up as the third of ten children. At age thirteen he got high for the first time: "First on marijuana, and then my older cousins introduced me to heroin, which led to armed robberies, which led to prison." Even though Carl's account may oversimplify causation, he is no exception when it comes to the role of drugs in his life. For most interviewees, drugs contributed to spiraling marginality. Walter describes it as follows: "I quit [school] because I got arrested for drugs. I was going to a trade school then, and if you missed class, you got behind, so I didn't go back." For other interviewees, drug use was not limited to marijuana. Sixty-one-year-old Frank, who dropped out in sixth grade, became addicted to heroin at an early age. He characterizes his childhood by physical abuse at the hands of his father, while his mother had to take care of his siblings and was not able to keep an eye on him: "When I got out of school, I was introduced to heroin. Because of a lot of things that went on in my life, you see, [. . .] [you want to] escape, we suppress a lot of stuff, and if you use a drug like heroin, there's just no more pain. It is just gone. You don't deal with this, you can't deal with this." Frank obtained money for drugs by breaking into cars and houses: "Heroin, back in the days, was cheaper. Ten dollars a bag would last you a long time. [. . .] There was no shortage of drugs, like there is now."

Melvin, a fifty-seven-year-old Caucasian lifer, presents a similar narrative. He is somewhat slow to respond, which can be attributed to a brain injury he sustained several years ago. He grew up in one of Boston's suburbs as the youngest of five children. "They all used drugs," he says. At age thirteen he was drinking alcohol regularly, and around that time he started on his mother's diet pills: "I found out that there were some amphetamines in there, they gave you a kick in the ass." He did not graduate high school, he says, because "they threw me out for being drunk all the time." His substance use progressed: "My favorite was barbiturates. And when I started using drugs, it became a mess. It started at age fifteen, sixteen, and I was just high all the time." At that time he also became involved in criminal activities: "Robbing drug stores, and robbing people to get drugs, that sort of thing."

Carl, Frank and Melvin each illustrate what the majority of interviewees told me about their childhood and adolescence, as reflected in table 4.1. Their childhoods were characterized by early signs of juvenile delinquent behavior, in many cases leading to contact with the authorities,

TABLE 4.1. History of criminal behavior and substance abuse among interviewed lifers (N=66)

	Non-incarcerated interviewees (N=28)		Re-incarcerated interviewees (N=38)		Total (N=66)[1]	
	N	%	N	%	N	%
Juvenile delinquent behavior						
No history of delinquent behavior	7	25	5	13	12	18
Delinquent behavior without system contact	5	18	11	29	16	24
Delinquent behavior with system contact (arrest)	16	57	22	58	38	58
Previous offenses						
No previous offenses	7	25	5	13	12	18
Some previous offenses (non-felonies)	5	18	6	16	11	17
Some previous offenses (felonies)	5	18	20	53	25	38
Range of previous offenses (felonies)	11	39	7	18	18	27
History of substance abuse						
	25	89	31	82	56	84

1. For two individuals, these characteristics were unknown.

including arrest and placement in reform schools. Four out of five interviewees had committed criminal offenses prior to the homicide. Nearly 38% of the interviewees had committed some felonies (N=25), and 27% (N=18) had been involved in a series of felonies. Again, prior use of substances among the interviewees was the rule rather than the exception.

Being Off-Time

Hypothetically, such bad starts in life could have been altered by life-course transitions such as becoming a parent, getting married,

TABLE 4.2. Family and employment characteristics among interviewed lifers at the time of the homicide (N=68)

	Non-incarcerated interviewees (N=30)		Re-incarcerated interviewees (N=38)		Total (N=68)	
	N	%	N	%	N	%
Living situation						
Living with intimate partner	10	33	12	32	22	33
Living with parents or other family members	5	17	14	37	19	28
Living alone, with roommate, or other	15	50	12	32	27	40
Intimate partner						
Married / in a committed relationship	12	41	18	47	30	45
Children						
	14	48	17	45	31	46
Employment						
Unemployed, not in school	16	53	21	56	37	54
Manual employment	7	23	9	24	16	24
Other employment	1	3	1	3	2	3
Other (in school, veteran)	6	20	7	18	13	19

and starting a career. Each of these events have the ability to act as turning points in a person's life, moving from a delinquent past to a non-delinquent future. Among the men and women I talked to, such events did not occur at a time when they could have had a significant impact. Rather, they became parents "off-time" relative to members of their age cohort who had never been incarcerated. The off-time occurrence of becoming a parent did not contribute to a life of conformity, but rather added to their already marginal socioeconomic status.

Mitchell, a fifty-three-year-old white man of large stature, obtained a marriage license at age fifteen. "I got my girlfriend's sister pregnant and I always take my responsibilities, you know," he explains. After his child was born, Mitchell dropped out of school. In the period that followed, he says, "All I did in those days was lifting weights, drinking, and kickboxing."

In our conversation in prison, Miguel shares a similar narrative. When he was sixteen years old, he got involved with a twenty-year-old girl and soon moved in with her. "She tried to guide me in the right way," he says, but admits he found it stressful to work a minimum-wage job and help pay the bills. Soon thereafter he went back to selling drugs. His girlfriend became pregnant with their son, but rather than abandoning a life of crime, he says, "I couldn't deal with any of that [e.g., working a minimum-wage job], so I abandoned that."

Raymond also had a child at a young age. When he was eighteen years old, he says, "I was married for a cup of coffee to my daughter's mom, four months before I went in [to prison]. And it was for, like, all of the wrong reasons, you know, I mean, I don't know how much you could love somebody at eighteen, especially amorously that way."

In the period preceding the homicide, most interviewees lived the "street life," characterized by substance abuse, hustling, and hanging out with like-minded others in their neighborhood. As reflected in table 4.2, most were (temporarily) unemployed, and made ends meet with crime and help from family and friends.

Their Crimes

Providing an Account

By design, all interviewees were convicted of a homicide. Not all of them were eager to share that part of their lives with me, and they employed strategies to avoid talking about it, using what Marvin Scott and Stanford Lyman called "mystification strategies."[9] In accounts like these, the interviewee admits that there are reasons for his actions, but he cannot tell the interviewer what they are. In its simplest sense, the interviewee would say, "It's a long story," and leaves it at that. Others referred to their attorneys or their legal documentation, or simply state, "It's all in my case file." Still others mentioned they did not wish to speak about the event because it was "such a long time ago." In such cases, I would rely on newspaper accounts and parole board documentation to get a general idea of what type of homicide they had committed.

Still, most interviewees were willing to share their account of what happened. The violent act they once committed, however, was incongruent with the way they saw themselves today. This finding is not unique. As early as 1957, Gresham Sykes and David Matza identified several linguistic devices, known as "neutralization techniques," that mitigate the guilt of criminal participation. In their original theory, Sykes and Matza discussed why juveniles experience guilt from engaging in delinquency, and how they neutralize this guilt by neutralization techniques. The most commonly used technique among the interviewed lifers was the denial of responsibility, summarized as "I didn't mean it." The guilt that accompanies having committed these crimes has the potential to produce a negative self-image. In order to maintain a perspective of oneself as "a good self," or to "save face,"[10] they must find ways to rationalize the action or neutralize the guilt associated with it.[11] Similar to other research on offenders,[12] the lifers I interviewed engaged in violence but distanced themselves from it by pointing to situations or circumstances that caused their actions.

Others attributed the lethal altercation to the victim in their crime. Consider the case of Leroy, for example, who highlights the arbitrariness of victimization: the victim could have been him. Leroy, a forty-two-year-old African American, grew up in a large family of seven children in a poor neighborhood in Boston. I talk to him in the middle of winter, in a cold prison interview room. His affect seems as cold as his surroundings, not showing any emotion or even a change in facial expression throughout our conversation. About his upbringing, he says, "My mother and father weren't really disciplinary. They were like, 'Get out of the house.' My father never used physical punishment, my mother did, so sometimes I would go to my father and tell him that my mom tried to lay her hands on me and that was that." Leroy was successful in his youth playing basketball and football. He was removed from school in the eleventh grade because of "major fight." As a result, he was not allowed to attend any Boston public high school, and hence ended up in a youth facility. When he was fifteen years old, he became involved in street life and participated in a neighborhood gang. In our interview in prison, he says that at that point in his life, "I was destructive, I had violence in me, and I had an addictive personality. I mean, I was drinking pretty much every single day and smoking weed." When he was seventeen years old he became involved in a residential shoot-out. He describes the event as one in which "several people got hurt and killed. The victim and I pulled a gun at the same time and I shot twice." He was arrested together with two codefendants, charged with second-degree murder, and incarcerated for sixteen years before being paroled.

Another interviewee employing this neutralization technique was fifty-eight-year-old Jay, who was born in the South and recalled a happy, relatively uneventful childhood, until his parents divorced and he and his brother were placed in a home. At age fifteen, influenced by peers, he began using drugs and soon thereafter stopped attending school. Together with his brother he started working at a shipyard, and in the years that followed he was convicted and incarcerated several times for breaking and entering. When he was in his late twenties, Jay tells me, "I needed to change my environment to change myself. I didn't have any concrete goals or higher aspirations. I had no respect for the law or other people's properties. I was uneducated [. . .] I had no self-discipline. I had no moral compass." He moved to Boston, where he met a girl. At that time, he "started feeling grounded." He had a girlfriend and worked for a company that gave him a steady wage. Still, at this point, he says, "I knew what I wanted but I didn't know how to take the smaller steps to get there." One night that winter they went to a bar. His girlfriend complained that the victim was assaulting her. "The alcohol spoke," he explains, which led to him "taking it outside." He went back to his car, grabbed a baseball bat, and hit and killed the victim. Jay was sentenced to second-degree murder and spent eighteen years in prison before being released on parole.

In their narrative, Leroy and Jay do not only pull in contextual factors (addictions, alcohol, etc.), but also point to the roles of the victims, whose precipitating behavior led these men to act accordingly. This is not to deny their involvement in the homicide, but rather to maintain and present the idea of a good self.

The Homicides

Contrary to the popular stereotype, these lifers are not hardened killers—their homicides were largely unpremeditated, and occurred in the context of bleak, often tragic life circumstances. The homicides could be largely divided in three types: homicides resulting from a robbery (38%) (the victims of which include store clerks, bystanders, or police officers), homicides resulting from an altercation (40%) (e.g., a fight over drugs, a bar fight, a fight at a party), domestic homicides (7%) (victims were family members), and other types of homicides (15%) (see table 4.3). There was no clear distinction in race when it came to the type of homicide in which individuals were involved. I will address these homicide types one by one. In robbery homicides, the main motive was to obtain money. These events were typically perpetrated with others, such as in the case of fifty-two-year-old Benjamin. When I talk to him at a reentry organization he seems to be doing well: his black hair is cut short, he is clean-shaven, dressed in a white shirt, khaki pants, and white shoes, and wears a diamond earring and a gold watch. After having served twenty-one years on a life sentence, he has been out on parole for ten years when I talk to him. At the time of the homicide, he lived in one of Boston's housing projects and made a living by dealing marijuana and cocaine. One night, he recalls:

> My other codefendant came around with a pistol, and we decided to go out and make some money. And so we did and the plan was to rob somebody with a gun, but, sometimes, you could have a plan and it just doesn't work out, you were just not on the same page. And, my codefendant was angry from earlier that day and so he ended up firing, shooting the victim [. . .] and that is how all that crime ended up that night. And, I say, four or five months later we ended up getting arrested when one of my codefendants turned state's evidence.

As Benjamin's case illustrates, drug-related altercations did not necessarily involve the use of drugs by the victim and/or perpetrator. Rather, these altercations arose out of drug dealings gone bad or drug territories being threatened. Consider the case of Miguel, for example. When he was twelve years old, Miguel came home one day to find his mother robbed of her drugs and money, and left seriously injured. All he wanted was vengeance. When he caught up with the robber, he says, "I beat the kid up with a bat and a pair of nunchakus and I ended up getting arrested." After his release he returned home, where his friends welcomed him like a celebrity. He adds, "From that point, I learned that to behave violently was to gain respect and recognition." In the years that followed he started selling drugs himself. He says, "I was violent, I

Table 4.3. Types of homicide among interviewed lifers (N=68)

	Non-incarcerated interviewees (N=30)		Re-incarcerated inter- viewees (N=38)		Total (N=68)	
	N	%	N	%	N	%
Type of homicide						
Robbery	12	40	14	37	26	38
Altercation	10	33	17	45	27	40
Domestic	4	13	1	3	5	7
Other	4	13	6	16	10	15

started experimenting with guns and I remember how powerful it made me feel. Having guns made me powerful. I showed it, and then I would use it." At age eighteen he became involved in a fight with a man who was selling drugs on "his" corner. The argument escalated and ended up in a shoot-out in which Miguel shot his opponent. He fled to another state but was arrested several months later.

Domestic homicides involved the killing of a family member. Thanh, for example, was convicted of killing his mother-in-law. He is a black-haired man of small posture. I got to know him through a small-scale religious reentry organization. We talk on a warm day in summer. It is his day off. He speaks fast, especially when we talk about issues related to the homicide he committed many years ago. He tells me how on the night of the event, he went to a party and came back drunk. "And I do not know how it started," he says, "but I had an argument with my wife about something and my wife was yelling." His mother-in-law was also present in the house, he continues: "I was so angry, at that time I couldn't stand the screaming and yelling anymore, and I was like, "Everybody, shut up, shut up!" And my mother-in-law, she can do that [yelling], so I was so angry that I grabbed a knife [and] stabbed her." He continues, incoherently, "And I said it and I did it, if you're not quiet, you know, and there was an altercation and I was so drunk." The victim died on her way to the hospital. Other examples of domestic homicides included child homicides and intimate partner homicides. Regarding the latter, the notion of gender is particularly pronounced, as in this type of homicide there is a blurred boundary between women's victimization and offending.[13] Of the female inmate population in the United States, a significant portion is incarcerated as a result of violence against their abusers in a defensive or retaliatory fashion.[14] Of the four women I talked to, only sixty-three-year-old Heather was serving a life sentence for killing her abuser. She is an atypical interviewee, in that she is a white, educated, woman working a white-collar job. In her office attire she makes a professional impression. I talk to her on a sunny afternoon in a university office. When first entering prison, she recalls, "Things just started to sink in, you know, I am here [in prison] to stay. But you know what? I am safe [in prison]. No one is going to beat me down, no one is, you know, try[ing] to stab me or shoot me or whatever, you know, I'm safe in here. And that's what a lot of women, when they go through domestic violence, when they go to prison, after they killed their abuser, they're safe. And that's what they think about." Holly, a forty-six-year-old, heavyset white woman, suffered abuse at the hands of her boyfriend, who also acted as her pimp. She was sentenced for killing a client who abused her during a sexual encounter. I interviewed Holly in a minimum-security facility. She simply states, "I have no empathy for men. Women are here because of the men." The other two women were convicted of their involvement in homicides committed together with men.

Homicides that did not neatly fit into the aforementioned categories included the case of Glenn, who explains, "My girlfriend's ex-boyfriend had molested her son. And she told me about this. And me and my brother, we went to her house and I had asked her to bring the guy over. And I killed him, I shot him. So, I shot a child molester." In prison, he was received as a heroic vigilante, which contributed to his justification for acting the way he did, he says.

Other homicides in this "other" category involved an interviewee who avenged his father's murder by taking the life of his father's killer; a homicide resulting from an argument at work; a homicide between fellow prostitutes; and other unique cases that could not easily be clustered. Again, despite the diversity of their crimes, what all interviewees had in common was that they were charged with and sentenced for murder.

Sentenced to Life

The overwhelming majority of the interviewees were convicted of second-degree murder, referring to homicide with malicious intent but *without* premeditation or extreme cruelty. First-degree murder includes homicide with malicious intent and with premeditation or extreme cruelty. In Massachusetts, individuals serving a life sentence for first-degree murder are not eligible for parole and hence, by design, have not been included in this study.

It was uncommon for interviewees to go to court for their crimes, as most of them took a plea bargain for second-degree murder. If they were convicted of first-degree murder, they would, after all, never see the streets again. Fifty-two-year-old Benjamin recalls how he took a plea bargain to avoid a first-degree murder conviction: "Well, my lawyer thought it was the best not to go through trial because they had a state witness. Like I said, I ended up with the second degree, well, pleading guilty to a second-degree life sentence and [I] ended up doing twenty-one years." Virgil, a forty-four-year-old man of Caribbean descent, was seventeen years old at the time he was sentenced. He spent seventeen years behind bars after killing his cousin in a mutual gunfight. He feels bitter about the plea agreement: "My lawyer misled me and my parents. I was a juvenile, and my parents weren't exactly fluent in English. He [my lawyer] told me to tell the judge to agree with everything. And, I really didn't know what was going on." Some older interviewees pleaded guilty to second-degree murder because they wanted to avoid capital punishment, which Massachusetts did not deem unconstitutional until 1982. Sixty-five-year-old Cory, for example, did not "pull the trigger" in his crime, but drove the getaway car as the crime occurred. Cory is one of the lifers with the longest time behind bars: since age seventeen, he spent the majority of his life locked up. In the early 1960s he took a plea bargain for second-degree murder: "At this time, they had the chair. We pleaded guilty to avoid the chair."

I should note that although all interviewees were selected because they had been convicted of a homicide, four interviewees had their cases overturned or their sentences commuted. Also, about half of the participants did not commit violent acts themselves, but pointed to their codefendant as the one who fired the gun or used the knife to kill the victim. This seems to be fairly representative for the national lifer population overall, as outlined by Marc Mauer and his colleagues at the Sentencing Project, who mapped the scope and nature of life sentences throughout the United States.[15] Under felony murder law, there is no requirement to prove that a person intended to commit murder or participated in a killing, only that he or she intended to commit the underlying non-homicide felony that resulted in a death.[16] This is also known as "the joint venture" theory, holding the defendant responsible for the conduct of a codefendant or any other actor. In other words, from a legal point of view, it did not matter whether or not they, in fact, pulled the trigger. They were sentenced to life in prison.

5

A Life Sentence

In the simplest sense, a study on the experience of imprisonment is about doing time. Over time, prisoners move through different stages of imprisonment. Both physical and temporal dimensions shape these stages: the type and place of confinement, phase of their sentence, and the sentence length.[1] To illustrate the experiences of confinement, let us first consider the case of Wesley.

Wesley is a heavyset, African American man. When I talk to him in a medium-security prison he is sixty-five years old. He wears two pairs of glasses: regular glasses and reading glasses; the one he is not using rests on his forehead. In the gloomy prison setting, he tells me about his life with great animosity. Wesley's childhood and adolescence resemble those of other lifers. He grew up in one of Boston's poor neighborhoods, in a family of five. At age twelve, he recalls, "I found myself having a hard time with school issues. [. . .] I started hanging out with people who were drinking and smoking marijuana and stuff." At age fourteen his behavior became increasingly problematic, at which point he says, "My parents were told that I needed to be sent to truant school, so that's where I went." It did not last for long, however, as he quit school a year later and then left home with his girlfriend, whom he married at age eighteen. In the period that followed, he slept "anywhere and every-where. [. . .] I kinda grew up in a poolroom."

He tells me how, in his late teens and early twenties, he acted as a pimp for his wife and another woman. He was dealing heroin, until "I became my own best customer." Addicted, at age twenty-one he became involved in a drug deal that resulted in a homicide. He was convicted of second-degree murder and was sent to jail: "I continued to deal drugs in jail, my wife's sister supplied me."

After being sentenced, he was incarcerated in Walpole State Prison, at a time when violence was at an all-time high. "I loved the drama," he says. "I loved the fighting. I had a desire for it, I welcomed it." After three years, he was transferred to a medium-security facility, where he was allowed to go on furlough. During these furloughs, he says, "I just got drunk for eight hours. And I went out for another furlough, and another one. I just drank, that's what I did for most of my furloughs. And I brought a lotta drugs back. That's what I continued to do: use drugs and sell drugs. I wouldn't sell it myself, 'cause I didn't want it to interfere with my furloughs, but there'd always be someone else willing to actually sell it. [. . .] I was living very well [in prison]."

Wesley was first paroled at age thirty-eight. He was re-incarcerated a few years later, for "a domestic with my wife." He has been paroled and re-paroled numerous times, usually for alcohol and drug charges: "I was doing all kinds of good stuff, but sometimes I had relapses."

When I talk to him in prison, he is involved in the Correctional Recovery Academy. He explains his motivation to become involved as follows: "I'm just sick and tired keeping going through this. I just need to make some changes. I'm a mentor now, and I'm helping other people by sharing my experiences. Because I got a lot to share."

Conditions of Confinement

The initial exposure to the process of imprisonment and prison culture is the county jail. As we have seen in the previous chapter, more than half of the interviewees (N=38; 58%) had prior experience with the criminal justice system, ranging from arrest to having done time before for other crimes—usually in county jail. This time, however, their incarceration did not end in jail, but continued for decades in state prisons.

The vast majority of interviewed lifers started their prison career in Walpole State Prison, which at the time served as a classification prison. Based on their criminal record, affiliations, conduct, and the nature of their crime they were either sent to a medium- or maximum-security facility to spend the first part of their imprisonment. In the years that followed, most interviewees "cycled" through the prison system, moving from maximum to medium to minimum security and prerelease. As we saw in chapter 3, however, there are exceptions to this rule, as not all lifers reported such a gradual transition. Consider Leroy, for example, who was imprisoned at age seventeen. He recounts that during his sixteen-year sentence, "I spent most of my time in the hole. I would fight with anybody, with other guys, with the [prison] police, with the administration, with everybody [. . .] [because] I didn't want to be there, I hated the place. I spent a lot of my time with short-timers, because of that." Leroy and others like him, who were angry and violent throughout the majority of their prison sentence, did not gradually transition through the prison system but spent the majority of their sentence in a maximum-security setting.[2] Another group that did not "cycle through" the system were the female lifers. Even though the United States penal system currently holds over 5,300 female lifers, they make up a small proportion (3.4%) of the total lifer population.[3] In many states, including Massachusetts, there is only one facility for women, requiring all classification levels to reside together in the same institution[4] and forcing family members to travel extended distances for prison visitation. In addition, while male long-term inmates may be transferred to take advantage of program opportunities or to be closer to their families, this is frequently not possible for female lifers. Because long-term female offenders will spend many years in just one prison, there are few ways to escape from personal conflicts or to find comfortable niches.[5]

Prison is an example of what the renowned American sociologist Erving Goffman called a "total institution":[6] a place of work and residence where a great number of similarly situated people, cut off from the wider community for a considerable time, together lead an enclosed, formally administered life. For a total institution to function, Goffman argued, the pre-institutional self needs to be replaced by a new institutional identity. This process is accompanied by a "series of assaults upon the self,"[7] or a "degradation ceremony,"[8] consisting of the shedding of a name and replacing it with a number; the removal of outside clothing and substituting it with a uniform; and the elimination of personal possessions. These processes together constitute the figurative killing of a previous identity, to make one's institutional self more malleable, more willing and able to conform to the rules and requirements of jail and prison life, and to do so as something less than a fully autonomous person.[9] The prison system, in short, takes the inmates' identities, as it removes their abilities to distinguish themselves.[10] The French philosopher and historian Michel Foucault even went so far to draw parallels between the prison and a machine. In his book *Discipline and Punish:*

The Birth of the Prison, he discusses the workings of the modern penitentiary, in which corporal punishment has been replaced by punishment of the soul. "Discipline is no longer simply an art of distributing bodies, of extracting time from them and accumulating it," he argued, "but of composing forces in order to obtain an efficient machine."[11] This process is expressed, Foucault holds, in the individual body becoming an element that may be placed and moved: the body as an object in the prison machine.

Prison is also an extreme environment because of its physical characteristics (such as cells, locks, and confined spaces), its sensory deprivations (deprivation of sound, color, and variety), and its restrictions on social and sexual intercourse. Moreover, as the British prison researchers Stanley Cohen and Laurie Taylor put forward based on interviews with long-term detainees, prison has a special psychological character as an authoritarian, punitive, and relatively permanent regime.[12] In prison, movement and association are intensively regulated and privacy is nonexistent.[13]

Loss of Liberty

Perhaps the best-known work on the conditions of confinement is that of Gresham Sykes, who in his *Society of Captives* described what he considered the five main "pains of imprisonment," or deprivations prisoners face upon entering prison.[14] At the time of writing, in the late 1950s, he likened the New Jersey maximum-security prison where he was conducting research to the Nazi concentration camps. Based on inmate interviews, Sykes's first deprivation entails the deprivation of liberty, which he considered as a double loss, "first, by confinement to the institution and second, by confinement within the institution."[15] In addition to isolating the prisoner from family and friends, and restricting the prisoner's movements, the loss of liberty implies that the prisoner is "never allowed to forget that, by committing a crime, he has foregone his claim to the status of a full-fledged, trusted member of society."[16] For many lifers I talked to, the deprivation of liberty reached further than confinement to the institution, as many were detained in solitary confinement at some point in their sentence, or what they termed a "prison within a prison."

For the lifers, solitary confinement referred to confinement of twenty-three to twenty-four hours a day in small cells that frequently had solid steel doors. When in solitary confinement they were under extensive surveillance and security controls; there was no ordinary social interaction with other inmates and very little programming. Even during "recreation time," inmates were by themselves in caged enclosures.[17] The isolation cell at Walpole State Prison, where many interviewed lifers spent part of their sentence, measured thirteen feet by eight feet. These cells were part of Walpole's Department Segregation Unit, which was later termed the Department Disciplinary Unit. Within each cell, a four-inch-thick concrete bed slab was attached to the wall opposite the door. A smaller slab protruding from a sidewall provided a desk. A cylindrical concrete block in the floor served as a seat. On the remaining wall were a toilet and a metal sink. Prisoners were given four sheets, four towels, a blanket, a bedroll, a toothbrush, toilet paper, a tall clear plastic cup, a bar of soap, seven white T-shirts, seven pairs of boxer shorts, seven pairs of socks, plastic slippers, a pad of paper, and a ballpoint pen. A speaker with a microphone was mounted on the door.[18] The widespread use of isolation is, almost exclusively, a phenomenon of the past twenty years. Even though as far back as 1890 the United States Supreme Court came close to declaring the punishment unconstitutional,[19] solitary confinement is still widely practiced today. It has become such an integral part of modern-day prison practices that the American sociologists Fleury-Steiner and Longazel termed it one of the new "pains of mass imprisonment"—together with containment (prisoners being treated as objects), exploitation (using prisoners for financial benefit), coercion (prisoners being forced to engage in sexual relations), and brutality (prisoners being subject to violent treatment by their captors).[20] Of these new pains of mass imprisonment, interviewees most often mentioned being subjected to solitary confinement.

Lifers were sentenced to Walpole's Department Segregation Unit for various periods of time, with some interviewees reporting spending years on end there. This unit is still in existence to this day. Many detainees are escapees or suspected gang members. Most lifers who spent time in solitary confinement, however, told me they were there because of nonviolent breaches of prison rules. A transcript Cory showed me, which listed the infractions that lead to being sent to the Department

Disciplinary Unit, supported these accounts. His infractions included being in the common area during count time, which resulted in five days in isolation. Not long before that, a pornography magazine was found in his cell, for which he was punished with ten days in isolation. He goes on to tell me that he was prescribed antianxiety medication, which he began stockpiling when he was feeling particularly anxious. As a consequence, he was given fifteen days in isolation.

Solitary confinement goes beyond ordinary loneliness. It has been well documented that without sustained social interaction, the human brain may become as impaired as one that has incurred a traumatic injury. Effects include anxiety, depression, anger, cognitive disturbances, perceptual distortions, obsessive thoughts, paranoia, and acute psychosis.[21] The psychiatrist Stewart Grassian provided clinical observations on fourteen of fifteen prisoners who brought a lawsuit against the commonwealth of Massachusetts for the conditions they experienced in solitary confinement in Walpole.[22] These observations included fantasies about revenge, fears that guards would identify weaknesses that could be exploited, and worries that they might be driven insane. Prisoners also reported symptoms such as hypersensitivity to noise, difficulties with thinking, concentration, and memory, disturbances of thought, and problems with impulse control. Donald, who spent five years and one month in solitary confinement as a result of his involvement in the Walpole uprisings, reported many of these symptoms. He remembers how in solitary confinement, "This interesting stuff happens. Uhm. The ventilator makes this noise [. . .] and if you focus on it, you can hear stuff, you can hear words and all this other stuff, and [. . .] the TV talks to you." After a few months in isolation, he also experienced visual hallucinations, seeing the colors on the walls changing. He started talking to himself, had panic attacks in which he screamed for help, and paced back and forth compulsively. He did not become fully aware of the effects of solitary confinement until he was released to general population more than five years later and could not hold a normal conversation. He explains, "What happens is, the cell door is a twenty-seven-inch-by-three-inch piece of glass. The door is about here to that wall away. All right, so when you come to my cell, this is all I see [holds hands on both sides of his face, partially obscuring cheeks]. I don't see body language, aight." Being out of the cell, he could not focus on the content of conversations he had with fellow prisoners or with his lawyer. "I never experienced anything like that," he says. "I was losing my fucking mind."

Loss of Goods

A second "pain of imprisonment," Sykes wrote, includes the deprivation of goods and services. Even though the institution supplies inmates with basic clothing, basic food, and maintenance of health, being deprived of the goods available outside prison constitutes a loss that runs deeper than a mere loss of comfort. As Sykes pointed out, "Now in modern Western culture, material possessions are so large a part of the individual's conception of himself that to be stripped of them is to be attacked at the deepest layers of personality."[23] In such a deprived situation, Glenn tells me how he adapted accordingly: "In this environment, I learned how to be dangerous. I learned how to get through the system. I learned how to be weasel. I learned to get what I needed." "What did you need?" I asked. "I needed clothing. I needed sneakers. I needed food. I needed to belong, to my peers back home. I needed to be part of that in order to survive." Depending on the security level of the prison, interviewees were allowed to have a certain number and type of possessions. Stamps, phone cards, and cigarettes were most often used in trading drugs or alcohol. Interviewees described ways in which they acquired goods they wanted, which most commonly involved marijuana or other types of drugs that typically came in via friends or friends-of-friends during prison visitation.

Loss of Relationships

In his original work, Sykes considered prison sex culture as rooted in the deprivation of heterosexual relationships, resulting in having sex with other men not only for pleasure, but also as a means to display power and control. In this line of reasoning, being "shut off from the world of women, the population of prisoners finds itself unable to employ that criterion of maleness, which looms so importantly in society at large—namely, the act of heterosexual intercourse itself. Proof of maleness, both for the self and for others, has been shifted to other groups and the display of toughness,' in the form of masculine manner-isms and the demonstration of inward stamina, now becomes a major route to manhood."[24] Recent prison research adopts a more nuanced view, taking away the dichotomy between rape and voluntary sexual encounters, and instead describing sexual acts in prison as a multifac-eted phenomenon. One of these researchers is the prison psychologist Craig Haney, best known for his work on the psychological effects of incarceration. He attributes sexual exploitation among prisoners to the fact that so many of the factors that are known to produce sexual violence in general appear in such concentrated degrees in prison set-tings, including the veneration of toughness, acceptance of aggression, restricted emotionality, lack of empathy, and distrust of others. Another explanation, he argues, revolves around sexuality: many men are con-fined in prison at an age when their sexual needs and wants are at their peak, yet there are literally no officially sanctioned outlets through which they can express or satisfy them. Ironically, Haney observes, as fear of sexual victimization increases, it leads men to act in "hypermas-culine" ways that make such aggression even more likely to occur.[25] In the prison world, according to the American psychiatrist and prison researcher Terry Kupers, "The failed or fallen man is the one who is not 'manly.'"[26] Hypermasculinity, or the exaggerated, aggressive form of masculinity, thus becomes a way to generate respect, intimidation, and material advantage.

Even though popular movies such as *The Shawshank Redemption* and jokes about "not dropping the soap in the shower" reinforce the idea that prison rape is the rule rather than the exception, research consistently debunks this common stereotype. The actual incidence of sexual victimization is relatively low. The occurrence of prison rape thus stands in contrast to the pervasive fear of victimization. Many in-terviewees reported that they had to avoid becoming the victim of what they referred to as "sexual advances" by "sexual predators," especially in the beginning of their prison sentence. Despite the arguably sensitive nature of this topic, interviewees talked about it spontaneously, in what Mark Fleisher and Jessie Krienert termed "prison rape mythology."[27] In their study, they drew on more than five hundred interviews with male and female inmates throughout American prisons. They contend that rape tales are inherent in the culture of prison and are shared by inmates, who may or may not believe them but will take precautionary measures just to be sure.

I talk about this dynamic with forty-four-year-old Cedric, who was first sent to prison in his teenage years. He tells me how in the beginning of his sentence, he armed himself to fend off aggressors: "[In prison], people got killed, they got raped. [. . .] I was young when I got in, like eighteen or so, and they think young guys are weak and you can manipulate them. But I knew a couple of people in there, like my older cousin was there, and they gave me knife, a shank, and they were like, 'This is your best friend, don't go anywhere without it.'" Other men who entered prison at a young age also referred to arming themselves against sexual advances from other men: the majority as a precaution, and very few actually as a result of such encounters.

In the interviews, two men mentioned being engaged in mutual voluntary sexual relationships while in prison. One of these men was openly gay outside prison, the other openly bisexual, and both established a long-term relationship with male partners that continued well after release. Several female lifers (of whom one was openly gay outside prison, the other only gay inside prison) admitted to having engaged in sexual relations while in prison but emphasized that these relationships were consensual.

Other than sexual frustration resulting from lack of intimate contact, the interviewees just as often referred to the loss of other (non-sexual) relationships. Over the course of their time in prison, it became increasingly difficult for them to maintain social support networks. Mailed letters are slow, and phone calls are astonishingly expensive. Visits from family and friends may be their best option for maintaining social support networks, but they are often limited. First, because of the very nature of the prisoners' sentences, friends and family move on with their lives on the outside or pass away. Second, although the majority of prisoners lived in urban areas such as Boston and Worchester, most major prisons are located in rural areas difficult to reach by public transportation. Massachusetts's isolated prisons are not unique. Data from the Bureau of Justice Statistics reveal that nationwide, more than half of prisoners live more than one hundred miles from where they lived before prison, with one out of every ten prisoners living more than five hundred miles away.[28] Given the costs of traveling, and the relatively poor backgrounds these individuals come from prior to their incarceration, their families generally cannot afford visiting prisons so far away. After waiting for hours, visitors usually meet with inmates in large multipurpose rooms, where they are closely watched and allowed little physical contact. Some interviewees, such as sixty-one-year-old Kyle, resented these circumstances to such an extent that they chose not to have others visit them. Kyle tells me how he met his wife in prison, when she came along with her friend, the wife of his fellow inmate. He says how he was surprised that she was eager to date him, a heavyset man who wears his long white hair in a ponytail, sports a long white beard, and has his arms covered in tattoos. He moved in with her and her stepson when he was paroled, but he was re-incarcerated after fourteen months. At the time of our conversation he has been denied re-parole twice. He chose to stay in touch with his wife by calling, instead of by visiting, he says with watery eyes: "I don't want her coming out here, it's so aggravating. I mean, you've seen how hard it is to get in here, right? The female [correctional officers] are lesbian, I mean some are, and they get to touch her more than I can. And they can touch me more than my wife can. And I am just not OK with that." Particularly for lifers and other inmates serving long sentences, visitation from family or friends on the outside can cause a continuous grief reaction with each visit. For these inmates, it becomes easier to do their time inside by requesting their family members not visit. This technique of compartimentalization has been reported as one way for older inmates to cope with long-term incarceration and family separation.[29] Thanh, for example, urged friends and family not to visit, because he wanted to focus on his life in prison rather than being confronted with life outside prison:

> In my life, at the time, I was just focusing on what I was doing, I didn't want to distract my mind too much, sometimes it [being confronted with outside visitors] affects you. They [his wife and daughter] came for the first two or three years, but I wrote a letter, I told my wife: if anybody loves her, cared for her, go on, because I don't want you to wait for me, I am facing an uncertain future. Fifteen [years] to life, that means the possibility I get paroled, or maybe not, maybe I spent the rest of my life in prison. And I told my wife to move on [. . .] I said, "You don't need to wait for me, you can go, you go on, you have my blessing and I will never,

I promise, I will never hold anything against that. And I'm happy for you because you had to suffer for a long period of time because of my actions." And finally my wife moved on.

Mitchell shares this experience. When he was incarcerated at age twenty-eight, he was married and had a son and a daughter. He adapted to prison life by "shutting the outside world out. No calling, no writing." Shortly after he was sentenced, he told his wife, "Go live your life while I'm in prison. You shouldn't be in prison with me. When I come out, we'll see what life looks like then."

While some of these men purposefully pushed away their intimate partners to protect them from future suffering, many men also told me they had plenty of "females" coming in to visit them, particularly early in their sentence or nearing their date of first parole. Usually, these women came in with a female friend visiting the friend's boyfriend. Oftentimes this resulted in a romantic relationship that continued post-release. This stood in stark contrast with the experience of female lifers, who did not receive intimate partner visits, let alone visits from potentially interested men. Tonya explains to me, based on her past experience in a coed prison:

One of the things that I observed during my incarceration was that men always had a lot of visitors. You know, there were women out here who would visit a man in prison, who would marry a man in prison, who will come and visit, you know women are more supportive. You know, for women in prison it was a little bit different. It was either the family supporting them and then we had a small minority who were in supportive relationships with males, but women in prison did not receive the same support as men received from women.

This vacuum of companionship, due to loneliness and isolation from loved ones, was in some cases filled by establishing intimate prison relations. While men joined gangs or other groups within prison as survival mechanisms, women tended to re-create domestic relations in "play families" or "pseudo-families." This stands in contrast to male prisons, where families actually involve biological family relationships (cousins, sons, etc.).[30] Pseudo-families in female prisons were first studied by a group of researchers in the 1960s and early 1970s.[31] The female prison culture described in these landmark studies has remained relatively stable over the decades;[32] in fact, their findings are still applicable today. Play families, organized voluntarily, are created rather than biologically determined. These families may or may not represent homosexual relationships,[33] and they endure as friendships rather than romantic liaisons.[34] Heather illustrates in a follow-up letter how in Framingham, the state's only female prison:

> There are families that develop between the inmates. Someone will take the father role, mother role, and they will "adopt" kids. The family dynamics reflect the same as when they were free. It might be an abusive relationship between the father and mother and the kids are left to choose sides or try to make things better between their "parents," real tears are shed because of this very real and natural (to them) setting. Whenever they have what they call "movement," which allows the inmates to go out into the yard, the families will come together at that time. They're not all in the same housing units so when they are able to be outside they congregate in their own groups until it's time to go back into the housing units. The way the "kids" are introduced into the family is as "this is your new sister" and no one disagrees with this process. They are accepted and if they fight with anyone of the other "siblings" the "parents" will step in. If one of the kids don't mind then it's up to the "father" to talk to that person. Some families do get along but when there are fights with an outsider they all fight together. These are families that are culturally conscious so you won't see a Latino taken in by a Caucasian family and vice versa.

It has been suggested that play families may be particularly prevalent among newly arrived inmates as a coping mechanism that helps them adjust to prison.[35] Play families were not as important for adjustment later in a female lifer's prison career. Later in their sentence, the female interviewees reported being involved in lesbian relationships, although only one interviewee reported to be gay outside the prison walls. This is in line with findings reported in other studies: lesbian relationships were perceived as attempts to reexperience a sense of closeness and intimacy.[36] Sexual relations were thus not so much regarded as a reflection of sexual preference but rather as an attempt to find emotional and physical comfort.

Insecurity

Upon entering prison, the individual prisoner has to reside with others who have a long history of violent, aggressive behavior. This constitutes the deprivation of security, which Sykes illustrated by a prisoner saying, "The worst thing about prison is, you have to live with other prisoners."[37] Living in such an environment brings about fear of victimization. Interviewees described that early in their sentence, they coped with this fear by showing themselves ready to fight, such as Scott, who was twenty-nine years old when he was convicted of second-degree murder. When I talk to him in one of Span's meeting rooms, he is fifty-two years old and has been out for four years. He still wakes up at night at every little sound, he says, just like in prison: "I always had to be careful, you never know what's coming through the door, when the door opens up in the middle of the night." He also tells me about his summer, describing how he had never been able to walk in sandals because throughout his incarceration he never took off his sneakers:

> I could not walk, I had these sandals, these massage sandals. Have you ever seen them? They've got like little, little rubbers that stick up and massage your feet. I could not even wear them, because my feet were so soft, because every day, all day you got to wear your sneakers, because you don't know [whether] there's got to be a fight or anything, do you know [what I'm] saying? So, my feet, for all those years, from all those years I was laced up, so you don't know [whether] someone was trying to start a fight, do you know what I'm saying? So my feet, so I couldn't walk on grass. The grass hurt my feet. I couldn't walk on that. It was crazy.

As time moved on, most interviewees reported getting adjusted to the prison setting, by having established contacts they could trust in times of trouble. This did not imply, however, that the prisoners could let their guard down. They were "on," day and night.

Loss of Autonomy

Finally, and arguably the most invasive pain of imprisonment, is the deprivation of autonomy: the capacity, condition, or state of acting or exerting power. Prisons are environments that limit control and deprive freedom.[38] In his work, Sykes described how the rigidity of prison life "reduce[s] the prisoner to the weak, helpless, dependent status of childhood." Prisoners steadily lose their capacity to exert power and control their destiny as they serve time in prison. Prison life is completely routinized and restricted, with few opportunities for prisoners to make decisions or exert choice in their daily routine. The prisoner's day is laid out from time of each meal, work, recreation, visits, and lockups.[39] This type of routine is followed day after day, week after week, month after month, year after year. Months or years of getting up at a certain time to certain signals, going about the day in a routine fashion, responding to certain commands, and repeating things in a similar fashion creates a deeply embedded set of automatic responses that cannot simply be "turned off" upon release. The prison researcher John Irwin and the sociologist Barbara Owen point out that years of following repetitive, restricted routines and of being regulated by an extensive and somewhat rigidly enforced body of rules steadily erodes the prisoners' sense of agency.[40]

In addition to these well-documented deprivations associated with imprisonment (fear, loss of relationships, etc.), hope and the loss of hope distinguish lifers from other inmates. In his book *Life without Parole*, Victor Hassine discusses his life sentence beginning in the early 1980s and the deprivations associated with it. He hoped that his living a life of helping others in prison and dedicating himself to prison reform would ultimately cause the parole board to consider clemency. When, after more than twenty years, he sent an appeal to the parole board, the members voted to reject it without consideration. That night, after hearing about the rejection, he checked himself into solitary confinement. In the morning his body was found, hanging by the neck.[41]

It is with these deprivations—confinement, the loss of goods, the loss of relationships, insecurity, the loss of autonomy, and, for some, the loss of hope—that prisoners must learn to cope.

Coping in Prison

It is not unusual for inmates first entering the system to have trouble adjusting to incarceration, particularly for lifers. As opposed to short-term prisoners, who typically wrap up their sentence after a few months or several years, lifers do not see the end of the tunnel once they enter the prison system. Each individual, however, copes differently with this (lack of) perspective. Consider Ray, a fifty-two-year-old, African American, balding man. He seems nervous during the interview, continuously tapping his finger on the table between us. Psychiatrists considered him mildly retarded, with an IQ of only sixty-six. In his first months of incarceration, he attempted suicide several times while awaiting trial. At that time, he says, "depression got to me, everything got to me, the waiting, my girl [. . .] I was all set to commit suicide. I had a rope around my neck. I was gonna jump and snap it and that would be the end." But the rope could not hold his weight. Neither would the shoelaces. He remained depressed for a considerable time but did not attempt suicide again.

Derrick, a sixty-five-year-old Vietnam veteran dressed in motorcycle gear, describes how he shut himself off from his environment when he first entered prison. He spent eighteen years behind bars for killing a man in a drug rip-off in the early 1970s: "I treated that like being in prison, like being in war, more or less. I conducted myself like I had been captured. So there's some of that stuff that you drift from the norm, you leave some of that reservation psychologically and you condition yourself." Derrick was not diagnosed with PTSD until years later: "Back then [. . .] PTSD wasn't even labeled. [. . .] They would put everyone as manic-depressive or schizophrenic. They didn't have it down like they do now." He adds, "Not to put sugar on it, but it's like, I liked crime, I was a psychopath at the time. I enjoyed the adrenaline at the time, but little did I know, I didn't know anything about PTSD at the time. So I was starting to do a lot of what I missed from the war business, and this military experience." Contrary to Ray, who had much trouble adapting to life behind bars, Derrick's military experience helped him, he says, in adapting to prison life. "I had that ability to go from zero to one hundred, to be in the middle of a conversation and say, 'Excuse me,' and get right into kill mode. But I could shut my emotions [. . .] and that was part of the military mindset. Detach yourself from really traumatic events and horrendous deeds to go right into being cold, ice cold."

As we saw in chapter 3, violence was the norm in prison life at the time these men did their time. Victor, like most other lifers, was first admitted to Walpole, the state's maximum-security prison. He spent a total of nineteen years behind bars. When I talk to him in Span's downtown office he has been out for sixteen years. He recalls how in Walpole, "The next things they got, you know, [. . .] they had a big shake-down. They shook down the whole prison. Barrels and barrels of rum and no visits or nothin' and they just shook down the whole joint and that's when they found pistols. . . . They found pistols; they found all kinds of stuff. Knives. Brass knuckles. Everything." Other interviewees told me similar stories, such as Brandon, who was incarcerated at twenty. He had been in reform schools since the age of thirteen, but prison, he says, was a whole different ballgame: "So you're placed in there with adults, and you know it was an entirely different environment, things were more . . . you had to be conscious of everything, how you looked at a person, how you spoke to somebody, how you conducted yourself. You know? In that type of environment, there was no playing games or anything like that. You had to be, you had to conduct yourself in a serious manner, because you were in there with grown men. And these grown men could get you." He says how prison made him "very hard and calloused. Because you have to be in order to survive. You're really either a lion or a gazelle, you know. You're a predator, or you're the prey. So it does that to you."

A small subset of interviewees reported that they experienced little or no trouble adapting to the prison environment. Victor, for example, describes how his entrance to the prison system was facilitated by people from his old neighborhood and by other lifers. He recalls the following about his first day in prison:

> V: When I went there I was down in the New Man Section and one of the guys came down and [. . .] brought me bowl of spaghetti and I ate, you know, and they said, "You be upstairs tomorrow morning— you comin' to the block with us," and I said, "OK." [. . .] It was a little crazy when I first got there it was like . . . They gave me a knife, you know they told me the rules: "Where we sit, what tables, you know any drugs, you deal with us. [. . .] Don't go to the others, you know, don't go to anybody."
>
> ML: And these were all people that you already knew from [back home]?
>
> V: I knew—I knew *of* a few of them but I just got to meet them now. You know and, uhh, we had our own little table up there. And basically, phew, that was it . . . that was like, you know [pauses].

ML: What do you mean exactly by "that was it"?

V: You know, I got comfortable. I got high. I was doin' my thing . . .

ML: Was it easy for you to obtain drugs while in prison?

V: Yeah. So we start getting the visits back and stuff starts comin' in.
And then, it's crazy like . . . you know like . . . you just get used to it.
You know, like, you get comfortable with it.

He further adapted to prison life by putting on a "murderers' mask": "You play a part and [. . .] you just let everybody know 'You don't mess with me,' you know, 'I got nothin' to lose. Doin' life so . . . I'm gonna do what I wanna do. Screw almost everybody.'" The tough attitude Victor portrays is not only a reflection of not having anything to lose, but also a result of the status these lifers had in prison. As opposed to sex offenders or "wife beaters," lifers enjoyed a special status within the prison hierarchy. Also, the acceptance associated with imprisonment, as expressed by Victor, does not mean that the inmate has become content with prison. Rather, he has become numbed to it.

Jailing, Doing Time, and Gleaning

In his classic work *The Felon,* John Irwin[42] describes the stages of a "prison career." He explores the struggles associated with each stage in the prison sentence and distinguishes three modes of adaptation to the prison environment: jailing, doing time, and gleaning. First, those who adapt to prison life by "jailing," have never acquired any commitment to the outside world. These individuals, Irwin argues, are state-raised youth for whom the prison world is the only world with which they are familiar. They are the men who seek positions of power and become prison "politicians." Donald, for example, used to be such a prisoner. Having spent the majority of his childhood and early adolescence in juvenile detention facilities, he thrived in prison as the chair of the Inmate Council.

Most interviewees, however, were "doing time." Particularly in the beginning of their sentence, "doing time" is an adaptation favored by those who still keep their commitment to the outside world and see prison as an extension of that life. Among interviewees, this included continued substance abuse and spending time "hustling" in the yard. Most interviewees described living this type of lifestyle in the early years of their confinement, such as Nathan, a forty-five-year-old, well-spoken, African American man. While he is eager to speak about his redemption and his current role in the community, he is reluctant to speak about his youth and his criminal history and refers to it only in vague terms. I meet him in his church office, where he runs a men's support group. The walls are lined with various certificates, pictures of him shaking the hands of community members, and children's drawings saying "Thank you." In somewhat therapeutic vocabulary, he says, "I would say my first three to four years was a big blur. [. . .] I did a lot of the same things that I did when I was in the streets, there was drugs coming in through different sources, so I was still smoking marijuana, I was still smoking cigarettes and still engaging in loan-sharking [. . .] all the same type of behaviors that you [adhere] to when you're in the streets."

For most men, the first years of their confinement were also characterized by acting out, as Ruben, who was convicted of murdering his girlfriend's abusive ex-boyfriend, illustrates:

> The first seven, seven and a half, almost eight years, I spent a lot of time in lockup, you know, I got into a lot of fights, I got on it with staff a lot, the administration a lot, I still stayed in school, I was still in college at the time, I still kept this job, you know, I still get programs but, but, like, I still had a lot of anger, built-up frustration, denial, I was still in denial for the murder, still in denial over the fact that I did something wrong and then it was, that was also bolstered by people around me, too, you know, when I explained the situation around my case they were like, "Yeah, man, he [the victim] deserved it! This guy was a piece of crap," you know . . .

After these first years of maladaptive behavior to the prison system, for Ruben and other men like him, misbehavior tends to diminish over time. After the first years of incarceration, which were typically spent continuing the life of the streets, the majority of interviewees adapted to prison life by looking at the potential of a future life on the outside. "The first two years are hard," says fifty-eight-year-old Andres, who served seventeen years. "After that, you get into a routine. You go work out and stuff."

After some years, most lifers tried to effect changes in their life patterns and identities, in what Irwin termed "gleaning."[43] They took the

~~first steps to bettering themselves or improving themselves through study or training.~~ Cedric, for example, was transferred from a medium-security facility back to a maximum-security facility after he had an argument with a correctional officer. At the maximum-security prison he changed his perspective on the time ahead of him: "When I was sent back [from the medium- to the maximum-security prison], I was about twenty years old, maybe twenty-one. And I had seen people leaving the prison. And I wanted to go home, too. So I started doing programs." When he initiated these programs, he says, "I left the troubles behind. I had to stay away form the knuckle-guys. [. . .] I started hanging around the older guys. And I started to see what they were doing and I wanted that, too. [. . .] I did every program they offered."

This process is not uncommon. When confronted with setbacks such as being moved to a higher security level, suicides of fellow prisoners, or the deaths of family members, many lifers made a switch from "doing time" to improving themselves through education and programming. For other men, making a switch was not preceded by an adverse event, but rather took place gradually, such as in Ruben's case:

> The transformation [to being incarcerated], for me, physically was fairly easy, mentally it was a little tough. Because my mind was still out on the outside, so I was focused on the outside and I was trying to control people and places and things, you know [. . .] I had no power over but, ways you don't know you still think that you control that, so I have that issue for a few years, you know, try to live on the outside and physically imprisoned. So once I got in line I said, "I can be in here, where my body is. I need to leave [the outside life] and I got [. . .] enrolled in school."

What Ruben, Cedric, and most other interviewees have in common is that in this process, they shied away from former friends or others who were not moving into the same direction, and sought out the company of individuals set on "doing the right thing." One of the men illustrating this dynamic is as forty-two-year-old Alan. I talk to him in a medium-security prison in the midst of winter. His thin-rimmed glasses are held together with tape; his left hand, revealing part of a tattoo, and his speech reflect the street life he was involved in prior his incarceration. He tells me, "You change when you align yourself with good people. I aligned myself with older guys." Over time, men like Nathan, Ruben, Cedric, and Alan planned their activities around long-term goals rather than seeking short-term excitements. At that point, they were not simply "doing time"; prison became their life.[44]

A Life Sentence

The lifers' perspective on imprisonment differs vastly from the experience of those serving shorter sentences. For lifers, sentenced to spend a major portion of their adult lives in prison, the mechanisms of incarceration become part of a permanent lifestyle. Imprisonment thus becomes a total life experience rather than simply an interruption in the offender's life.[45]

In line with findings reported elsewhere, until lifers are given a possible date for release they are in a state of continuous uncertainty about how long their imprisonment will last.[46] The essence of this position is that lifers are not tourists in prison; they are not just "passing through."[47]

Both male and female lifers considered themselves as separate from the younger generation of short-term prisoners. Early in their sentence, they may have disclosed personal information to other inmates, but after some time they no longer confided in other prisoners. Also, as reflected in other studies,[48] they tended to associate with older prisoners, as younger inmates served sentences that were too brief for true bonds to develop. They regarded younger generations as rude, disrespectful, and inconsiderate. Their life experiences were too different, which made it difficult for the two groups to identify with each another, as Holly illustrates: "I had to share a cell with this other woman who was crying that she was sentenced to three months and I was like, 'You cry over three months, I have years ahead of me.'"

Short- and medium-termers may be able to keep some things going while inside. Wives and friends can be maintained. Property can be looked after and jobs lined up upon release, but for lifers the prospects in each of these domains are bleak.[49] What further distinguishes the difference in coping between non-lifers and lifers is that for the latter there is no set release date. In Massachusetts, "second-degree lifers" are eligible for parole after serving fifteen years of their sentence. This does not guarantee their release after fifteen years, however. As a means to cope with this uncertainty and ambiguity, many lifers developed a "here and now" perspective. In the literature, this perspective resembles coping strategies employed by physically disabled patients.[50] What sets lifers further apart from those serving shorter sentences is both their association with those in a similar predicament and their active avoidance of "trouble" with both other prisoners and staff. This finding is not unique to the Massachusetts lifers I interviewed. The prison scholars Hans Toch and Kenneth Adams studied disciplinary records of thousands of inmates from New York State and observed that long-term prisoners consistently had lower infraction rates than did other inmates. Long-term inmates in their sample also demonstrated a more settled and mature attitude, were more accepting of their situation, and tended to view their prison activities in the context of more extended time perspectives.[51]

In terms of the associations they make, lifers hang out with other lifers. Interviewees reported seeking out other lifers from the same race and same geographical area. The Irish American Glenn, for example, says that in prison, "I've always stayed with lifers, lifers from my neighborhood, like Cambridge and Charlestown. They became my family." The Italian American Victor recalls the first time he was made aware of being part of a larger lifer community in prison: "So . . . you had to wait in line to get on the phone and he [a fellow lifer] was in charge of it and it was funny because when I was in line he says, 'You. Come up here.' And [he] made me come in front of everybody and I felt funny doin' that and I says, 'I don't wanna cut the line,' and he says, 'Who do you wanna call?' And that's what it was like, and you know, in right away you know. Ego is everything." In addition, most lifers put forward that, within the prison pyramid, they and their fellow lifers occupied the top, while sex offenders occupied the lowest strata. Derrick elaborates on this hierarchy:

> More severe than a woman abuser would be a child abuser. Or a child rapist, or what have you. Now if I'm going to get pissed off at you because you don't treat women right, how in the hell am I gonna treat you if you're bothering little kids? So if I'm gonna give you a hard time just 'cause you're bothering pretty girls, pretty women, what am I gonna do if you're violating little children? So I got my own rules here. But it's not just me, any of the old convicts you talk to will maintain that.

Being at the top of the pyramid because of the nature of their crime and the time they had ahead of them implied that lifers enjoyed more privileges, such as access to goods and services, than did other inmates, in order to maintain what they called "a comfortable life." Derrick recalls how in the first years of his sentence, "I made my own booze in prison, I got alcohol smuggled in, I was like on a high echelon as far as the hierarchy in there. I was pretty high up, so I could get things smuggled in there."

Over time, lifers became more involved in work and other structural activities, and less involved in casual socializing with other inmates—findings not unique to this Massachusetts sample, but also reported elsewhere.[52] These lifers developed strategies for making their stay as comfortable as possible. They avoided confrontation that resulted from involvement with other inmates and hence received less disciplinary records over time. Similar to findings among British prisoners,[53] the lifers I talked to were not strongly tied to other prisoners. This made them less emotionally vulnerable, and less likely to be drawn into the kinds of disputes that would jeopardize their progression within the system. One of these interviewees, forty-year-old Juan, decided early on in his seventeen-year term that he wanted to stay out of trouble at all costs. His decision was reinforced when he saw other inmates being put in "the hole":

> So [. . .] seeing that [inmates put in the hole], I was like, you know what, I don't want that to happen to me, I do not want to be here [in prison], but I have no choice, so I'm going to try to make it as easy as possible. And I went in with that mind-set and, after seeing a couple of fights and seeing things happen to people, I was like, it's not worth it. So, that's what I set for myself real early. And I think that's what helped and, you know, going through the time and not get[ting] into trouble.

The process Juan describes can be attributed to both aging and maturation. Such maturational effects are more prevalent among long-termers compared to prisoners serving shorter terms.[54] Criminological research has long demonstrated that maladaptiveness peaks at a young age and declines as people age, both inside and outside prison.[55] On the other hand, fewer infractions over time could be attributed to becoming adapted to the prison system. Edward Zamble, a research psychologist known for his work on behavior and adaptation in long-term inmates, has pointed to the role of special conditions of long-term confinement. Unlike the weak relationship between behavior and consequences that the system presents to most prisoners, misconduct really does result in tangible reductions in the quality of life for long-term prisoners. Even though a short-term prisoner may suffer punishments for misconduct, the end is always in sight, and it is possible to drift through a prison term characterized by a finite succession of days, Zamble argues. In contrast, lifers see an indefinitely long period in which they have to navigate institutional rules and bureaucracy. As a result, they began to make progress through the system, albeit slowly. ~~Lifers in general have low rates of infractions—disruptive behavior brings with it punishments that disrupt the routines lifers value.~~ By organizing their routines around avoiding trouble, lifers take charge of their lives in the precarious world of prison and thereby make their lives more secure.[56]

Even though most lifers I talked to looked for ways to keep themselves busy mentally and physically, not all lifers engaged with other inmates socially. These inmates retreated into their own worlds and avoided contact with the prison system's social network. In line with findings reported in earlier work,[57] those individuals gradually lost interest in the world outside the prison walls and focused only on their time inside. They created a niche for themselves—even though they were physically in prison, their cognitive focus was elsewhere. Kyle illustrates this dynamic. He fills the room at the maximum-security prison with his presence. In my notes, I scribble, "Oozes hostility." In our conversation, he describes how during his confinement "I didn't want people to talk to me [. . .] I just wanted to be left alone." Nothing much has changed, he says, since his last incarceration: "I talk to five out of the sixty-eight people in my block. They are mostly lifers. One guy is deaf. [. . .] I stay in my cell with the door closed. I play cards with the deaf guy. I love being alone." Prisoners like Kyle cope by what Stanley Cohen and Laurie Taylor termed "retreatism" or resignation:[58] they wanted to be left alone, by the authorities and by other prisoners.

Prison as a Home

What further sets lifers apart from the general prison population is their fear of becoming "institutionalized." Prisoners and correctional staff use this term to describe a process involving the loss of interest in the out-side world, viewing prison as home, and, in general, defining oneself totally within the institutional context.[59] Institutionalization is more likely to arise when inmates' needs are ignored or squelched in institu-tions.[60] Perhaps the most all-encompassing aspect of institutionalization is the loss of the ability to make independent decisions. When you are in prison, you don't make decisions for yourself. Prison gives the state almost total power over the prisoners, or as the French legal scholar Charles Lucas eloquently wrote:

> In prison, the government may dispose of the liberty of the person. [...] He may regulate the time of waking and sleeping, of activity and rest, the number and duration of meals, the quality and ration of food, the nature and product of labor, the time or prayer, the use of speech and even, so to speak, that of thought, that education which, in the short, simple jour-neys from refectory to workshop, from workshop to the cell, regulates the movements of the body, and even in moments of rest, determines the use of time, the time-table [...], which, in short, takes possession of man as a whole, of all the physical and moral faculties that are in him and of the time in which he is himself.[61]

Almost two centuries later, the interviewed lifers described the very same tendency. Derrick summarizes this process as follows: "That's the thing about prison in general, is that sort of helplessness, when some-body else is in control of your life." The fact that all inmates were sub-jected to this removal of self-efficacy does not mean all of them coped in similar ways. Typically, in the early years of confinement, interviewees protected their sense of self—knowingly or unknowingly—by refusing to cooperate with prison rules, trying to escape, and seeking confronta-tion with both other prisoners and staff. Most interviewees gave up this strategy after a while. Others, such as Cedric, were conscious of keep-ing their sense of control, and thereby their sense of self, throughout their incarceration. Cedric spent fifteen years in prison for stabbing a drug dealer. I interviewed him in prison, after he was re-incarcerated for a technical parole violation. When we speak, he has been back be-hind bars for over a year. He was given a three-year setback at his parole board hearing. "Have you ever been afraid of being institutionalized?"

I ask him. "I am only here physically," he replies. "Mentally, I'm on the street. I never let the [Department of Correction] take that from me. I think that's why I adjusted so easily."

It is, however, a fine line to walk between maintaining a sense of agency, or control, on one hand, and sacrificing individual willpower to be an obedient prisoner. Prisoners who strive to upset the system by exerting too much control are transferred to other institutions[62] or are deemed "unruly" and subjected to disciplinary measures,[63] including solitary confinement—as discussed above—perhaps the most frequently executed measure. In addition to navigating the conditions of their confinement, over time these lifers learned how navigate the process that could lead to being paroled. This is where we will turn next.

6

A Productive, Law-Abiding Citizen

As we have seen so far, prison did not simply act as a "deep freeze,"[1] in that offenders were immune to adaptation over the many years of confinement. When I asked them what role prison had played in their lives, a large majority of interviewees replied they had changed into a new, "improved self" in the course of their life sentence. One of these men is Frank.

I met Frank, a white, sixty-one-year-old man dressed in a crisp-looking shirt and khakis, on a sunny day in spring. Before the interview, he walked around the area where he grew up. He told me about his childhood, how his father went to prison for armed robbery. He got in trouble early in life, he says: "I just decided to quit school in sixth grade. [. . .] For many years I used the abuse and neglect as excuses to do the things I wanted to do." Delinquent behavior resulted in him being sent to Shirley Industrial School for Boys, which he describes as "pretty brutal." In the years that followed he developed a heroin addiction, for which he was committed to Bridgewater State Hospital at age seventeen, for a period of two years. After that, he says, "When I got out of Bridgewater I still kept doing the same thing and then I eventually, me and a few friends robbed store for eighty dollars and they caught me [and] by the time I went to trial the judge gave me twelve to fifteen years." He continues, "This was the kind of life that I [had] chosen and especially being illiterate, I mean I really couldn't apply for jobs and stuff. [. . .] I just procrastinated in prison all those years."

He got out after twelve years, at age thirty-two: "I did manage to move on, and met a girl, she had a five-year-old daughter, and [got] married. And I lived up [north of Boston] and I was really illiterate, I could not read or write." Several years later they had a daughter. Even though he continued to use drugs and alcohol, he was able to obtain a job. A conflict at work eventually led to him killing another man, he says: "And I ended up going back to prison for twenty-two more years. I shot somebody. And I went to prison." He recalls, somewhat emotionally, "When I was arrested for this crime, my wife stood right by me, with the kids there, in court, and then when I went to prison, I was thinking about how I grew up. And I always blamed my father, I always blamed my community where I grew up. And here I was, saying, 'I'll never be like them,' and I have become just like them. I left my two daughters and my wife by themselves to fend for themselves, and I am in prison now."

Frank spent another twenty-two years behind bars. At first his wife and daughters came to visit regularly, he says: "Almost every week, and then, I convinced her to come every two weeks because it was just too much. And then by the time the thirteenth year was there, maybe twice a month, maybe once." When he failed to make parole after fifteen years, he and his wife separated.

Faced with a number of years ahead of him before he would see the parole board again, he recalls, "I had a choice: either go back to the yard and to the blocks and hang with the guys that I used to, or follow another way [with] educational programs within the church. Counseling, and things like that, so I went into that direction." After a spiritual retreat organized by one of the religious groups in prison, he described himself as "changed." After his parole was rejected the first time, he says, "What I did was, I got involved in a couple of programs called Alternatives to Violence, Emotional Awareness, this Jericho Circle program, I just stepped it up. [. . .] And I just acquired this massive programming."

At the second parole board hearing, he tells me, "They made me file all the programs that I done, [and] at the spur of the moment, had me take out segments and apply it to my recovery. So, once they were done with that, they asked, "How is it that you come about this?" And I told them, and I said, "I never changed." And you could hear a pin drop [. . .] because you know, the only way that you could get on parole is to show that you really changed. And I told them that I didn't change because I didn't have to change. I said, "I have been trying to change for twenty years, and I never succeeded, because I realize now that the change that you were looking for came out of me, to stop pretending to be something that I wasn't. You know, I just took this mask off. I have been going around, all these years, showing everybody else someone that I wasn't. I was not a tough guy, I am none of these things. But, you know, if you have people believe that you are something that you are not, then you can go on in life. I just stopped doing that, and I just started progressing into other areas, education and spirituality." At his second parole board hearing, Frank was granted parole.

His time on the streets, however, did not last for long. After two months he was arrested and re-incarcerated for driving under the influence. When I interviewed him on that sunny day, he had just been re-paroled for six months. He worked as a store clerk in a nearby suburb. "The future, for me is obviously, I am not going to live in an apartment by myself," he says. "A structured environment that lets you grow and not just keep you undercover for parole."

Prison as a Turning Point

Personal change did not happen overnight. In line with other studies, the initial step among the interviewed lifers was "openness to change"[2] or "orientational change"[3]: a realization that first, their criminality had been an unproductive enterprise, and second, that this situation was unlikely to change. The Irish sociologist Barry Vaughan argued that criminals' attempts to change are based on the shame involved in reviewing the past and deciding that a fundamental adjustment to criminal inclinations is required which can only be achieved by dedicating oneself to a new ideal. Other scholars have pointed to intense feelings of loss when subjects are faced with long-term imprisonment, evoking an existential moment in which someone questions his or her very existence. Cut off from their preexisting social networks and meaning systems, the self appears to be in a state of fragmentation. It is at this point that the first signs of self-change begin to emerge.[4]

At some stage, the lifers in this study realized that a life of crime was a dead end. In line with previous studies, these individuals came to the belief that there was an alternative to offending.[5] Among the interviewed lifers, both the non-incarcerated as well as the re-incarcerated groups expressed coming to such a realization.

An Epiphany

For some, this realization was gradual in nature, while others described it as an epiphany, or a "spiritual awakening," which typically occurred four to seven years into their life sentence, as Ruben, whom I introduced at the start of this book, illustrates:

> I went into the hole, [. . .] for about three months and my niece came up from Florida to visit me. [. . .] And she was, she had tears, I could hear the tears in her voice, I couldn't really see them, but I could feel them and hear them, she just wanted the best for me, she really looked up to me, she wanted the best for me, and she just wanted me to come home, without the same attitude that I went in with or worse. And it hit me hard, you know, coming out the hole, time to reflect on things in my life where I was going, what my possibilities were when I came back out. And at that point I made a conscious decision to really work on one change in my life, a change of mind-set, into working on my case and then work on things that would get me out on the streets.

In the period that followed, he says:

> I really focused on finding all the self-help I could get, you know, within the prison walls. I did a, I started doing anger management, I started doing therapy, I focused a little bit more on schoolwork and pretty much just stayed away from all the drama, hanging out with different people. You know, I became a loner, that is exactly what I did over the next four or five years. And in doing so, all the guys just watching, staff was watching, administration, they notice a change in me also, they also noticed how nonviolent I became. [. . .] So, within the next three years, like I said, I just focused on trying to get my mind right, and staying mentally imprisoned, but at the same time trying to learn new things [that were] happening out there, new changes.

These "epiphanies" varied widely. Miguel, for example, says, "My real change happened when my cousin was killed. [. . .] He idolized me. [. . .] He would kiss the ground I walked on. He would tell his friends, like, 'That's my cousin!' [. . .] He ended up following in my footsteps." His motivation to change was further triggered when he realized that the one who came to his cousin's help in the shootout was the brother of the man Miguel shot to death eighteen years earlier.

Still others, such as Clarence, experienced these epiphanies in a spiritual or religious context. He describes how, after realizing that he would not get out anytime soon, "It was a very, very revealing moment for me. [. . .] My sister whispered over to me and she said, [. . .] "Brother, do you believe in God now?" [. . .] And it hit me in such a way that now I'm a Christian and I believe in Jesus Christ. [. . .] It went through me like a lightening bolt, and I felt what I said when I said yes, and I meant what I said, and I went on from that moment. I believe in that moment, I was saved." Mike shares a similar experience: "I became aware of God in Walpole. I just gave up. I just felt this cloud swallowed me up." What Ruben, Miguel, Clarence, and Mike all have in common is that they came to these new insights when they felt they had hit rock bottom: in solitary confinement, faced with the death of family members, or realizing the weight of their life sentence.

Not all of those who described having experienced a cognitive transformation experienced this shift during their life sentence, but rather after being released for some time, such as Derrick:

D: I went out, and after I got out, I still was interested in crime. This time of year I got out, I was going to rob an armored car. Highly armed with a lot of people. [. . .] See that's one thing, my dearest friends in prison [. . .] they were criminals, too. Criminals who had the best reputation, respectful people. So, a lot of them people, the mafia, and other people, gangland and them, they killed my friends after they got out. Shortly after they got out, they got killed. So I can see [what the consequences would be], if I stayed in that lifestyle. Now, I'm getting ready to do an armored car [. . .] robbery. So there was some kids there just because it's Christmastime. So kids were walking by just when it's about to come down, they were like goofing on my disguise. So because there was that decimal of a possibility if the thing comes down there, they would be in the path of fire, I aborted the mission. Therefore I caused dissention among the team, we worked for months planning it. [. . .] I had two big-ass powerful weapons, but I'd be the first contact, I'd be the first one to grab them and the other people there. So there was that proximity for an accidental round, even if that guard shot the little kid. So from that point on, I never done crime. Just when I says, even if I was about to make a million dollars, that's not worth them little kids getting hurt. So from that point on I said nope.

ML: So this came after prison, not in [prison]?

D: Yeah, so what I'm saying is these people who see the light, I came out as aggressive as I went in.

Still others described experiencing a cognitive shift when they were re-incarcerated. Hakim is one of them. After spending eight years in prison for a homicide for which he denies involvement, he was brought back behind the walls for another homicide. The second time, he says:

> I got sentenced to life and I did thirty-six years. Straight. [. . .] Those thirty-six years that I did straight, I finally was able to come in to my own instead of having my own identity. I was not Malcolm X; I was not all those other things that I thought I was. It kind of, really, it took a long time, during those thirty-six years, because going to prison you have to enter your goal, you come in with a life sentence, now you have to somehow—you go off [and] your consciousness will change, and you finally get it. [. . .] The real crux was a spiritual awakening for me because I had gotten to a point I was starting to accept the fact that regardless of all the good things that I was doing, I may never come out of prison. I had to resolve, in my own mind, that [if] I never got out of prison, I was not going to go backwards in terms of how my character had been. I was grown.

What all the individuals describing a cognitive shift had in common, regardless of timing, was that once they made the decision to move away from their old lives, they described consciously distancing themselves from delinquent peers and surrounding themselves with a supportive and positive social network. Not all interviewees described this cognitive shift as a "spiritual awakening" like Hakim experienced. More frequently, they came to a point that they decided it was time for them to change their lives. Darrell shared his prison experience with me in a bus terminal. When we first met, he lived in western Massachusetts and took the bus to Boston to come talk to me. With his leather biker jacket and green Boston Celtics sweater, he did not stand apart from his fellow travelers. He was incarcerated for twenty-seven years before he was paroled. He was out on parole for three years and sent back for another six years. When we talk, he has been out for four years. Almost two years after our initial conversation, I hear that he has been re-incarcerated for using drugs and drinking. When I ask if he experienced a "spiritual awakening," he says, "I've never had a spiritual awakening, um . . . I just, I just had a change in mind-set, a change in attitude. Um, when I went to prison there were probably forty people from my hometown, so like it was almost like going home when I walked into Walpole. And I made the decision that I needed to step back from them and go off on my own direction. In my own way."

"Were they not pursuing a similar path?" I ask.

Um, no. They were pursuing a path of, of, what we would call "gangsterism." I mean, you know, they, um, they ran a loan-sharking ring and drugs, and they were involved in a lot of violence, you know. I needed to step away from that in order to make the changes that I needed to make for myself. Ah, there was no issue with that, they understood, you know . . . they just weren't ready to change, they didn't wanna change, and some of them were never getting out anyways, so it didn't make any difference. But, I had the goal, not on my own because I made friendships, but I just had to step away from, because it was the type of atmosphere [. . .] I had to back away from it, you know, and make new relationships.

New relationships were prisoners involved in education, programming, and self-improvement. These were usually older prisoners or fellow lifers. Forty-one-year-old Keith illustrates a similar dynamic: "I knew that I [. . .] had to stop repeating everything I was doing. If that had to mean push away from these [delinquent] friends, as a start, that's what I was going to do, and that's what I did. [. . .] Other inmates supported me [by saying], 'Don't listen to the negativity, keep [your] focus.'" Inmates supporting this shift acted as mentors for younger inmates. Over time, interviewees themselves became involved in inspiring others to turn their lives around and move away from the gang lifestyle that characterized their first years inside.

Vehicles for Change

The sociologist Neal Shover has described this new perspective as a "watershed" in individuals' lives. They decide—either in a "spiritual awakening" or through a gradual process—that their earlier identity and behavior are of limited value for constructing the future. Once these individuals experienced an "openness to change," a "hook for change" becomes fundamental in continuing this process.[6] For some, such as Tyrone, a fifty-two-year-old African American re-incarcerated lifer, this hook was of religious nature. I talk to Tyrone in a maximum-security prison. He is very excited to share his story. "You've got the perfect guy for this," he says at the start of our conversation. He tells me he is unique, different from the other guys. He says, "I like telling my story. I get comforted knowing that I'm possibly doing something good for someone else, someone like me." He tells me about his time inside after he committed a robbery homicide at age nineteen:

> In the first five to ten years of my incarceration I still thought little of my spirituality. But [then] my cousin who is a pastor started coming to the prison in which I reside in to support the inmate faith. [And he] sent someone to tell me to come to church and I would leave whatever activity that I was doing and attend church that Sunday morning. And after church I had the opportunity to speak with him and he begin to preach to me about the Lord and to never stop believing in God. I came to look at myself in regards to how can I go about my day in a manner [that is] peaceful and humble. The transformation was without doubt the burning of my aggressive nature. I had so much suppressed anger inside my soul and [. . .] I realized that I had so many loved ones constantly in my life pray[ing] for me. Yes, I changed for my loved ones at first, then I realized that I liked the humble [me] and I studied [. . .] to achieve my goal to change. It truly felt good to have people come up to me and say, "Man you've changed," and I rarely prayed on my knees, I always thanked God [. . .] for giving me the strength and courage to change. [. . .] The reward was so gratifying [and] I would be in my cell later that day smiling ear-to-ear know that I made someone look at me in a different light. [. . .] So I started doing AA/NA and various other groups and sharing my experience with fellow inmates. The responses I received were very rewarding.

My spirituality usually played a big part in me changing my beliefs and negative behavior. I had a reputation for being a tough guy who was very skilled at street fighting. As few people wanted to be on my bad side. And for those who got to know me, [they] were amazed that they could hear as much about my bad disposition and encounter a person who was the total opposite. [. . .] I must say that God has changed my life tremendously.

Tyrone is not the only one mentioning religion as a vehicle channeling their change. Such was the case for Thanh, who summarizes, "In [prison], a lot of good things came to me. God came to me. It doesn't matter what I have done in the past, God looks at me as a person and my future. Two or three years [after I came to prison] it was entirely different, I felt it. Closed [it], [it] was final chapter of my life." Thanh is now actively involved in a Christian reentry organization.

Similarly, Walter reports that when he was two years into his twenty-seven-year sentence, he realized he did not want to continue the life of the streets. I talked to Walter in prison, a few days before he turned sixty. He is a heavyset man who comes across as depressed and tired. He had his re-parole hearing several months ago and is eager to get an answer, although he is not hopeful about the outcome. His expectations seem justified: later, I learn that he received a three-year setback because the board found that he lacked "motivation and productivity on parole." He describes how during his twenty-seven-year sentence he became a member of the Nation of Islam, which further contributed to his initial desire to change. He describes how the Nation "is a way of life. You're submitting your will to Allah. It made me a better person. Islam helped me understand people." He continues, "You respect everything that God created. You don't pay attention to everything going on in the penitentiary. You hold yourself to a higher set of values."

Claiming to have found God behind bars can be met with considerable cynicism. Prisoners who "find religion" are thought to be putting on an act to impress parole boards or gain public sympathy. However, as Shadd Maruna and colleagues have shown,[7] becoming a convert in prison gives the experience of imprisonment purpose and meaning, empowers the largely powerless prisoner by turning him into an agent of God, provides the prisoner with a language and framework for forgiveness, and allows a sense of control over an unknown future. While for Tyrone, Thanh, and Walter religion served as a "master narrative," in which they felt God was directing their lives, for others it was not necessarily the religious element that made the difference but rather the structure it provided. This particularly accounted for men who became involved in the Nation of Islam, such as Nathan, who tells me, "The Nation of Islam always stressed discipline, and they stressed education, and they stressed change. [. . .] And they encouraged questioning everything. And that's how you learn, you question everything. [. . .] And I knew at that time, that if they ever let me out, that I would never come back to prison again. [. . .] I was changed."

Men such as Nathan utilized in-prison programs and education as mechanisms for further transformation. They emphasized that their cognitive shift was not a matter of simply aging, but the result of the hard work they put in to transform themselves. Education in many different forms was vital to interviewees, Nathan continues: "Involvement in different types of programs helped me to start looking at different aspects of myself. [. . .] The support groups, psychotherapy, self-help, helped in the sense that listening to other people's stories, particularly men who were older than me, helped me to realize how similar my . . . that my story wasn't unique." For him, it was a combination of in-prison programming and the sharing with older inmates that supported him on his road to transformation. Such a dynamic is echoed by Ron, a blond, bisexual man of medium build, who was twenty years old when he committed a homicide that resulted in him spending the next twenty-seven years behind bars. He is forty-nine years old at the time I meet him at a medium-security prison. He has an optimistic outlook, especially considering his circumstances, and considering the five-year setback he received at his most recent re-parole hearing. Ten years into his sentence he became involved in a prison program aimed at introspection, encouraged by a fellow inmate: "I wanted to change, and maybe he saw in me that I wanted it. I took the program not knowing what to take out of it," he asserts. "I really thought of myself as an awful person. I saw these other men [in the program], who showed forgiveness and I wanted that, too." He describes how the prison program taught him to be alone: "First, I lived with my parents, and then I lived with this older man, and with [someone else]. I was afraid of being alone [. . .] I took that from my mother. When my parents divorced, she did not know how to deal with being alone, and I incorporated that." He received additional cognitive behavior therapy, "to change other thoughts I had [. . .] such as 'I am dumb.' But eventually I completed all but some credits for my bachelor's degree. So I wasn't dumb, I could do this. [. . .] It takes some studying, but I can do this." For men like Ron, participation in programs gave him a vehicle for change, which in turn encouraged his identity transformation process. He participated in the program several times and noticed a cognitive shift in his attitude over time: "Each time I completed the program, I learned something else, something new."

Those who participated in furlough or work-release programs emphasized their importance as catalysts for change and preparation for release. Programs facilitate the development of what Giordano and colleagues have termed a "replacement self"[8] that may be seen as superior to, or at least more socially acceptable than, the identities previously held. Melvin, for example, became involved in an electrician's program while he was in prison. When he was in minimum security, he worked as an electrician's helper in the nearby town: "That's when positive growth really started happening for me. And it made me feel really good and it built my self-esteem, you know."

Interviewees who completed such programs emphasized that they themselves were doing the work: the programs were mere facilitators in their self-initiated change. Thanh, who has been out on parole for a number of years, describes a similar experience:

> The [reentry] program helped me, but I have to help myself. You know, just like when you read a book but you don't remember anything, you do not practice anything even if you went to a hundred programs, you would not be serious. It is not enough to read a book about recovery but thinking about partying. [. . .] The program doesn't help if people do not really have the desire, a lot of programs do not help people do the same thing. If people do not have the guts to admit [. . .] the kind of honesty to say that they were wrong and need to change and sometimes they expect everything to change. No, *I* have to change first. [emphasis in original]

In sum, prison programs in various forms constituted vehicles for change for many interviewees: they offered a blueprint for behavior and facilitated the development of an alternative view of self that was seen as fundamentally incompatible with criminal behavior.[9] Not all interviewees, however, solely pursued educational and training programs in prison as vehicles for change. For some, "doing programs" was motivated by post-release employability, to pass the time, or to increase their chances for an upcoming parole board hearing, such as forty-year-old Vincent admits: "The reason I went to programs wasn't necessarily to learn anything. It was to get out of prison." When he became involved in the programs, he says, "I bought into it [. . .] I got an opportunity to go to college in prison, I got an opportunity to read, there's . . . You can't replace that with anything and once I realized that I was able to do great things, I began doing 'em. I began starting programs, I began standing up for what I believe is right." Today he considers himself as fundamentally different from the person he was when he first went to prison.

Similarly, fifty-one-year-old Norman admits that participation in programs was not merely driven by the desire for change. With his shaven head and tattoos on his face and neck, he presents a tough appearance. He seems cold and distant at the beginning of the interview, but along the way he opens up. Asking him about participating in programs, he asserts, "I didn't just fake it to make it. I did it both for improvement for myself, and for improvement of parole." Because this is, in the end, what all interviewees strived for: being paroled. In order to do so, they had to present their case in a compelling, convincing narrative, in which the notion of personal change played a major role.

Developing a Narrative

In short, the large majority of interviewees presented new, "improved" selves that no longer cognitively or emotionally cohere with offending. This is not unique to the lifer population, as previous studies on offenders of lesser crimes reported similar narratives.[10] Maruna termed this narrative the "redemption script," with three elements at its core: the idea of a core self, generative motivations, and a sense of agency.[11] It has been argued that the presence or absence of such a narrative determines success versus failure after release. I will address these redemption elements one by one, to see to what extent this script can explain why some lifers stayed out of prison while others returned behind bars.

Core Self

First, a key element of the redemption script is the idea of a "normal," "core" self: despite what others think of the ex-offender, there "lurks within him a core of being that is normal."[12] To maintain the idea of a normal core self, Maruna holds, the ex-offender refers to his criminal past in terms of "failure events."[13] In doing so, the ex-offender uses neutralization techniques, most commonly denial[14] or diffusion of responsibility,[15] such as justifications, excuses, and other explanations for past shortcomings—typically blaming past behavior on the effects of drugs or alcohol.[16] Among the interviewees, as we saw in chapter 4, these denials and justifications were commonplace. Paradoxically, their denial of the offense is still compatible with their present idea of "having changed"—even though they denied being involved in the homicide, they acknowledged living a life characterized by crime and associated behaviors, such as forty-one-year-old Arthur, who pointed out, "It's probably a good thing I came to prison, because if I didn't, I'd probably be dead." Arthur describes himself as an "Oreo," descending from a Caribbean father and a French mother; he has a large tattoo bearing her name on his forearm. He is likeable and comes across as intelligent and well spoken. Similar to Arthur, the large majority of interviewees (both non-incarcerated as well as re-incarcerated) diffused responsibility: they presented "failure events," in which they attributed past criminal behavior to emotional and physical neglect, resulting in drug and alcohol use, which in turn resulted in juvenile delinquent behavior. As we saw in chapter 4, many attributed criminal behavior in adolescence to having weak bonds with parents. This includes forty-one-year-old Keith, who was convicted of his involvement in a gang fight that ended deadly. He indicates how "I grew up in the projects in a single-family home with my mother. I never met my father. [My family] introduced me to drugs, alcohol, and violence, at an early age. [. . .] I was drinking probably a beer, beer and a half by like eight or nine [years old]." Others attributed past criminal behavior to peer influence. Rather than making a conscious choice to become involved, they were pulled or pressured into the life of the street, as thirty-seven-year-old Ernesto discloses when I talk to him one month after he was paroled from a seventeen-year-long sentence. When I ask him with whom he associated, he leans back, takes a deep breath, and says, "Before I started hanging in the streets, I used to be an honor roll student, I used to be considered a mama's boy. I played baseball. That was like one of my favorite sports." He describes how he was reunited with his mother at age nine, after being raised by his father. When he moved in with his mother, he says:

> I met an individual who lived on the other side of the street next to me. [. . .] And I met him, and then he used to come around all the time. [. . .] And he came right through the back door. And he was like, "Do you have a plate or whatever?" And I'm like, "A plate?" He's like, "Yeah, a plate and some baggies." So I'm like, "Alright whatever," so I gave him a plate and some baggies. And he pulled out, which at the time, I didn't know what it was, but he pulled out this rock, like this rock substance. And he started cutting it on the plate. And I'm like what is that? He was like, "It's cocaine, it's crack." I'm like, "Crack?" I'm like, "What are you gonna do with that?" And the only thing I knew about crack was from *Scarface*.

This was his introduction to crack. Soon afterward, he noticed his friend had $110 sneakers "that his mom did not give him." He adds, "I asked my mom for $110 sneakers, but she was like, 'What?'" When he started selling, and started associating with his friend's friends, he alienated himself from his baseball friends. At a certain, point, he says, he could buy those sneakers. When his mother asked him about this, he would simply answer that he got them from his new friend: "My mom, she believed that, she was happy to have me around and did not ask more questions." After a while, he remembers, "things got more serious. Now it was me buying these rocks [. . .] and it's all about, let's go sell some drugs and get money."

Like Ernesto, most of the interviewees reported having been involved in the "street life" in which they used and sold drugs. However, it was clear from the interviews that their street personality involvement did not represent their "core self." It was only their behavior; it did not reflect who they really were. Even though they engaged in violent behavior, they did not consider themselves violent people. They stressed that they became involved in those activities because of environmental factors such as pressure from a group or growing up in an impoverished area where crime and drug use were rampant.

Almost all interviewees thus emphasized that this was how they *had behaved*—by the time they faced the parole board, they were different men, having shed their old, delinquent selves and transformed into the people they were supposed to be all along. The majority of men and women I talked to described how they were now different people as compared to who they were when first incarcerated. The central feature of their narratives, such as Nathan's, was the use of past tense when referring to the "old self": "If you ask some people to explain me back then [. . .] I've never done anything wrong to my friends, or my family, but if I didn't know you, I didn't care about you. It was 'I, I, I, I, I, I, I.' I had this warped sense of being that was just wrong." By using religion, by being disciplined and reading self-help books, he says, he changed his life. Nathan is an extreme example in considering himself as a project. He monitors his day-to-day behavior like a scientist would study rats. By constantly evaluating and reevaluating, he aims to write a manual to success in life: "I am hoping that I can put it into some kind of commercial product and I can sell it. So that's my hope. And hopefully that it can be something that any human being who's interested in accelerating growth and not taking twenty years to be great and you can be great in five years if you really commit yourself to it, can use it."

Even though Nathan could be regarded as being on one side of the spectrum, what he had in common with most of the interviewees was that they portrayed their former offending self as a false identity, denying that it was their "real self." This false identity runs parallel to the concept of the "feared self": an image of what the person does not want to become, or turn back to.[17] Tonya defines the contrast between her old self and new self as follows: "Ten years ago, I would say, 'Fuck everything and everybody.' [. . .] Nobody gives a fuck about me, so why the fuck should I care about anybody else?" Today, she says about herself, "I am a better person. I'm a stronger person, nothing can break me down."

Criminal justice scholars have cautioned that we should be critical concerning the mere presence or absence of the self-ascribed "personal transformation."[18] Arguably, having been able to stay out—for longer or shorter periods of time—is inextricably linked to each individual's capacity to position themselves through their narratives as heroic transgressors successfully struggling against the many hurdles of reentry. The fact that offenders face tangible incentives, such as release on parole, for portraying themselves in a particular way (say, as innocent or remorseful) reinforces the view that their stories mainly serve a remedial function.[19] From a critical point of view, along these lines, the parole board hearing and other events in which the narrative is presented thus serve as publicly validated performances through which a sense of self arises.[20]

These lifers thus presented a narrative that enabled them to reconcile discrepancy ("I used to be bad") with unity ("Now I am good") through positioning their present self as another person.[21] Because they have to face a parole board, opposed to others simply "wrapping up" their sentences, lifers in particular are called on to explain themselves and thereby to reconcile multiple selves—usually, the bad person they were with the good, responsible agent they must now be. Tyrone, for example, indicates that at the time of the homicide, "I was a hostile, confused, scared young man. [. . .] At age nineteen, I was Satan's angel. Today, at fifty-two, I'm God's child. [. . .] When I left the streets, I was a mess. But when the guys I grew up with see me, they say, 'Whoa! What a change!' They're probably still doing what they were doing back then." Here, Tyrone represents what the sociologist Lois Presser[22] terms "the paradox of the narrative": it not only reassembles events into a meaningful whole, but it also creates a distance between the narrator in the present ("God's child") and his or her life in the past ("Satan's angel"). Thus, as Presser has aptly noted, a change *to* a moral self was really a change *back* to a moral self.[23] Through his narrative, Tyrone is able to recognize his past as qualitatively different from his current self. In the eyes of these lifers, their current self is their only "true self."

Generative Motivations

A second element in the redemption script, Shadd Maruna described, includes generative activities, or the idea to "give back."[24] In the redemption script, generative motivations include a sense of fulfillment—perceiving one's existence as meaningful. Generative activities thus serve at least a dual purpose: they can provide offenders a sense of fulfillment in life, and can help clear one's conscious associated with previous criminal acts.[25]

Both non-incarcerated and re-incarcerated interviewees expressed how they were involved, or wanted to become involved, in generative activities during or after their release. These activities were mostly centered on their life stories, and how they could help others with the life lessons they learned. Clarence, who is now in charge of a reentry organization, tells me, "Who better to support a person who was incarcerated than another person who was incarcerated and has done well and can share that experience, you know? And so I've done that for several years [. . .] I go into the prison into the [. . .] County House of Correction as well as other houses of correction. [. . .] I have my own curriculum, I go there [. . .] and engage the guys. I have a group of about thirty guys that I engage." Similarly, Raymond emphasizes how helping others has shaped his identity. His appearance—he is dressed in a suit, behind a desk—stands in stark contrast with the sixteen-year sentence he served: "Um, the way I dress doesn't define who I am, you know. How I interact with you, how I perform my job, and how I help you not only get from homelessness into permanent housing, by helping you develop the skills in order to maintain it, that that defines who I am. Not this suit, not those Timberlands, and not those . . . [laughs] modestly baggy jeans."

For those who are re-incarcerated, the subject of their generative motivations typically included younger inmates. Fifty-two-year-old Joel, for example, whom I meet in a minimum-security prison, first became engaged in public speaking at schools and colleges during his twenty-seven-year confinement: "If only I could touch one kid, prevent one kid from going through what I have been through." When he was out on parole for two and a half years, he was involved in religious activities and made many friends through the local church. Now that he is back in prison for violating the conditions of his parole by having alcohol present in the house, he has been living "less like a person, and more like a Christian." When I ask him about his outlook for the future, he answers, "I want to go back to my church and help people."

Similarly, Cedric, also became involved in generative activities while in prison. He started several inmate programs to help others: "I started Relapse Prevention, Anger Management, and the Young Fathers Program. I never had a father in my life, but I wanted to be there for my kids." Others wanted to "give back" professionally, like Hakim, who studied law in prison and became a jailhouse lawyer. He says, "I became a student in legal stuff, and I was filing briefs. [. . .] I had a reputation with the lawyers that worked here, because I was always involved with [the] prisons' Legal Advice Report. I was the president. So, when inmates sue the state, I represented them against the state."

Being involved in generative activities, as was the case for Clarence, Raymond, Joel, Cedric, and Hakim, strengthens the new, conformist, and pro-social identity they assumed. These activities made them feel smart, important, and progressive. Other examples of such activities include working in the law library, joining prisoner's rights movements, and helping others, in turn, with their transformation process. Similar to findings reported elsewhere,[26] interviewees described the fulfillment they obtained from being able to contribute to a social establishment— for example, by public speaking activities or by becoming a counselor or mentor—which they had long seen as their adversary. These generative activities helped them deal with the shame and guilt of their past behavior and serves to reframe their identity: shedding their past and making way for a new, reinvented self.

Agency

A third part of the classic redemption script consists of a sense of agency, or the capability of individuals to act independently and to make their own choices within the social structure. The abovementioned examples illustrate that both groups of lifers expressed the main components of the redemption script: they reflected having a good "core self," and they were involved in generative activities. In short, those who were re-incarcerated at the time of the interview did not differ in these two aspects from those who were out on the streets. Instead, the two groups differed in terms of their sense of agency. Even though both groups were able to acquire a narrative that made them eligible for parole, they differed in terms of reflecting the possibility to exert control over their future. Agency was thus not a requirement for individuals to express "transformational power" and create a narrative of change. To gain a full understanding of the dynamics underlying "agentic," of "self-efficacious" action, and how this operated differently in the two groups of lifers, let us first consider the parole board process and the struggles these individuals faced upon release. We will return to the notion of agency in chapter 10.

Acquiring a Narrative

The finding that both non-incarcerated and re-incarcerated interviewees presented prototypical reform stories can be traced back to the role of post-prison programming that encourages therapeutic discoveries and emotional disentanglement from ex-offenders' "old" selves.[27] Hence, we find its presence among both non-incarcerated and re-incarcerated interviewees.

Another explanation for the omnipresence of these narratives can be found in lifer groups in prison, whose members help one another prepare for parole board hearings. These programs and interactions thus aid in the creation of new identities, produced through the autobiographical work these lifers engaged in for so many years. Fifteen years into their sentence, second-degree lifers are legally entitled to have their first parole board hearing. According to the Massachusetts Parole Board guidelines, the decision to parole an inmate serving a life sentence is guided by several legal standpoints. First, an inmate can only be paroled if it is reasonably probable that he will not reoffend, and his release is compatible with the interests of public safety and the welfare of society.[28] The parole board will assess whether the inmate's period of incarceration has been of sufficient length to "protect the public, punish him for his conduct, deter others, and allow for rehabilitation."[29] In answering this question, an assessment is made of the facts of the crime, victims of the crime, other convictions, and criminal conduct. The second guideline asks whether the inmate is rehabilitated, which is reflected in the degree of remorse and understanding of harm caused by the crime. The third guideline focuses on a realistic post-incarceration plan, reflected in indicators of future behavior of the inmate "as a sober, law-abiding, employed, productive person who is making positive contributions to his family and his community."[30] In answering this question, board members consider the length of time the inmate has been rehabilitated, the degree of support from family and friends, the likelihood of employment after release, plans for housing, the inmate's plan for reentry with recognition of factors contributing to previous criminal behavior and, finally, receptiveness and commitment to conditions of parole. Further, parole "cannot be granted merely as a reward for good conduct in prison."[31] The guidelines make explicit that the decision to grant parole is ultimately left to the board, implying that there is no presumption for or against parole at fifteen years.

At his hearing, sixty-nine-year-old Mike addressed these aspects explicitly by stating, "I am looking for professional help so I can deal with the triggers for addiction. I need to be able to identify my stressors and deal with them without alcohol. I do substance abuse work through my church. The church has filled by needs and I truly believe God has removed this barrier from my life."

Other aspects that are considered according to the official parole board guidelines include institutional conduct and participation in institutional programs and, finally, the "inmate's demonstration of rehabilitated character and reformed behavior." To prove their changed character, defendants at hearings pointed to their transformed selves while consciously taking responsibility for past behavior. Mike, for example, stated, "I am proud of myself that I changed myself, I am not a criminal anymore. Thank God, because I was a horrible young man." In Mike's hearing, the parole board found what they were looking for and granted him parole to a long-term residential program. At these hearings, lifers such as Mike appeared to have constructed their version of events to meet the board's requirements for parole. Even though making excuses by pointing to external causes for behavior is normal and frequently healthy, in doing so parole-eligible prisoners would risk being accused of cognitive distortions[32] or an inadequate attribution style. Behaviors frequently do have external causes. Instead, in each of the hearings I attended, lifers pointed the finger at themselves.

Board guidelines for paroling an inmate are well-known among lifers. The parole board publishes these guidelines, it says, "for the benefit of inmates who hope to obtain another chance, supporters of inmates, victim families and surviving victims. [. . .] Inmates should know what standards they need to meet and how cases will be evaluated."[33] With the help of lifer groups in prison, lifers adapt their narrative according to these guidelines. In my interview with Glenn, we talk extensively about the role of lifer groups in prison. Like many others, Glenn became involved in a lifer group to help him prepare for his upcoming parole board hearing: "They taught me how to create long-mid-short-term goals. They taught me how to use a word processor.

They taught me what to say, and what not to say. They planted the seed and allowed it to grow."

The lifer group also organized mock hearings in preparation for the hearing. I ask Glenn if it is possible to acquire a narrative of personal change before facing the parole board, without necessarily having undergone such a transformation. "Well, yes you can. I am the living proof of that," he admits to my surprise. Lifers such as Glenn have been schooled in presenting a narrative of redemption, change, and "giving back."[34] I have a similar discussion with sixty-three-year-old Carl, whom I interview in prison. He attributes his initial release at age fifty-five to the presence of prison programs. Even though he completed educational programs and hardly received any disciplinary reports, he was denied parole four times. For his fifth hearing, he said, "I completed the [Correctional Recovery Academy] program. And it taught me to use the phrases [the board] wanted to hear." After his fifth hearing, at which he presented a sound narrative, he was paroled.

Lifer groups and mock hearings were not helpful for all interviewees, and not all lifers had a positive attitude toward these groups and their activities. Frank, for example, volunteered to participate in a mock hearing, but after seeing several hearings, he says, "I realized that it is not helping anybody." He felt that his fellow volunteers in the lifer group were becoming actors: "They weren't really interested in how they could help the person see the board. They were just performing and these guys that were sitting in front of these mock parole boards, they would not get anything out of it. So, when they went to the [real] parole board, they were confused."

While the above-described guidelines for granting parole seem straightforward to some, others argue that standards for release are, at best, ill defined and irregularly applied.[35] The board's grant to release, criminal justice scholars argue, is not based on "a detailed clinical assessment of treatment effects that parole theory and model are based on."[36] Instead, the decision consists of an interplay between a variety of political, personal, and administrative factors about which parolees and the public are misinformed. The net result, critics put forward, is "a public that is frightened about a perceived threat from the paroled offender and an incarcerated population frustrated about the perceived caprice within the parole process."[37]

A recent review of empirical studies showed that, despite decision-making guidelines, parole release decisions remain irregularly applied. Rather than considerations laid out by guidelines, release decisions throughout U.S. states are found to be primarily a function of institutional behavior, crime severity, criminal history, incarceration length, mental illness, and victim input.[38] A survey study among 351 U.S. parole board members showed that they hardly consider an inmate's physical health, age, and prison conditions in their decision to grant parole.[39] Still others find that none of these factors is explanatory, and point out that the decision made by the board is largely random.[40] When parole is denied based on the hearing and supporting documentation, lifers in Massachusetts can receive one- to five-year setbacks. Hence, the lifer can never believe in the certainty of an eventual deliverance from his incarceration, as he is reminded time and time again that release is a privilege and not a right.[41] For those who are able to convince the parole board that they can be "sober, law-abiding, employed, and productive individuals," their life behind the walls ends and a new life starts.

7

Life after Life Imprisonment

When Heather was paroled from a life sentence she was picked up by her son, who was now an adult. When we talk in a university office, she has been out for fifteen years. She describes at length the initial impact of reentering the world she left so many years ago:

> I remember, coming out [. . .] and you know, it's the first time I actually breathe different air and I could smell different smells, with my back against the [. . .] [prison] building, and I was just standing there and [my son] was like, "Are you OK?" And I was like, "Yeah, I just want to stay here for a minute." Because I was afraid that the cops would come out and run after me again, you know what I mean? You know, that they would put the handcuffs on me, that it wasn't real. We just stood there for about half an hour, forty-five minutes, and some kid, what [do] you call those? Skateboards. He was coming down [the road] and I could hear this skateboard going really, really fast and I turn around like that and [my son] is like, "Are you OK?" and I says, "Yeah, but if anyone runs up to you in prison you have to turn around and be ready to fight." You know, it was just sounds, and smells, you know stuff like that.

After years of confinement, Heather moved from a state of incarceration where the pace is slow and routinized, the events monotonous but familiar, into a chaotic and foreign outside world. Heather's observation mirrors that of other lifers. The transition from inside to outside involves a particularly stark contrast between "inside" rules of behavior, interactions, and expectations, to the "outside" world, with a logic of its own. When I asked interviewees about their experiences when first released, many pointed to cars, buses, people, buildings, roads, stores, colors, and noises that they had not experienced for decades. Glenn, who was incarcerated for twenty-two years, phrases his initial experience being out as follows: "Everything had changed. Highways, streets, totally different roads. I was a stranger." Interviewees released in more recent times also mentioned rapid technological advances that were made in the time they were incarcerated. One of these men is Cody, a sixty-nine-year-old Caucasian lifer whose arms are covered with tattoos. His age is reflected in his face; his sunken cheeks point to long-term drug use; he has edema in both hands. I talk to him in a medium-security prison, where our time to talk is cut short because of "movement": I was not allowed to stay during moving time. In a letter, he follows up on the interview: "The toughest part about going out for the first time is the culture shock. When I went out after thirty years, I was amazed at all the new technology that was out there. Stuff like computers and cell phones. I think some guys are overwhelmed by all the new things. Sometimes they give up and go back to their old life of crime because it feels comfortable to them. It's all the feel-comfortable thing."

Going back to a life of crime because they cannot deal with smart-phone technology seems to be an oversimplifying account of why some stay out and others go back. What Cody seems to get at is the ill pre-paredness of being out in the free world that brings about discomfort. Advocates for reentry of lifers point out that throughout the 1970s, 1980s, and 1990s, the Department of Correction did not emphasize reentry ser-vices for the inmate population. Inmates would receive fifty dollars upon release and a bus ticket home. If an inmate had post-release supervision, reentry services were left to parole or probation. Over time, this changed to a more gradual reentry process in which an inmate would first report to a transitional house, where he would stay for several months. I talk about this process with Ruben, in Span's office downtown. Ruben had been incarcerated for fifteen years before being granted parole. He was transferred from prison to a transitional house in Boston:

This guy came in and did the intake, showed me the room, did a tour with me, and he's like, "There's a store nearby, and you can buy your bedsheets, buy your towels." And I was like, "OK," and I walked down [. . .] the street, which is maybe two blocks, and I got to the corner and I just broke down, you know, I couldn't go any further, you know, I just broke down and I just, I just felt isolated, like, you know, I felt as if I was placed in a foreign country, I didn't know anybody, nobody knew me, I didn't know my position, my role. You know, there was no structure, there was nothing, it was just like, it was like being tossed, it is hard for me to describe, but it is just like being tossed in some plains were you have no survival skills, no tools, no nothing, you know.

He returned to the transitional house, not having been able to go down the store. He adds, "For me, it was just overwhelming, it was just too much to go from being behind the wall, you know [. . .] being out in society now, not having a role, not knowing anybody, you know, not feeling like you can trust anybody, that was a shock for me. And remember I was estranged from my family, not from all of them, but from most of them, so I felt really alone." Even in the months that followed, he says, "I just became so overwhelmed, all these impressions, I wouldn't leave the house for days, I wouldn't talk to anybody, I was barely eating and I lost a lot of weight. [. . .] I could only be around people for twenty to thirty minutes, especially in crowds, I just felt so, so weird or different from people." This caused him to isolate himself from others. It was not until several years later, when he was re-incarcerated and paroled for the second time, with the help of much programming, that he was able to cope and build a life for himself on the outside.

Immediately upon release, interviewees wanted to enjoy ordinary, taken-for-granted pleasures of the outside world: walks on the city streets and long-denied delicacies. The first thing Aaron did, for example, was to walk the four miles from the place he was released to his wife's house. His wife recalls that in the days and weeks after, "Everybody kept asking me what he was gonna eat when he got out [laughs], what he wanted to eat . . . But it's like the only thing he wanted to do was walk. You know, like somewhere that's not on a track, going around and around."

As reported elsewhere,[1] in the days and weeks that followed their release, most interviewees became aware that the most ordinary actions were dropped from their repertoire of automatic maneuvers. Alan was twenty years old when he was incarcerated, and thirty-five years old when he was released on parole. He described how coming home after his fifteen-year-long sentence was "a culture shock. I didn't know how to work the remote control, to work the washing machine, or how to write a money order." Holly, who served sixteen years, shared such similar day-to-day aspects. In prison, she says, "We have a choice to be good or bad, be locked up in isolation or to be in your unit. [. . .] Getting outside, it's a billion choices." She recalls going to the supermarket for the first time after she was paroled: "I didn't know how to buy stuff. How to buy meat. I didn't know. It comes down to relearning those baby steps again." Seventy-year-old Donald, who spent forty years behind bars, faced similar difficulties in making mundane choices in the outside world when he was first released:

> My brother brought me to CVS, to get cosmetics and stuff, and in the prison, you have one toothbrush, a white toothbrush. So, you could have medium, soft, or hard bristle. All right, that was it. That was the choices. When he brought me to CVS, there were two shelves, at least two feet long, of toothbrushes, every shape, size, and color. Some of them looked like you could mine coal with them, you know what I mean? And I was incapable of picking out a toothbrush. I mean, I couldn't do it and I told my sister, I told her, "Just grab me a medium bristle." And she looks and is like, "It's right here." And there's maybe three feet, two shelves of medium bristles. And I said, "Look, I don't care what it looks like, just grab one of 'em, all right, that I could brush my teeth with, all right?"

Virtually all interviewees illustrate the initial troubles of reentry into a chaotic, foreign world. A changed city landscape and technological developments are but the tip of the iceberg; most interviewees described the making of mundane choices, such as Donald illustrates, as a major struggle. Although all released lifers experienced this facet to some degree, most endured it and reoriented themselves. After years of anticipation, planning, and dreaming, they left the confined, routinized, and slow-paced setting of the prison and stepped into the streets as an adult citizen. For some, becoming accustomed to the outside world took years, and still continued at the time I talked to them. Forty-one-year-old Arthur is an exception. He was seventeen years old when he was incarcerated for a homicide, and he spent an equal number of years behind bars. He claims that he felt as if he never left the streets: "I had a positive force guiding me through my transition from prisoner to civilian. The transition was surprisingly quick and within a week, I was adapted to society." The adaptation did not last for long. After six years, he was re-incarcerated for not being at the address he said he was when his parole officer came to check on him. Unlike Arthur, for most interviewees, adapting to a changed environment, coping with parole, and getting started toward a gratifying lifestyle is at least difficult, and for some it proved to be impossible.

Places of Return

The vast majority (86%) of interviewed lifers returned to the urban or suburban neighborhoods they originally came from, or that were similarly characterized by low median income, high unemployment, and high crime. These were often disadvantaged neighborhoods that lacked the economic and social resources that contribute to public order, such as opportunities for employment. What makes these relatively impoverished areas unique, according to the renowned sociologist William Julius Wilson, is that the people who live and work there are isolated politically, socially, and economically. In his work *The Truly Disadvantaged* he detailed how these poor, racially segregated neighborhoods are characterized not just by high rates of crime and unemployment, but also by an array of other problems.[2] Even thirty years after Wilson's writing, it is still in these neighborhoods that the effects of incarceration are felt most strongly. The options for support for ex-offenders are limited to whatever resources their neighborhood can provide.[3]

One out of five lifers returned to the same neighborhoods they lived in when they were arrested, which were generally poor urban areas.[4] Even though previous research found that ex-offenders returning to neighborhoods with higher rates of disadvantage were significantly more likely to be arrested after release,[5] among the interviewees no such relationship could be established. As Maps 7.1 and 7.2 illustrate, most non-incarcerated (indicated as white circles, or "desisters"), as well as most re-incarcerated interviewees (indicated as black circles, or "non-desisters"), returned to neighborhoods that were similarly disadvantaged in terms of median income and murder rate. As the size of the black and white circles reflect, the majority of interviewees returned to urban areas in the Boston, Springfield, and Framingham region. In Boston, neighborhoods of return mostly included Roxbury, Dorchester, East Boston, and Charlestown—areas characterized by a relatively low median income and a high violent crime rate.

Map 7.1. Median income in return locations for desisters and non-desisters.

Most interviewees, however, explicitly said they avoided going back to the neighborhoods they came from, such as Glenn, who did not want to move back to Somerville, where he lived prior to his incarceration: "I avoided the city like fire avoids water. [. . .] I got out of the city. I didn't want the city, I didn't want Somerville and all that." "Why not?" I ask. "There were twenty to thirty men in Norfolk [State Prison] from my town that I knew, growing up. And they were doing a great amount of time [for violent crimes]." Glenn avoided going back to his "old" neighborhood, where the risk of associating with old friends who chose a life of crime was too high. Instead, he decided to move to a small town in rural Massachusetts.

Some theorists argue that returning to the same neighborhood creates a cycle of re-incarceration: the environment that created offenders to do wrong in the first place is still there when they get back.[6] None of the in-

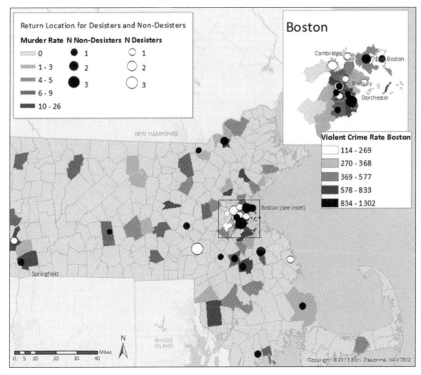

Map 7.2. Violent crime rates in return locations for desisters and non-desisters.

terviewees, however, explicitly attributed their re-incarceration to their places of return. When he was released after fifteen years, forty-two-year-old Alan, for example, chose not to move back to the neighborhood he lived before imprisonment, and instead moved in with family in the suburbs: "Although later on, I learned that that was a fallacy. You know how they say, 'You can take a man out of the ghetto, but you cannot take the ghetto out of a man?' Well that was me." He has been back in prison for various violations. One of these included credit card fraud. He explains how he was in need of money, and "someone presented it to me, and it was around the holiday time. And there was food, two cars, and my sister wasn't doing well, and it was all coming down on me, being a family man, at the same time." The credit card fraud involved him taking the role as a driver: "They told me, 'Just drive. We're not going to hurt no one.'" He was getting $500 for every time he participated. Two months later he was arrested and re-incarcerated. His most recent re-incarceration resulted from using cocaine.

In sum, the majority of lifers returned to impoverished, high-crime neighborhoods: those who were able to stay out, as well as those who were re-incarcerated. In other words, neighborhood factors alone do not provide a sufficient explanation for why some returned to prison while other stayed out on parole. For most lifers, as we will see, more prominent factors than neighborhood characteristics played a determining role in successfully staying out on parole, or returning to prison.

Roadblocks to Reentry

Sixty-nine-year-old Mike was released at age fifty-seven. He had been incarcerated for thirty-two years before being paroled. I talk to him in a medium-security prison in rural Massachusetts about his reentry process. He sighs and says, "Don't ever release a man without a piece of ID. I went to the DMV, and this is post-9/11, and they wanted two pieces of identification, and all I had was a paper from parole with my name on it. And they told me to go to the Social Security Office. And I told them, 'I've been property of the state for thirty-two years. I don't have anything else than this paper.'"

This wrenching quote and the desperation he must have felt at the DMV desk illustrate at least three aspects in the reentry of men like him. First and foremost, the penal institution has "owned" him for thirty-two years. "Owning" is more than "housing" or "detaining." It is the penal institution having full claim, power, and authority over you. Others, not you, decide where you sleep, what you eat, when you can work, where you can walk, what you can say: the list endless. Second, Mike's quote highlights the sharp contrast between the prison world (in which he exists by his inmate number) and the outside world, where he does not exist until he has a valid ID. Third, once that "ownership" stops—in Mike's case after thirty-two years—how are we to expect these men and women to start living a life without any tools to help them? In contrast to earlier days, at the beginning of this century the Department of Correction started to provide reentry planning for the inmate population. Each inmate nearing reentry is now offered a Reentry Workshop.[7] This program involves substance abuse treatment, employment readiness, social support, housing planning, financial awareness, and budgeting. Although this workshop is a vast improvement from the vacuum of services several decades ago, it alone is not able to remove one of the major hurdles faced by released lifers: the felon label and the implications this stigma has on finding housing and employment.

The Felon Label

The fact that these individuals are now paroled does not imply that they can simply start a new life afresh: other than having to abide by the conditions of parole, legal barriers prevent them from obtaining basic needs such as housing, public assistance, driver's licenses, and eligibility for student loans and food stamps, and they are denied the right to vote.[8] The French sociologist Loïc Wacquant, who is well-known for his work on the ghettoization and the development of punishment in the United States, has termed this set of barriers as "panoptic measures," which reach further than official "rap sheets" limited to the eyes of law-enforcement personnel.[9] Nowadays, a person's Criminal Offender Record Information (or CORI), reflecting that person's criminal history, can be requested by non–criminal justice agencies such as schools, day care centers, home health aides, youth athletic coaches, and municipal government agencies. Someone will have a Massachusetts CORI if they have, at any point, been charged with a crime in a state or federal court in Massachusetts, regardless of whether the case ended with a conviction, a finding of not guilty, charges were dismissed, or another outcome.[10] In recent years, Wacquant argues, the routinization of background checks curtail the life chances of former convicts and their families by "stretching the effects of judicial stigma on the labor, housing, and marital markets as well as into daily life."[11] Many new laws have further amplified sanctions for ex-prisoners by restricting access to public services, privileges, and benefits, including public housing and public employment.

Aside from legal barriers and stigma associated with the felon label, nowadays, virtually anyone with an Internet connection can find information about someone's conviction history without his or her consent or any guidance on how to interpret or use the information.[12] The widespread availability of this information, together with legal barriers, serve as obstacles for ex-offenders to reconnect to the institutions that have been demonstrated as important in the desistance process, especially work and family. Thus, current policies regarding ex-offenders may produce unintended criminogenic effects by further damaging offenders' already weak social bonds and cutting them off from promising avenues for desistance and reintegration into communities.[13]

Together, these new laws and policies lead ex-inmates to be trapped in what the civil rights lawyer Michelle Alexander has termed "a closed circuit of perpetual marginality."[14] In her book *The New Jim Crow: Mass Incarceration in the Age of Colorblindness*, she argues that these restrictions amount to a form of "civic death," sending the unequivocal message that "they" are no longer part of "us": once labeled a felon, the badge of inferiority relegates ex-inmates to a permanent second-class status.[15] Both Alexander and Wacquant understand such measures as part of a larger phenomenon of American racism against African Americans. In their studies, they consider these restrictions as aimed toward the exclusion of African Americans from general society.

Among all interviewees, regardless of their descent, the stigma associated with having been incarcerated exceeded legal access to mainstream society and economy: social stigma further inhibited them from establishing social relationships. Previous studies have outlined three types of managing the stigma of being an ex-offender. These include hiding the fact that one has been in prison (secrecy), avoiding social interaction (withdrawal), and education (preventative telling).[16] In deciding if, and when, to disclose, ex-prisoners must weigh the costs and benefits of disclosing. The benefits of disclosing include not having to worry about hiding it, finding others who can help or express approval, and promoting a sense of personal power. In contrast, the costs of disclosing include being excluded from opportunities such as employment, and worrying about what people are thinking about you.[17] The interviewees mostly adopted secrecy and preventive telling (for those who use their ex-offender status in counseling work).

One of the men actively avoiding talking about his prison past is Ron, a lifer who served twenty-seven years for a homicide he committed when he was twenty years old. His teeth are in bad shape, but overall his blond hair makes him look younger than his forty-nine years indicate. He comes across as friendly, intelligent, and well-spoken. When I interviewed him, he had recently returned to prison, after having been out for ten months. In those months, he says, "I carried the shame of the crime." When I asked what he meant by this, he explained, "My shame still influences my behavior. When I meet new people, I avoid telling them that I've been to prison. I don't lie to them, I am just afraid of telling them and how they would react." Others, such as fifty-two-year-old Ray, found themselves telling, what he terms, "a different version of the truth." In our conversation in a minimum-security prison, where he follows the CRA program, he talks about his time on parole and how he met women through websites. He brags about the number of women he dated: "Everybody in the program is jealous because I got all these girls." He adds, "Right now, I'm looking for a laid-back woman. I don't want no party woman. And no kids, either. Then there's more lovin' for us." He does not share his past with anyone, he says: "People are scared of you. People are scared of people like me doin' life. So I don't tell nobody. Except for the mental health guy." I ask, "You don't tell the women you met and dated, either?" "No. That will scare 'em off. I'll tell them that I went to jail and that I'm on parole, but that's it." Others, like fifty-two-year-old Irish American Scott, are able to share their history with their intimate partners but find that their felon label "sticks" in associated social settings. When we first talk, he had just moved in with a woman who has two teenaged children. He tells me, "Now, the kids have seen my [ankle] bracelet. So now they think I'm a weirdo or something. I ain't telling them nothing about my life. It's none of their business, really. So, now the fourteen-year-old daughter is judging me, saying that I'm no good at this and that and that I should be in prison." He tells me they fight over her children. He feels he is making an effort by buying clothes and other goods for her and her children, while her children do not approve of him because of his criminal past. Several months later I call him to see how he is doing. He moved out, he said. They had too many fights. It simply wasn't working out with the kids.

Scott is not alone in this. After their release from prison, all lifers faced the stigma of the felon label. It affects multiple facets of life, including—but certainly not limited to—housing, employment, and social relations. They usually hid their "real story" from acquaintances and coworkers, evading questions about their past, or responding to probing questions with vague statements like "I've been away for a while."

Like other offenders, these lifers were fully aware that their personal attributes would be devalued and that they would not be treated "like anyone else," but rather as failures or pariahs.[18] In prior work, it has been suggested that avoiding disclosure serves two interrelated functions: it minimizes the potential threat to one's self and enables the ex-offenders to connect with others.[19]

Others, such as the "professional exes" (those that make a living based on their prison experience), used their past in their daily lives to help other similarly stigmatized people. They do this by sharing their experiences, becoming a role model and mentor, and making a career of helping others who are not as far along in the process of recovery or transformation.[20] For these ex-offenders, their past became a new part of their identity. Prior research suggests that this can even allow stigmatized individuals to overcome their felon label and reconcile with society for their past crimes.[21] Even these lifers, however, found it difficult to establish traditional roles as parent, intimate partner, and breadwinner—not only because the stigmatizing label of being an "ex"-prisoner, but also because they were "off-time" in creating these social roles.

A Place Called Home

In the majority of states, public housing authorities make individual-based choices about an applicant's eligibility that include considering the person's criminal record as well as evidence of rehabilitation.[22] Obtaining a safe place to live is important, as researchers consistently find that released prisoners without stable housing are more likely to return to prison.[23] Restrictive lease agreements, however, inhibit individuals with a felony record as well as their families from both private and public housing.[24] As a result of these restrictions, many ex-prisoners, including the lifers I talked to, frequently moved from place to place in their first years in the community.[25] Among the interviewed lifers, many were dependent on a good word from family or friends. One of these lifers was Thanh. After spending months in a transitional house run by a small religious community, he obtained a one-bedroom apartment in a small town south of Boston. He tells me, "With housing, it's tough, because they know your [criminal] records and they have a right to refuse that, you know, they do not want a criminal in the building, it is tough. One of the volunteers [from the religious community] called the landlord and explained my situation and he was OK with it."

For many interviewees, obtaining housing involved relying on other people and playing a political game. Because of his age, seventy-year-old Donald qualified for senior housing. Based on his criminal record, however, he did not. He describes the necessary legal knowledge and politics he had to navigate to be admitted to public senior housing:

> My friend tried it first. Now, what you do is, you fill out the application, you give it to this one woman, she calls you in and puts the information together. She's going to deny you because of your CORI [Criminal Offender Record Information], aight? They don't call it a rehearing, they call it a reconsideration, aight? Her boss, you go to see him, and now you can bring witnesses and all this other stuff in. And he's gonna deny you, because of the CORI. They have a three-person panel, two staff members, and a resident. The staff always controls the vote, 'cause it's two to one. No matter what, aight? So [my friend] had about ten people, including a cop and whatnot, to speak for him, so he gets in. So now I go into it, and I see the woman, she denies me, I see her boss, he denies me, and when it's going to the next level, the head guy overruled him, and in the overruling he lists the [college] degrees [I got in prison]: "Solid," he said. Right, so demonstrated rehabilitation, all right. So now it was very hard to get housing. So me and [and my friend], we slid through, because we demonstrated rehabilitation. And if [the panel] didn't give it to us, we could record it, and they didn't want to go in that direction, [so they] just gave us the housing.

Thanh and Donald have been lucky. Those who did not have friends and family with such ties often stayed in sober houses and transitional homes for years on end. It should be noted that not all interviewees strived for complete independence. Sixty-one-year-old Frank, for example, who has been in and out of reform schools and prison since age twelve, admits, "I don't want to be picked up after years of prison and be dropped out here, I won't do too well." After his initial release, he took a big step by moving into an apartment by himself. He lasted ten days before he was rearrested and sent back to prison. Now, he says, "I have to go to a long-term reentry program with a follow-up program after that, and then I have to live in a community setting where I am dealing with people who know my situation. You know, if they would ask me if I was institutionalized, of course I was institutionalized!" Most interviewees, however, could not wait to catch up with the years lost, and became impatient when administrative hurdles prevented them from moving forward quickly. Legal hurdles and finding a place to live, however, were hardly the only restrictions to becoming a full citizen—obtaining employment was arguably the biggest challenge of all.

"Don't Hire Me"

Employment is an important component of the reentry process. Employment, in general, satisfies a basic human need to be self-sufficient.[26] Even more than a steady source of income, jobs can provide a sense of structure and responsibility to former prisoners as they return to the community. Unfortunately, many released prisoners will face a difficult path in finding and keeping employment,[27] which can be traced back to two major factors: the supply side and the demand side.

On the supply side, most offenders leaving prison are under-skilled relative to the general population: they lack much-needed work skills, educational qualifications, and a stable history of employment.[28] This is particularly problematic for lifers, as vocational and educational programs in prisons (to the extent that they are available) are typically designed for short-term inmates.[29] Few efforts are planned to involve inmates in a sustained effort of learning and growth over many years. Hypothetically, a lifer could select from these training programs "cafeteria style" and emerge from the sentence with an odd combination of certificates in plumbing and small engine repair, and an associate's degree in sociology.[30] Even with a completed program, former prisoners face a bleak employment future because of low educational attainment, high rates of previous unemployment, and little work experience in jobs that provide a stable career and a livable wage.[31] For the most part, prison has not given individuals new skills that they could use to launch a conventional career.[32] This dynamic is illustrated by Holly, who applied for dozens of jobs after being paroled but was not successful: "I felt I had this sign on my head saying 'I'm an ex-con. Don't hire me.' [. . .] I had this interview in which they asked me what I could add with my experience, and I was like, 'What?! I've been taking trash out [in prison] for the past sixteen years, what do you mean experience?'"

Holly and most interviewees like her reported difficulties in convincing potential employers to hire them, given their lack of experience. Cedric was another of these ex-prisoners. He served fifteen years before being first paroled. He did not have any work experience before he was incarcerated at age eighteen, and he did not complete an educational program while in prison. When potential employers asked him about work experience, he said he always wants to sit down with potential hirers rather than "check the box" indicating a prior criminal record. In these one-on-one conversations he would say, "All I'm asking for is a fair chance. Just give me thirty, sixty days and see if it works out. I will work hard." He adds, "Thing is, I learned in jail that honesty is the best thing. I was always honest." His honesty paid off: after working for a temp agency, he obtained full-time work at a concrete company.

The most frequently mentioned reason for not being able to acquire a job, however, was the demand side: employers are very reluctant to hire those with criminal records, as reflected in the widespread use of criminal background, or CORI, checks.[33] Both re-incarcerated individuals and those under parole supervision at the time of the interview spoke about the dominance of the "felon label" when seeking employment. It has been well documented that employers appear to discriminate by type of conviction, such that violent offenders are thought to be least deserving of second chances.[34] Through laws against hiring or licensing, ex-felons are barred from up to eight hundred different occupations across the United States. Such bans were initially warranted for occupations directly tied to offending history. Child sex offenders, for example, should not be employed to work with children. Often, however, as the criminal justice scholars Shawn Bushway and Gary Sweeten point out, employment bans are blind to offense type.[35] Even if people like Cedric are able to overcome employers' reluctance to hire felons, many former prisoners are legally barred from some of the economy's fastest-growing fields, including education, child care, private security, nursing, and home health care.[36] By virtue of their record, offenders face an especially narrow range of job opportunities. Fifty-seven-year-old Melvin, for example, was able to secure a job as an electrician after release. However, this did not last for long, he says: "I was an electrician on the street, and I worked in buildings and stuff, and for my last job, I had to go into schools. And they didn't want me there, even when I came to the schools at night, because of my felony background. It made me feel pretty low." When he was not able to obtain new work due to CORI checks, he struggled to obtain medicine for an existing brain injury. He continues: "I took up a minimum wage job, but they shut my health care down, and I went out and shot dope to stop the headaches." One day, he recalls, "they showed up at work for urines. And I knew mine was dirty so I just left. And I turned myself in two weeks later."

For Cedric, there thus was a direct causal link between his re-incarceration and his failure to land a job. Because he did not have health-care coverage, he was unable to acquire medicine. He reached for an alternative all too familiar to him, which resulted in his re-incarceration. Despite the adversities men like Cedric described, the majority of interviewed lifers succeeded in acquiring some form of paid employment. Table 7.1 indicates that the majority of released lifers (52%) obtained employment as a manual worker post-release. This mostly implies employment in construction or manufacturing—industries that require little customer contact. The willingness to hire ex-offenders, in line with other studies,[37] appeared to be weakest in retail trade and other service sector businesses. Fifty-two-year-old Benjamin, who had been out on parole for ten years and worked as a painter, explained to me why construction was the number one choice for many ex-felons: "One thing about the construction industry, though, they don't do CORI checks. [. . .] I mean, because oftentimes I guess if you're on a [construction] site, it's not like you're actually involved with civilians, walking and passing by, you know what I'm saying? [. . .] So basically, you're just on a site. None of the trades that I know of do CORI checks." Trades that interviewees were involved in included painting, plumbing, brick laying, carpentry, and electrical work.

It should be noted that women specifically are reported to be less likely to obtain full-time or part-time employment in the first years after release.[38] Even though prior literature suggests that this may be due to women having a higher unemployment rate prior to admission to prison, female lifers I talked to mostly pointed to a lack of job training while in prison. Others consider being a woman working in a tradition-ally male profession as the main hurdle to employment. Fifty-year-old

TABLE 7.1. Employment status among released lifers post-release (N=68)

	Non-incarcerated interviewees (N=30)		Re-incarcerated interviewees (N=38)		Total (N=68)	
	N	%	N	%	N	%
Employment[1]						
Unemployed, not in school	5	17	5	13	10	15
Manual employment	8	27	27	71	35	51
Counseling	14	47	3	8	17	25
Other (in school, creative job, or white-collar job)	3	10	3	8	6	9

1. These jobs should not be regarded as permanent. As reported in other studies, the majority of this population changed jobs several times before their current job, in line with findings reported elsewhere (Coker & Martin, 1985).

Doris, for example, obtained plumbing and glazing licenses in prison but found it hard to get jobs in those fields. She appears strong, fit, and masculine. Her looks, however, seem to be deceiving, as she tells me she, too, suffers from gender discrimination: "You're not likely to hire me for a men's wage in trading jobs. I would get fifteen dollars an hour, whereas there is no way a guy would get as little as that." She obtained a job at Stop and Shop packing groceries. She did some "things on the side" without paying taxes on the money she earned, until her parole officer found out and she quit those side jobs. She tells me how "I went back from $500 a week to $150 a week. That was hard. I had to apply for food stamps. I went into the office with tears in my eyes, and the woman wouldn't give them to me, and I remember saying 'You don't understand. I am hungry.'" Whenever she could not come up with the rent, she says, "I started making phone calls to people to ask them to help me out." She managed to keep her head above water, despite a small monetary income.

Another complicating factor for lifers specifically, compared to those serving shorter sentences, is their age: older individuals in general experience age-related discrimination in the labor market, and lifers specifically may find it more difficult to get a job after having spent decades behind bars. As we saw in chapter 2, life-course theory suggests that employment can act as a turning point in the criminal career: informal social controls of the workplace encourage conformity, as workers are likely to experience close and frequent contact with other individuals leading a conventional lifestyle. At the same time, job stability, commitment to work, and a meaningful change in routine activities also lead to desistance from crime.[39] Although interviewees emphasized that they did well when working jobs where they were considered valued employees, the relationship between employment and staying out of prison was as not straightforward as expected. On one hand, this can be attributed to a changed economic landscape: while the Bostonian men in Sampson and Laub's study mainly held solid manufacturing jobs, the interviewed lifers live in a time when such jobs are not as ubiquitous. On the other hand, the lack of such a one-on-one relationship between doing well and employment can be traced back to the "off-time" occurrence of transitions into adult roles. Many interviewees reported that they had not gotten further in life—building careers, forming families, purchasing houses, and taking on other adult roles—due to their stay in prison. Rather, they emphasize the sense of being behind schedule, such as Hakim. He was fifty-eight years old when he was paroled from his most recent sentence: "I am not getting any younger, I am transitioning into—I am sixty-three years old—I am transitioning into a career at a point in my life where most people my age would be retiring. I am just starting with a career! I need some time to start paying off these [student] loans and debt that I'm in from that." He has $50,000 in student loans, which causes him much stress and sleepless nights, especially because he feels he is failing to financially take care of his wife and his siblings, who are about to be evicted from their house. His wife, however, has been very supportive. He tells me he wants to become a public speaker—other than wanting to "give back" by sharing his story, he hopes to earn some money to help cover the bills.

"MAKING GOOD" PROFESSIONALLY

As table 7.1 reveals, one out of four interviewed lifers was employed as a counselor in an ex-offender program or as a paralegal for a prisoners' rights organization. They had acquired legal skills while in prison or had been heavily involved in post-prison programming. Those who held jobs pointed out that work provided them with a sense of identity and meaning in their lives, a concept also known as "the helper principle": helping helps the helper.[40] Unlike the coping strategies of concealment or avoidance associated with stigma, being involved in advocacy work involved some form of "coming out."[41] This was particularly pronounced among those finding their way into the field of social work, such as Ruben, who describes his work as a counselor:

> Using my story, my experience, and just like building the bond, I can see a lot of the clients, they can really identify with me, even though I don't have the big degrees, and all that, but because I have the experience, they can create a bond. They know what I am coming from and I understand a lot better where they are coming from, as opposed to the case managers, a lot of time, they are like, "They are an asshole, and this and that," but once I, you know, talk to that person and read their charts, I am, like I explained to the case managers, like, "This is what they are going through." So, it works for all of us better. I can help the case managers address their clients and clients can always come to me and feel safe and [we] have that trust thing with each other where's it's not an issue, you know, once we start talking, "Well, you have been through what I have been through, so I can trust you," so that trust just oozes itself, it vanishes for that moment in time, so it's been really good.

He finds his work "fulfilling, you know, so fulfilling, because I know that I am helping someone." This finding is not unique. Previous studies on ex-offenders pointed out how ex-offenders use their past to "make good" from the bad by applying their experiences to a professional setting in which they help others.[42] In the literature, these individuals are known as "professional exes":[43] individuals who have exited their deviant careers by replacing them with occupations in professional counseling. Their new, legitimate career embraces their deviant history. As Brendan Marsh showed in his recent work on drug-addicted offenders, much like sober individuals in Alcoholics Anonymous, generative activities can also be therapeutic for offenders, which helps them maintain a path of desistance from crime.[44] Consider the case of Derrick, who had been incarcerated for eighteen years: "Yeah, when I was counseling, I would use my negative as a positive to help others. I would say look, like for instance, somebody would say, 'Well you don't know what it's like.' I'd say, 'Well let me tell you something, I believe I do know what it's like.

I think I even know better than you know.' So, I mean, a lot of people, it worked out pretty well. Because there would be nothing that people could really tell me that would shock me."

The interviewees did not "just" become paralegals and counselors; because of their experience they considered themselves, in Maruna's terms, "super-counselors."[45] Because of their prison experience, they were more capable than others to provide guidance and support. Thanh describes how he talked to reentry program participants: "I helped a lot of people, I talked with a lot of people, you know. [. . .] Like, in the [reentry] program, a lot of guys came to ask me, they say, 'When I talk to you, it's different than talking to a counselor, because the counselor doesn't know what we went through.' [. . .] All the things that they went through, I went through, so it's easy for me to talk to them, because I am more understanding, I'm not afraid of them, but more understanding."

For lifers like Ruben and Thanh, doing this type of work is part of "making good," fulfilling a role that is inherent in their newly found self. Again, as we have seen in chapter 6, much like sober individuals in Alcoholics Anonymous,[46] these generative activities are arguably therapeutic for ex-offenders, which in turn helps them maintain a path of desistance from crime. As mentioned above, this is also known as "the helper principle," in which the helper benefits from helping. Assuming this role can allow ex-prisoners to overcome their "felon status" and reconcile with society for their past crimes.[47] Among these professional exes, the transformation process began with themselves and ends with the transformation of others.[48] In addition to those interviewees who were "making good" in paid positions, many interviewees acted as volunteers or became self-employed "motivational speakers," like Keith:

> [My] long-term goal is to stay out of prison, continue to be a contributing member of society. I do a lot of programs where I go speak to teen centers and youth centers. Actually, ironically in fact, the police will call me and say, "I'm running an anti-violence program at such and such youth center, do you think you can come and speak?" And I go there and I tell my story. [. . .] I want to continue to do that. [. . .] I can't make up for the eighteen years that I missed, but I can at least continue to do good for whatever time I do have.

These activities reinforce Keith's newly found identity as a key example for troubled youth. This type of employment strengthened ex-offenders' sense of control and purpose in life. On a day-to-day basis, they were reminded that they were now an example to others, which in turn may have reinforced their ability to stay out successfully.

Putting Down Roots

"The longer you're away from society, the harder it is to fit in. I was forty-four, being at a cookout, everyone was married and had kids. I didn't fit in," fifty-two-year-old Joel says. Thirty-one years ago, he killed a female friend. Looking back, he describes himself at that time as "angry as hell at everybody." He was first paroled in 2007, returned one year later, was re-paroled again, but returned behind bars one and a half year later for having alcohol in the house. His younger roommate threw him a party, at which underage people were consuming alcohol. He blames his ex-girlfriend for his re-incarceration. Joel says she was the one who notified the parole office about the party because she had a grudge against him for breaking up with her.

By being in prison for decades, these lifers have been removed from structures that favor maturation and provide sources of informal social control, such as employment, marriage, and parenthood. Prison, in this view, has disrupted the "journey of going straight."[49] As we found in chapter 5, interviewees who had an intimate partner at the time of arrest typically lost contact after the first years in prison. The same accounted for contact with their children, who were either born after the interviewees were incarcerated or were too young to visit independently of their mothers. Scholarly work consistently points to the role of social support provided by family members as a condition that motivates offenders to immerse themselves into more conventional life domains.[50] Factors that appear to have the most impact on post-release optimism are family relationships and family circumstances while incarcerated.[51] While offenders are in prison, visits from family and friends provided support networks. Strengthening pro-social bonds for incarcerated offenders may be important not only because it can help prevent them from (re-) assuming a criminal identity, but also because many released prisoners rely on family and friends for employment opportunities, financial assistance, and housing.[52] Thus, while it is widely recognized that visitation from family members significantly decreases the risk of recidivism,[53] for the interviewed lifers, visits from significant others were rare, and for some they became nonexistent over time. The question, then, becomes whether these lifers are able to reestablish such relationships after release. Are they able to find an intimate partner that provides them with a source of informal control, become a parent, and reestablish ties with other family members? In other words, are they able to successfully "catch up" after having been removed from society for decades?

Good Girls and Bad Girls

Of those who had an intimate partner upon release, the majority had met their significant other while they were incarcerated. With the exception of one, none of their wives "stood by them" throughout their life sentence. In most cases, relationships ended several months or years into confinement. As reflected in table 7.2, less than half of the total sample was married at the time of the interview; several characterized their relationship as ambiguous, being somewhere "in between" (25%) involved and not involved. Approximately one-third did not have an intimate partner at the time of the interview. The low marriage rates among these lifers could be attributed to the demographics of the sample: black men are less likely to be married than are white men,[54] and ex-prisoners in general have lower marriage rates.[55] In addition, the large majority of our sample was incarcerated at their marriageable age. For men in the general population the average median age of first marriage is twenty-nine.[56] Therefore, in terms of marriage as a factor for desistance, many may have missed the critical phase in which intimate partner relations are typically established and, accordingly, could have acted as a pro-social force. In line with this reasoning, contrary to what we would expect from studies based on those serving shorter sentences, none of the interviewees mentioned an intimate partner as a reason for (periods of) successfully staying out of prison.

Rather, most interviewees pointed to several reasons *not* to become involved in intimate relationships after release. They mentioned that many programs for ex-offenders actively discourage such involvement for at least a year post-release. They prioritized their own recovery over

TABLE 7.2. Relationship status among released lifers post-release (N=68)

	Non-incarcerated interviewees (N=30)		Re-incarcerated interviewees (N=38)		Total (N=68)	
	N	%	N	%	N	%
Intimate partner						
Married / in a committed relationship	10	33	18	47	28	41
Ambiguous	7	23	10	26	17	25
No intimate partner	13	43	10	26	23	34

the involvement of an intimate partner, as fifty-year-old Raymond illustrates: "The worst thing would be to get into a committed relationship that I knew I wasn't ready for. [. . .] I think we need to grow into that. And part of that growth process is coming to terms with certain things about ourselves. I think in order to have a healthy relationship, with a partner, I think you really need to be [. . .] accepting of who you really are not who you want to be." Raymond divorced the mother of his daughter when he was in prison. After his release he became acquainted with several women, some of whom he was dating at the same time. "I am not a Canadian goose," he jokes. Recently he moved in with his long-term girlfriend, determined to be in a steady relationship.

Juan, who has been out for one and a half year when I talk to him, agrees, adding that "it should be at least a year" before engaging in an intimate relationship. When I ask him why it should be at least a year, he elaborates:

Because the first year is like a whirlwind, things are just going tsjuu-tjsuu-tsjuu [imitating the sound of a whirlwind], you know what I mean? The first six, seven months, you are still getting established. [. . .] It is judgment, too, I am going to be frank with you, most men when they get out of prison, what they want is, there's only one thing on their mind, and that is: How can I get a girl? And that is all that they are concerned about. I am not going to lie, that was me. But fortunately that didn't [happen], you know, it creates bad judgment because all they are looking at is, "That looks nice, I want that." [. . .] But they don't know the woman, they don't know her, they don't know her attitude, if she's OK up here [pointing to his head], you know, what her motive is. [. . .] He needs to be careful about the woman that he's dating or seeing, and so on and so forth, because, just because someone is nice-looking doesn't mean that she is good for him. That would be my advice.

After the interview, I find out through another interviewee that Juan's "one-year rule" is not just random: he recently got involved with a girl and plans to move in with her. Finding an intimate partner, especially one without a troubled past, does not come easy. In our conversation, Glenn describes his relationships with women over the past few years. He first got married when he was in a minimum-security setting: "I met her here [in prison], through someone else. It was a marriage of convenience, I think. For both of us. She had a child and wanted a father figure for her daughter. And I needed someone to progress socially. It was kinda adolescent, there was no sex involved." When he was caught drinking, he was put back to a medium-security prison. Three months later his wife filed for divorce. The second time he got married, he says, "I met her [in prison] here, also. I was married for twelve years. But when I was on the point of getting out, she confessed to me that she had been unfaithful." Neither of these marriages involved sexual contact. He admits to feeling insecure after being released on parole when it came to approaching women: "I was terrified. I didn't know how to meet women. I didn't really have a social life. [. . .] Being locked up since I was eighteen, I didn't have any real sexual experience. I mean, a little, with girlfriends. But then it just stood still, for all those years. Nothing." When he was released on parole he met a woman at an AA meeting. She was an alcoholic. They were together for four years and got married. She died of liver cirrhosis soon after. Some time after, he met his current girlfriend trough a motorcycle club. "She's gorgeous," he says. Even though he is now in prison, he says, "She wants me to come home and marry her. But I'm not sure if I want to do that. I mean, I have this poisonous touch, you know, three strikes."

Theoretically, the attachment of an intimate partner is what provides individuals with a "stake in conformity," making them reluctant to engage in crime because they might hurt or jeopardize their relationship.[57] The fact that interviewees did not attribute their short- or long-term successes to their intimate partner does not necessarily mean that their intimate partner did not play a role in the desistance process. It could thus be argued that those who became involved in an intimate relationship did not attribute their desistance to their significant other, but rather to themselves, and were "desisting by default."[58] That is, they would have made commitments to a new relationship without much forethought, and "went straight" without realizing it. This concept is based on Sampson and Laub's findings.[59] The married men in their sample had—unknowingly—invested so much in a marriage or a job that they did not want to risk losing their investment. The interview material in this study, however, does not seem to support this point of view. Making use of the life-history calendar, insofar they were engaged in a relationship, those who went straight typically met their intimate partners *after* having made the choice to commit to a noncriminal lifestyle. Recall Ruben, for example, who made "a conscious decision to really work on change" after spending time in solitary confinement. Several years after having committed to a new identity, he met a woman through church. He describes her as follows:

> We had a lot in common, you know, our past, you know, our goals in the future, where we were both headed, you know, we just kind of clicked and I love being around her and I have someone to go and someone who understood me and believed in me, so, and it worked, we're making it work [laughs]. [. . .] So, she supports me, and I support her, and she is patient. Still, I am still going through issues, I still have some baggage from prison, but I'm still working on it, I'm still doing therapy, so I'm still working on a lot of issues that I have, some of it dealing with closure, I don't think it's ever going to end, and then some of it is just personal stuff from prison, and I'm still dealing with, still trying to get out of my system and you know, but, but the main thing for us is like success.

They had recently married. Not all interviewees were as fortunate as Ruben to be involved with an intimate partner with a normative orientation. Many became involved in an intimate relationship soon after their initial release, which they typically referred to as "playing catch-up": compensating as quickly as possible for "lost" time. Among this group, rather than intimate partners acting as a potential deterrent, interviewees attributed failures while on parole to circumstances involving their intimate partners. Jay, for example, had been out for two and a half years, he says: "I had my place. It was in the harbor, the top floor on a corner, overlooking the harbor. I had a flat screen. But I went to work, alone. I make my meals, alone. And I went to bed, alone. I was doing well but I wanted a companion, someone to share with. I actually felt lonely." At the same time, at his work in construction, "I had people around me who were using. Like, after work, they ordered chicken wings and a couple of six-packs. I didn't smoke, didn't drink. I felt strong." Then, he says, he met a woman and soon moved in with her:

> She wasn't as grounded as I was. She was using and I felt confident in my sobriety. I was like, "See, she is using, but I'm clean, I'm good, I'm strong." And one day, I remember, she set a cigarette down in the ashtray and [. . .] before I knew it, I would go to the store, buy a pack for her and buy a pack for myself, too. And I would buy her a bottle and get two beers myself. So I was on a little slippery slope. Before I knew it, I was smoking weed with her and started using alcohol.

He was re-incarcerated several months later when he was pulled over and his girlfriend's prescription drugs were found in his car. He was re-paroled after a year, but he violated his conditions of parole again when he took Valium for pain he experienced from a recent knee surgery.

The literature is quite unequivocal about the positive influences of the intimate partner relationship for released offenders: it provides these men and women with a secure social niche, which in turn encourages the ex-offender to engage in other socially conventional activities, reinforcing a noncriminal identity.[60] For women, the advantages of becoming involved with an (ex-)felon are somewhat less obvious. Research on "prisoner's wives" shows that the correctional institution can grant women a surprising measure of control and leverage in their dealings with men, structures for enacting the gendered roles of nurturer and caregiver, and substitute sites for domestic and conjugal life that are preferable or easier to manage than the chaos and stress of the family home.[61]

It was not unusual for men to meet their wives through fellow inmates or family, sometimes as an explicit romantic arrangement. Others met their intimate partners through prison programs. These women were, as reported elsewhere,[62] usually engaged in prison matters for religious or political reasons. Joel started dating a prison group counselor while incarcerated, and moved in with her after his release. When the relationship threatened to go sour, her motives for becoming involved with him became clear: "She called my parole officer all the time, making all sorts of allegations. She said to me, 'I want you back in prison, there our relationship is safe.'"

For some women, the sociologist Megan Comfort suggests in her work on women with husbands, fiancés, and boyfriends on the inside, men's release from prison disrupts their autonomy and household control. It may further engender feelings of resentment and powerlessness in their partners, especially if the men anchored them in the relationship during the incarceration period with assurances that their circumstances would improve.[63]

In short, none of the successes, but rather some of the failures, were attributed to the role intimate partners played in prisoners' lives postrelease. "Catching up" on lost time often proved to have a negative, rather than positive, influence.

Parenthood

Another part of life that receives much attention from life-course theorists is the role of parenthood. Assuming the role of parent is thought to benefit the reentry transition process, as it aids in the development of pro-social identities.[64] Having children and envisioning a "possible self" as parent and provider has been shown to increase the optimism among soon-to-be-released offenders and, hence, the likelihood of them doing well after release.[65] Parenthood can thus have a deterrent effect on future criminal behavior. Even though more than half of the interviewees had children (see table 7.3), the majority did not take on a parental role either before or during incarceration. While incarcerated, most men lost contact with their children. As in most male facilities, at the time these men served their sentence there were very few parenting programs, increasing the threshold for men to maintain contact with their children. Most male lifers did not reconnect with their children after being released. Fifty-one-year-old Norman is one of them. He was eighteen years old when he was incarcerated and his girlfriend was three months pregnant.

TABLE 7.3. Parenthood among released lifers post-release (N=66)

	Non-incarcerated interviewees (N=29)		Re-incarcerated inter- viewees (N=37)		Total (N=66)[1]	
	N	%	N	%	N	%
Parenthood						
Children	18	62	19	51	37	56
No children	11	38	18	49	29	44

1. The parental status of two individuals was unknown.

Now, he says, "Me and my kids, we don't have a relationship. I'm never able to be their dad. I don't think I can ever be a father figure." Those interviewees who had children were incarcerated when their children were very young; by the time they were released, their children had reached adulthood. For the men especially, parenthood occurred "off-time" relative to members of their age cohort who were not incarcerated: while the average U.S. man fathers his first child in his mid-twenties,[66] most interviewees were incarcerated during this potentially critical time of family formation and remained childless, or had fathered a child at a very young age before they were incarcerated. For those men, becoming a parent at a socially inappropriate age solidified their already marginalized identities. Others, such as fifty-two-year-old Ray, became parents while incarcerated but were never able to build a relationship with their child: "Before I got to prison I had this woman. And I didn't know how much time I was gonna get. She found out she was pregnant after I got arrested. [. . .] She said she was gonna have my baby, and I told her, 'You gotta find somebody else.'" He has never been in contact with his child.

Some men, like Ray, never took any initiative to play a role in their children's lives. For others, personal visits from their children were difficult to maintain during incarceration. This was due to the distance between the place of incarceration and the child's place of residence; the associated costs of travel; and, particularly for fathers, the willingness of mothers to facilitate visitation between incarcerated fathers and their children. With the exception of one, none of the interviewees maintained relationships with the mothers of their children while incarcerated—hence, contact with their children became virtually nonexistent. This complicated the parental relationship some wanted to reassume after release, as forty-year-old Miguel puts forward: "Lots of things I wasn't privy to [. . .] things with my daughter. While we were living in the same house [after release], she felt uncomfortable, I felt uncomfortable. [. . .] She had a lot of anger and resentment towards me. She would call me a 'telephone father.' [. . .] When I moved out to go and live with my girlfriend, she felt like I was abandoning her all over again." Miguel tried to re-create a relationship with his daughter after release, but conflict followed instead. One day, when he was driving home, he saw his daughter and her boyfriend fighting in the street. She was four months pregnant at that time. He pulled over and tried to intervene, he says, but the fight escalated. He called the police, who showed up and suggested that his daughter should get a restraining order if she does not want her father to be involved in her life. She secured a restraining order, and Miguel was sent back to prison. His daughter subsequently withdrew the restraining order, to no avail. At his most recent hearing he was given a three-year setback. At the hearing Miguel said he wanted to make amends with his daughter. One of the parole board members re-marked, "You gave up your parental rights when you took [the victim's] life." Now, he says in resignation, "This is good . . . neither of us are ready to have a relationship. I feel totally powerless with her. I can't help her. I'm forced to be in here. [. . .] I'm seeing my life disappear. [. . .] My home life is completely destroyed." Similar to those who married after release, those who became fathers after release indicated they had gone through a meaningful life transformation prior to meeting their inti-mate partner and having children. Others, who became involved with an intimate partner who had children of her own, described the presence of stepchildren as a complicating factor, rather than a positive one. We saw this before in the case of Scott, whose relationship ended because of the troubled relationship with his girlfriend's children.

In short, the majority of those who had children prior to going to prison were estranged from their children, while others never had children. In this regard, it is important to state the obvious: as in other spheres of social life, gender matters. Although female offenders expe-rience a range of relationships with individuals on the outside, one of the most significant relationships for an incarcerated woman are those with her children, especially during her imprisonment.[67] Compared to male interviewees, female lifers played a central role in the care of their

TABLE 7.4. Elements of "success package" among released lifers post-release (N=66)

	Non-incarcerated interviewees (N=29)		Re-incarcerated interviewees (N=37)		Total (N=66)[1]	
	N	%	N	%	N	%
Employed	24	83	32	87	56	85
Employed & intimate partner	9	31	15	41	24	37
Intimate partner & children	7	24	7	19	14	21
Employed & intimate partner & children	6	21	6	16	12	18

1. These factors remained unknown for two individuals.

children prior to incarceration. While men concentrate on "doing their own time," relying on inner strength and their ability to withstand outside pressures, women remain interwoven in the lives of significant others. This particularly accounts for relationships with their children and their mothers, who usually take care of their children.[68] Earlier studies found that both male and female inmates suffer from the pain of being separated from their families, but the separation seems to be more detrimental for women.[69] The female lifers I interviewed also voiced this pain. One of them was sixty-year-old Tonya, whose mother took care of her daughter while she was incarcerated. Throughout her sentence, she says, she was concerned for her daughter: "You know, you [be]come a little less important when you have children and we have to provide for them, and then your mission, you know, [. . .] [is] being able to feed your children." One of the major challenges they faced was to reestablish relationships with their children. Heather, whom we saw at the beginning of this chapter, describes that "it's just time" spent in prison that complicated the relationship with her sons after release. Similar to male interviewees, the time behind bars had created a distance between her and her children that could not be bridged.

Jim, a fifty-nine-year-old African American man on parole, shares a similar experience, and has now decided not to be involved with three adult sons: "I distanced myself from them. My sons, I cannot tell them what to do and how to do it. I just play it safe." One way to explain the lack of a relationship between "doing well" and traditional forms of social control arguably lies in the sample on which the original theory of informal social control was based. While a large percentage of the men in the studies by Sampson and Laub[70] were both married and held a full-time job, the interviewed lifers in this study show various combinations of relations, employment, and parenthood (see table 7.4). Only 18% of the sample had the total "traditional respectability package"[71] in that they were married, employed, and took up a parental role.

Families and Surrogate Families

So far, we have focused on the influence of newly assumed social roles as an employee, an intimate partner, or a parent in the reentry process. Another important facet to consider is the role of preexisting family relations. These should not be considered as a "turning point" in the life course, in that they may provide the ex-offender with a new, prosocial identity, but rather a "*returning point*."[72] These preexisting social bonds, such as family ties, are thought to be fundamental in the desistance process. In this dynamic, the offender ceases criminal behavior in order to compensate for the supportive role of the preexisting relationship. Based on self-report surveys of eight hundred men and women preparing to leave prison, Christy Visher and Daniel O'Connell showed that those who maintained a strong family support while incarcerated had a higher degree of optimism—a factor strongly related to successful reentry[73]—upon release: they may view family reunification as a reason for hope, which may in turn engender a strong commitment to a more positive self.[74] Due to the long period of time these lifers were incarcerated, the influence of such preexisting relationships was not as pronounced as may be expected. Rather, both non-incarcerated and re-incarcerated interviewees indicated that many of their parents, siblings, and extended family members died while they were incarcerated or passed away shortly after they were released. I ask Tonya if she had family support when she was released, and she answers, "No, my family was in [the Midwest] and I was here [Massachusetts]." Her brief answers set the tone for the interview; she is not keen on talking to me at all, but is simply doing a favor for Lyn, who introduced me to her. "Have you been in contact with your family while you were in?" I ask. "My family has passed on. We are talking thirty-two years ago . . . My mom passed, couple years ago, my grandmother passed, I didn't have any siblings, so . . ." Doris is more forthcoming in sharing her experiences. She recalls that she felt out of place in family settings: "I felt I did not fit in these family events. I felt like I didn't belong, like I wasn't there for twenty-five years and concessions were being made to put me back in the pitch and I didn't feel comfortable with that." The only family member she is in contact with is her mother, whom she calls three times a week: "I drive her crazy. I just want to check up on her, make sure she is doing OK, [especially since] I am the only living child of my mother." Her three brothers passed away: one as a result of ill health, one due to an accidental drug overdose, and one by suicide.

Many lifers who did have living family members frequently pointed out that they did not act as pro-social role models in the desistance process. As we saw in chapter 4, many interviewees emphasized the absence of father figures in their childhood, adolescence, and later in life: fathers were incarcerated or, more commonly, never present in the interviewees' lives. Others pointed out that parents and siblings did not constitute a significant source of support because of drug use, incarceration, or involvement in crime. Still others expressed that they needed to work hard to improve relationships with their families post-release. Not infrequently, they felt that family members had given up on them, and they needed to prove to them that they had redeemed themselves, as forty-five-year-old Nathan illustrates:

> When I got out, I wanted my family to embrace me, to welcome me, to understand that I was gonna do the right thing and be a person that I now need to be, a healthy responsible person, and they weren't sure. They wanted to see it. People who you've hurt in the past, they want you to demonstrate that you're a changed person, long enough that they can rebuild and regain some trust. [It wasn't until] the second or the third year of doing the right thing and being out in society, my whole family started looking at me differently.

Now, he describes himself as a family man, engaged in every type of family activity, organizing get-togethers and acting as a father figure for his younger cousins. However, he says, it takes time and hard work. This sentiment is shared by the Irish American Vincent. He is in charge of a local job agency. As part of the job, he engages in public speaking for ex-prisoners. When he speaks to groups about the problems associated with reentry, he always cautions his audience that they should not expect their families to receive them with open arms: "You know, expecting your family to believe that you're no longer that person that was taken out of their living room in handcuffs—is that really fair to do to your family? You've gotta convince them through hard work and compassion and understanding where they're from. Obviously, if you're known to be violent and do you want . . . do families necessarily want to bring you in amongst the kids in the family to adopt your moral beliefs . . . until they know for sure that you are better and working hard?"

The interviewees did not express a common pattern in terms of how to deal with family relations after release. Some, such as Frank, found it emotionally too difficult to deal with family members because they did not fully understand what he had been through in prison. "You know, you just cannot, after fifteen or twenty years, maybe even after seven years, you cannot go back to your family. It is just too much," he insisted, "for them, and for you, because you are setting yourself up for a serious, serious mess. They are not equipped to deal with people who have been imprisoned for a long period of time." Others, such as Cedric, argue that family could be of great support: "Family can help you to come to that path. They can guide you through it." When I counter that family typically has not spent time in prison, and hence cannot know what the experience may be like, he maintains, "They may not have gone through what you've gone through physically, but mentally, they were there with you."

Still others went as far as to blame their re-incarceration on the lack of social support from family members. Randall, for example, was incarcerated for twenty-two years before being paroled. He started using heroin after he realized soon after his release that "a whole generation was gone: my parents, all my aunts and uncles, some of my brothers and sisters. [. . .] It is just a mind-blowing experience. [. . .] I came from a loving family." The extended family he left behind more than twenty years ago had passed away. He explains his heroin use as follows: "I had an emotional relapse, this generation thing, going home and this culture thing. [. . .] The culture I was raised in, big, extended, loving family, values and everything, gone."

TABLE 7.5. Involvement in post-release programs among lifers (N=68)

	Non-incarcerated interviewees (N=30)		Re-incarcerated interviewees (N=38)		Total (N=68)	
	N	%	N	%	N	%
Not partici-pating in any program	3	10	2	5	5	7
Participating in some program	27	90	23	61	50	74
Substance abuse program (AA/NA)	12	40	21	55	33	49
Religious program	5	17	1	3	6	9
Employment program[1]	3	10	4	11	7	10
Counseling[2]	20	67	7	18	27	40

1. In Boston, the most frequently mentioned employment programs included STRIVE, the Moving Ahead Program, and the Suffolk County Sherriff's Department "Job Club."
2. In general, two types of counseling could be distinguished: counseling offered by an individual counselor, and organization-based counseling, such as offered by Span.

Rather than referring to family members, many interviewed lifers received support from alternative social groups, such as substance-related programs (AA/NA), religious groups, and other post-release programs (see table 7.5). In some cases these social groups acted as surrogate families. Thanh, for example, became involved in a Christian organization during his incarceration and stayed involved after release. He attributes his successes, such as finding housing and obtaining employment, to the social structure offered by this organization: "[Religion] is very important, it helps me to change a lot. Because that's, you know, faith gives hope and hope gives life. And I need to have faith in God and faith in the people surrounding me. [. . .] I heard other people say, "I don't trust nobody," and you have to trust other people. The [religious] community has a lot of good people and they helped me realize, they left me with some kind of unconditional love—[even though] they knew what kind of crime I committed."

Others, such as forty-year-old Juan, point to post-release long-term residential programs that acted as a substitute for a social network long lost. When he was granted parole after seventeen years, he says, he had "no family, no nothing, no nothing, no wife, no kids." He tells me how life confronted him with the fact that he had no social network whatsoever:

[A fellow prisoner asked me:] "What are you going to do? You have nobody." And, you know, that scared me because if you don't have anybody, then, you know, that affects the recidivism aspect of, you know, the revolving door, you know, am I going to get out? Am I going to make it? Am I going to succeed? Or am I going to come back in? And that plays a major part in it. Having a social network on the outside is extremely important and, this guy said, "Why don't you go down to [the priest's] office and go see" [. . .] So, I went down there, assuming that it was going to be short, and they embraced me, and took me in with open arms. [. . .] Here I am, asking for help, and they are just taking me in, and then on top of it, finding the place to live, giving me a full-time job, you know, just, eternally grateful for them.

Today, he is working in a small-town local shop. He receives much support from his religious community. Such positive experiences were plentiful but not prevalent among all lifers. Female lifers pointed out that reentry initiatives tend to focus on men, as Tonya bitterly points out: "I think [it] is very different for men, just because they're not parents, you know, when they come out of prison, plus there's more resources for men when they come out of prison. Even today, when they get out, they don't have to get their children, no they just go on living their lives."

To sum up, life after life imprisonment, for many interviewees, has been a jungle, one with its own rules and structure. In talking about this research with others, I often bring up the comparison with Wolfgang Becker's movie *Good Bye Lenin!*[75] The movie is set in Berlin in 1989, and reflects the life of a mother and her son. Months before the fall of communism, the mother suffers a near-fatal heart attack and falls into a coma. She awakes eight months later but is severely weakened both physically and mentally. Her doctor asserts that any shock might cause another, possibly fatal, heart attack. Her son then realizes that the discovery of recent events—that her beloved nation of East Germany as she knew it has disappeared—would be too much for her to bear. Hence, he sets out to maintain the illusion that things are as before in the German Democratic Republic.

What these lifers, and the mother in the movie, have in common is that they are strangers in their own land. For these lifers, the life they knew upon entering prison is no longer there. They have to relearn how to navigate a place once called home. In this chapter we have taken a closer look at what may be termed "sociological" roadblocks of reentry: finding a place to live and obtaining a job. Contrary to what we might expect based on the life-course approach to crime, factors such as intimate relationships, parenthood, and family relations did not constitute areas of support, but rather areas of additional challenges. Now, let us change our scope from these sociological effects to another level: the psychological effects of long-term imprisonment.

8

Residual Effects of Imprisonment

So far, we have addressed numerous difficulties lifers faced upon reentry, ranging from poor employment prospects and housing to troubled family relations. The effects of imprisonment do not stop there. As we have seen, these lifers constitute a group that is exposed to the pains of imprisonment over a long period of time (see table 8.1). The long-term effects of exposure to powerful and traumatic situations, contexts, and structures mean that prisons themselves can bring about psychological problems resulting from prison trauma. The findings on the effects of long-term imprisonment on mental health, however, are conflicting. In their literature review, the Canadian prison scholars James Bonta and Paul Gendreau held that "from the available evidence and on the [psychometric] dimensions measured, there is little to support the conclusion that long-term imprisonment necessarily has detrimental effects."[1] Similar results have been reported by the criminal justice scholar Timothy Flanagan, who reviewed several studies on deterioration in intellectual functioning as a result of long-term confinement.[2] Flanagan hastens to add, however, that there are reasons to believe that long-termers face problems and challenges different from those faced by inmates serving shorter terms, and that these stresses may not be adequately measured by studies designed for populations other than lifers.[3] In addition, the aforementioned studies do not include inmates with very long prison sentences, but rather consider "long" sentences as those longer than five years. More important, however, none of these studies[4] assessed the effects of imprisonment *after* release. Another factor that may contribute to the underreporting of harmful effects of prison conditions can be found in the context of the time of these studies. In the post-1970s perspective, prisoners were portrayed as much worse and tougher than the penal institutions to which they were being sent. Politicians and policy-makers implied that since prisoners' bad characters were too resilient to be changed for the better in these settings, these

TABLE 8.1. Length of time served on a life sentence before initial release (N=68)

	Non-incarcerated interviewees (N=30)		Re-incarcerated interviewees (N=38)		Total (N=68)	
	N	%	N	%	N	%
Life sentence characteristics						
Total years incarcerated for homicide						
≤ 15 years	11	37	5	13	16	24
16–25 years	14	47	22	58	36	53
≥ 26 years	5	17	11	29	16	24
Average sentence length	18.6 ± 7.7		21.8 ± 6.2		20.4 ± 7.1	

settings could not harm them either.[5] That is, according to the prison psychologist Craig Haney points out, as the origins of criminal behavior were increasingly portrayed as rooted in the unchanging character of prisoners, "liberal" concerns over the potentially harmful effects of prison conditions came to be seen as exaggerated and misplaced.[6]

More recent studies on the effects of imprisonment, in contrast, do report on the predominance of mental health problems, specifically involving posttraumatic stress disorder (PTSD), among both incarcerated and released individuals.[7] PTSD was first introduced in the third revised version of the *Diagnostic and Statistical Manual of Mental Disorders*[8] as an anxiety disorder and is characterized by persistent reexperiencing, avoidance of stimuli, hyper-arousal, and emotional numbing. The prevalence of PTSD has been found to occur as much as ten times more often among released prisoners compared to the general population.[9]

In their study on nineteen long-term wrongly convicted and politically motivated prisoners, Ruth Jamieson and Adrian Grounds found that many of the men changed in personality following years of confinement. They had marked features of estrangement, loss of capacity, moodiness, inability to settle, and loss of purpose and direction. They were withdrawn and unable to relate properly.[10]

Craig Haney suggests that the immediate pains of imprisonment may thus produce lasting problems that persist long after prisoners are released.[11] Many prisoners, including the interviewed lifers, come from socially and economically marginalized groups and have suffered many adverse, traumatic childhood and adolescent experiences. This is particularly true for women. Compared to male prisoners, female prisoners are more likely to suffer from mental illness and have a higher prevalence of HIV/AIDS, sexually transmitted diseases, and chronic illness.[12] The mental health needs of female prisoners, including female lifers, are often complex and frequently symptomatic of a history of abuse,[13] self-harm, homelessness, poor physical health, low self-esteem, and problematic personal and family relationships. This situation is often intensified by the high levels of drug and alcohol misuse and co-morbidity promoted by the prison environment.[14]

The atypical backgrounds of male and female inmates compared to the general population include many risk factors that tend to increase their vulnerability to stress. This may render them less able to cope with the high levels of stress they are likely to encounter in prison.[15] Psychiatric assessments of long-term prisoners have found that their most serious psychological problems are typically manifested only after they re-enter society.

The majority of both non-incarcerated and re-incarcerated lifers reported struggling with mental health issues post-release. While some entered the prison system with mental illness and found that their pre-existing conditions were worsened by the stress of confinement, most interviewees reported that the symptoms they experienced predominantly stemmed from their incarceration. The prolonged duration of incarceration implies that these men, as reported elsewhere, were unable to avoid witnessing some traumatizing events.[16] Strikingly, the symptoms they described were not limited to PTSD, but also included institutionalized personality traits, social-sensory disorientation, and temporal alienation (the idea of "not belonging" in social and temporal settings). Taken together, this cluster of mental health symptoms can best be described as the "post-incarceration syndrome."[17]

Posttraumatic Stress Disorder

The first facet of the suggested post-incarceration syndrome comprises chronic PTSD. The interviewed lifers most prominently reported recurrent distressing dreams, hyper-arousal (e.g., sleep disturbances), persistent avoidance of stimuli, and emotional numbing. Recurrent distressing dreams mostly involved the prison experience, as Daniel, a fifty-three-year-old biker currently on parole, recalls: "When I got out, I was tormented by nightmares that I was still in prison. I'd wake up sittin' and screamin'. Cold sweat pouring down my face, literally, and my pillow soaked. [. . .] They were all prison nightmares and some of them were me . . . seeing myself waking up in prison. [. . .] Those were really bad when I [first] got out, they were almost debilitating." Daniel's hardened appearance contrasts with his mental vulnerability. Tonya experiences similar nightmares: "I do have nightmares about going back to jail [. . .] that's like my nightmare, my nightmare is I'm in jail." Frequently, these nightmares diminished over time, but for many they never disappeared completely.

A second feature of PTSD—hyper-arousal—mainly included sleep disturbances, which interviewees such as seventy-year-old Donald attribute to a disturbed sleeping pattern in prison. He reports that in prison, he woke up "every time [the correctional officers] make rounds. Forty-five minutes to an hour [. . .] you wakin' up, alright. To this day, I do not sleep a straight night. I wake up every forty-five minutes to an hour." Additionally, signs of hyper-arousal included startled responses, at times accumulating into full-blown panic attacks. Jeffrey, who has been on parole for fourteen years after his release at age fifty, still suffers from these attacks: "Like, you know, I take the [metro] ride here, and if I get into crowds or I'm in open spaces or things like that . . . it brings on panic attacks. And the panic attacks bring on the seizures. But, 'cause to me, it's like I can't go outside and walk around the compound because I'm in wide open spaces and there's nothing around me to like to hold onto if I start feeling panicky." Because of the nature of his symptoms, combined with diagnosed hepatitis B, he is on disability. His wife takes care of him. They live a quiet life in a rural community.

A third aspect of PTSD—persistent avoidance of stimuli—was reflected in interviewees evading places and situations to avoid feeling uncomfortable or, in the worst case, experiencing a panic attack. Jeffrey, who actively avoids the subway, is not the only one. Keith, another interviewee, also mentioned that he tried to avoid crowded spaces: "Going into the subway, when the door opened and the people poured out: instant panic attack. [. . .] I wasn't used to people in my space. It was overwhelming; it was hard to breathe, and [I had] to get away from them."

A fourth PTSD trait reported by the majority of the lifers was emotional numbing, a coping mechanism in which they had created a permanent and unbridgeable distance between themselves and other people. Haney has referred to this coping mechanism as a "prison mask."[18] In prison, these men and women inferred that revealing too much about themselves provides others with knowledge that can be used to exploit them. In response, the emotional and behavioral "prison mask" is unrevealing and impenetrable. While this mask may have been self-protective during incarceration, it becomes maladaptive post-release, as forty-year-old Vincent, a lifer from Irish descent, explains: "It's just, you, in prison, you learn not to show your emotions. You don't wanna be weak, you know, you need to be strong, you need to continue to be strong, and always strong. [. . .] Those coping mechanisms in relationships is where I struggle, is where I fall short. And it's like you just, you, you don't wanna show that emotion, that vulnerability, that is the damage of prison. [. . .] You're always trying to protect that vulnerability." Interviewees described difficulty shedding this mask post-release. In the decades spent in prison they created a permanent and unbridgeable distance between themselves and other people. Others found that the risks associated with open, genuine communication were too great. Their prison experience led them to withdraw from authentic social interactions altogether, and they sought safety in social invisibility. Similar to findings reported elsewhere, ex-offenders became as inconspicuous and unobtrusive as possible by disconnecting completely from others.[19]

Institutionalized Personality Traits

In addition to the "typical" PTSD features, interviewees mentioned that prison had changed them in profound ways, as Sean describes when I talk to him in Span's office downtown: "I do kind of act like I'm still in prison, and I mean, you [are] not a light switch or a water faucet. You can't just turn something off. When you've done something for a certain amount of time [. . .] it becomes a part of you." When I ask him if prison changed him, Glenn replies, "When I first got out, I was very, very manipulative." "Do you think this is a residual effect of having been in for so long?" I ask. "Well, I haven't shed it to this day," he says. "I know this [prison], but I do not know that [society]."

The most common personality trait described by interviewees as a result of incarceration was "paranoia," or finding it difficult to trust others and feeling vulnerable to attack, as Benjamin explains: "You cannot trust anybody in the joint. [. . .] I do have an issue with trust, I just do not trust anybody." To delve deeper into this notion, let us return to Ruben. When I ask him if he experienced difficulty trusting others, he replies:

Ohh, the trust issue—in prison, yeah [laughs] that's a big issue, with trust, you know, especially coming home [. . .] if you come from the streets, it's hard to trust people you know, you have your close circle, that's where the loyalty comes from—having your people in a circle. Everyone outside, you don't have loyalty to, you know, you don't trust them, you know, in prison that is amplified. [. . .] You know, the thing in prison is not to trust anybody because people will [. . .] knock you asleep and they will come to you. You know when I got in, guys were being vicced [victimized] on a regular basis, raped on a regular basis, you know. [. . .] Raping you for going around, they'd be buying candy, or they'd be buying you canteen or buying you clothes or trying to befriend you, and then you owe them and then they say, "Oh you cannot pay me back?" You know, and you cannot pay the guy back, so we feel obligated to, so many guys, there was a lot of, well, I'm not sure there were a lot of things like that going on behind the walls. So, the issue was big for me, I didn't trust anybody, I ended up meeting a couple of people over the years I became really close with, but the trust issue was always, you know, a factor, it's always a factor, you know, like, I hang out with you every day, but I don't trust you. Be in the same vicinity with you, you know, I wouldn't, you know, I got to watch you, I'm still watching you. And so when I came home, there was the same issue. [. . .] When you got a lot of lies compounding over the years and years and years, dealing with people, you put some walls up.

And then there were incidents when [. . .] my street was really quiet. I was used to being imprisoned, in prison everything is noisy. When stuff became quiet, something's wrong, something is about to go down, and that mentality was still in me, so when I was at home and everything is quiet and peaceful I was like, "This is so quiet," walked around the house I was just so tense [. . .] just expecting something to happen, you know, like something's going to happen, it was too quiet, something's going to happen, I would get out, walking around the streets, checking the backyards. I became very paranoid, you know [. . .] I couldn't shake some of those things when I came home and I was like, "Some of this stuff has really affected me," you know, baggage from prison into the streets.

When I ask Glenn about his experiences, he acknowledges, "I relive it, every day, every day, I cannot get rid of it." He recounts an experience at the supermarket, when someone approached him in a rude way, for no particular reason: "And I was ready to punch him in the face with a can of beans." Realizing what he was about to do, he said, "I was just like, 'What is happening to me?' Those were the defense mechanisms you learn in here [prison], because here, there sometimes is no time to talk." Similarly, Keith also talks about being "on edge" in the outside world: "Yeah I guess like the constant feeling of, I don't wanna say paranoia, but you're always on edge when you're in prison. You're always feeling like someone's gonna attack you."

The inability to trust others was also reflected in the inability to engage in social relationships post-release, as Ernesto puts it: "I'm not defected to where I'm crazy. But I think that I maybe be defected socially, in some way." I ask him, "Can you give an example of that, defected socially?" He says, "Yeah just like, just me not being able to get close to people. That's what it is. Um, I'm kind of like, kind of like detached, you know?"

The prison mask, combined with the inability to trust others, was also reflected in difficulties in intimate relations. Ernesto tells me:

> [In prison] you have to distance yourself, so you always have to keep on putting up walls and putting up barriers, every single day. You have to build like this shell around you, to protect you from your environ-ment. So if you keep on doing this for so long, then once you get let out, it's kind of difficult to bring it down, because it's ingrained in you. [So,] one of the things [my girlfriend] has a problem with is like [. . .] you're unemotional. And I tell her, I'm like, "Listen I'm defective right now, I'm messed up right now."

In addition to thinking of others as untrustworthy, another institu-tionalized personality trait was hampered decision-making, which the majority of the interviewees experienced. This could be traced back to the erosion of personal autonomy in prison and the way prisoners adapt to this erosion.[20] In prison, it seems increasingly "natural" that others routinely decide things for them. Even though the majority of interviewees had difficulties making decisions when they were first released, for some it took a long time to be able to make fairly mundane decisions. Clarence captures this best when he says, "in prison you really don't have to think. Not about your day-to-day activities." He continues, "As soon as you get out, there's all these sort of decisions . . . and now you're bombarded with all these decisions it's like what, what, am I supposed to do here, you know? [. . .] You know, and that's scary [. . .] to many men it can be daunting, you know, for many it can be frustrating and sometimes men go back to prison just because they're so frustrated they just can't handle this too much. It's just so much easier to just sit back and say, 'OK.'" Nowadays he feels he has regained control over his day-to-day actions and uses his prison experience professionally in counseling young men in their reentry.

Social-Sensory Deprivation

A third set of symptoms—in addition to PTSD and institutionalized personality traits—included spatial disorientation post-release as a result of social and sensory deprivation while incarcerated. Clarence, for example, observes, "For years it was very difficult on me to go somewhere and come out the other way, I'm lost. I have to turn around and come back the same way and try to figure how I got there and come back the same way 'cause I didn't have a sense of direction."

Many prisoners navigated the prison walls year after year. They felt lost in open spaces, devoid of walls. In addition to being deprived of spatial stimuli, many interviewees reported effects of deprivation of normal social contacts. They emphasized difficulties in social interactions post-release, such as judging people's intentions. This did not have so much to do with trust, as discussed above, but rather with the way people communicate in prison versus the outside world. Even though men who spent much time in solitary confinement often spoke about social deprivation, solitary was not a necessary condition to find social interaction difficult post-release. The effects of sensory deprivation became visible once interviewees walked the streets after release. Inside prison, physical contact meant physical harm, and hence interviewees adapted accordingly. This form of coping became maladaptive on the outside, as Ruben aptly puts it:

[In prison] you have to be respectful or you [are] going to have problems, you know, you bump somebody you don't say, "Excuse me," or, you know, just little things, like holding the door for somebody or say, "Excuse me, mind your own business," you know, not being in somebody's face, not stepping on anybody and, like, all those little things like that that mean a lot—that can be life or death behind the walls. Out here, you know, people, they are just so busy with their business, they bump into you and they don't say, "Excuse me." So when I first came home, the issue of riding the buses, riding the train, people bumping into me and not say[ing], "Excuse me," and how people are staring at me, you know, automatically I am like . . . I felt threatened, I felt [. . .] I immediately became, got into defense mode. You know all the time I was pretty much in defense mode, so, and now I am like, I'm like, when the defense mode comes in, ready for action, so, and everything else just shuts down, my thinking, my reasoning just falls down.

At times, Ruben says, the lack of trust in other people, the restlessness of being outside, and the unpredictability of other people's behavior became too overwhelming: "So that was a big issue with me and I knew people [were] hard for me. [. . .] And I isolated myself so much. But there was a point, there was a point that was so overwhelming, so horrible for me, and [I] asked [my parole officer] to take me back behind the wall, to turn me in, and she told me no, she told me it was not going to happen." It took a total of six months for him to be re-incarcerated for a parole violation: "A drug case. Somebody had some pills and some cocaine in the car with them. And because I was a passenger, they charged all of us." Back in prison he felt at home. He was re-paroled several years later.

"I Don't Belong Here"

In addition to the features reported above, the effects of incarceration also included feelings of alienation, reflected in the idea of not belonging in social settings after release. Before going to prison, sixty-year-old

Marvin worked as a seasonal bartender. He was a well-liked employee and made a decent living that allowed him to shop in department stores downtown. He was incarcerated after killing a friend in an alcohol-infused fight. He had served sixteen years and had been on parole for a little less than a year at the time we talked. He tells me:

> One of the things that was really overwhelming for me is that I found my-self in Macy's one day and it was the first time, maybe a month after I had gotten out. And I always shopped at Macy's or Saks or another high-end store, you know, and I got there and I had this overwhelming feeling that I did not belong there. And I was borderline tears and paranoid and it just all hit me at once. It was nuts and it took every ounce of me that I did not blot out of the store because I knew that if I was running out of the store someone would think something. So I like, slowly left [. . .] I felt I had "felon" written all over me. I felt as though "criminal" was written all over me, [that] I was a bad person [and] that people could see that.

Feelings of alienation were also expressed in interviewees' belief that their current situation was only temporal and that good things can be taken away at any moment, as Nathan points out: "Part of coming out of prison was the idea that eventually, I'll be back there. [. . .] When I was out and good things happened to me, I always thought that 'this cannot last for long.' When good things happened to me, I always thought that 'eventually, this will be taken away from me.' [. . .] I thought of freedom as a temporary thing."

The idea that the life they built for themselves outside the walls can be taken away at any moment, particularly after incidents with other lifers, resonates in intimate relationships. We turn again to Ruben, as he describes how he finds it difficult to deal with the "liminal status"[21] in his relationship:

> And that's one of the things, just one of the problems I have in the re-lationship with my wife—is that I am always, always, early on, I used to always do it but now I'm not forcing it on her, tried to prepare her, because I'm a lifer, prepare her, it's beyond my control, it's a lifer. I cannot do anything, I can't do anything right, but still be taken back, you know what I mean, [I could be] brought back behind the wall. Like I said, it's

political, this thing that happened a year, a year and a half go with that Dominic Cinelli. [. . .] But, when that happened, you know, I was like on eggshells. I was on eggshells.

He is still with his wife, but each and every day he reminds himself that he can be pulled back behind the walls. As reported elsewhere, for men like Ruben relationships are tempered by their awareness that future re-incarceration is always possible.[22]

As Haney points out, the extreme stress that results from incarceration, and long-term incarceration specifically, is problematic because it appears to have direct, adverse consequences on prisoners' mental health.[23] These findings suggest that post-incarceration syndrome constitutes a discrete subtype of PTSD that results from long-term imprisonment. Recognizing this syndrome as a subtype of PTSD may allow for more adequate recognition of the effects of incarceration and, subsequently, treatment for ex-inmates. This is particularly important because both before and after release inmates rarely have anywhere to turn for help.[24] On one hand, the thick and largely impenetrable psychological barriers that divide prisoners from guards and the prison code itself preclude them from seeking protection from staff. Several interviewees expressed concern about the lack of adequate therapy or counseling for long-term incarcerated individuals, particularly after release. Mental health professionals are often poorly equipped, in both knowledge and skill, to deal with the unique dynamics of the prison culture. Treatment staff frequently do not have direct access to actual mainline experiences, which limits their ability to prepare prisoners for transition back into society.

Daniel, who had been repeatedly assaulted during his twenty-six-year sentence, elaborates: "I go to a counselor and tell them some of those things, you know, just some of the stuff that I mentioned here and see their jaw drop, like, 'You have no idea what I'm talking about, do you? You can't even freakin' relate.' [. . .] It's frustrating, you know? I don't go to counseling, just can't find anybody that I'm compatible with." Daniel has been officially diagnosed with PTSD. He was in counseling for seventeen years, throughout his incarceration and three years after. However, he no longer seeks counseling because he feels no one can relate to his experience in prison.

Others, such as Vincent, had issues seeking counseling because of their parole status, and experienced intense fear that seeking help could potentially them back to prison: "There's the problem. When you're on parole, you gotta be very careful with that. You don't want them to think that you're not stable, in any way." "Because your parole officer would know about you getting treatment?" I ask him. "Right," he replies, "right. And they could essentially send you back just because they feel like you're unstable." Glenn shares this view. He says that while he was on parole prior to being re-incarcerated, he attended mandatory counseling: "I wasn't comfortable talking to their counselor. 'Cause he's not concerned about me, but about them [the parole board]. I want to find my own." Joel, in addition, points to a mismatch between the type of counseling offered and the lifer population: "People need stability. But in the two years I was out, I had two parole officers and three counselors. That's not stability. It takes time to build a trust relation, especially with a counselor."

Vincent, Glenn, and Joel are not unique in their observations. The sociologists Sara Steen and her colleagues, studying the parole revocation process, found that parolees with mental health needs committed significantly more technical violations.[25] Navigating the dynamics of parole often clashed with the lifers' need for appropriate mental health counseling. Meeting therapy requirements and abiding by parole regulations at the same time is, however, just one of the many skills needed to avoid being sent back to prison for technical violations. Next, we will take a closer look at the question of who was able to stay out of prison after reentry, and who was not.

9

Going Back

With the exception of six[1] interviewees, all lifers were on lifetime parole. Norman, who was re-incarcerated after an altercation with his wife, has been back in prison for two and a half years when I talk to him. He tells me, "When you get parole, you have to change your whole personality. You almost forget who you really are. You want to be out of there so bad." Similar to the initial impact and getting used to the outside world after decades of incarceration, he adds how getting used to being on parole required additional adjustments: "You cannot show weakness in here [prison]. Because people will take advantage of that. But while on parole, you have to humble yourself." About the conditions of his parole, he says, "I'd smoke weed every day if I could. But I can't." For him, the major difficulty in being on parole is not so much abstinence from drugs but paying the eighty-dollar parole fees, also termed "supervision fees," per month: "When I got out again in '09, I built up a debt of four-hundred-something dollars. And the guy just didn't understand that I had to go out and find a job and had a hard time, and couldn't pay the money all at once." He had to convince his wife to pay the fee on his behalf in order to stay out on parole. Eventually, after a few years, he was re-incarcerated after a fight with his wife.

Bernard, a sixty-nine-year-old re-incarcerated lifer, reported that due to his various medical conditions, he had trouble sleeping, but given his parole conditions he was not allowed to take any sleeping medication. He was very much aware of the strict conditions to which he had to adhere: "I couldn't risk it [taking sleeping medication], because I'm thinking, 'What would the parole board think about this?'" Bernard is an elderly man I meet in an empty, cold cell in a maximum-security prison. The only furniture is a plastic folding chair across from an iron chair chained to the floor. Bernard sits on the iron chair, his walking stick leaning against his swollen leg. He had most of his teeth pulled because of diabetes. He apologizes for his appearance, and for not having shaved prior to our meeting. He tells me how he ended up behind bars for a verbal altercation with his neighbors.

Navigating the Conditions of Parole

Among the interviewees, the parole agency's efforts to govern were frequently met with subversion, resistance, and hostility. Three general themes arose in prisoners' difficulties in abiding by the restrictions of parole. First, they had trouble finding and maintaining employment of which their parole officers would approve. Second, they found it difficult to participate in 12-step programs. Lastly, they encountered difficulty with the prohibition against associating with others with a criminal record. These restrictions strongly regulate and structure parolees' daily lives. Several scholars have pointed out that in its current form, the institution of parole "extends the gaze of the penal state and regulates and governs a group of marginalized people returning to their communities."[2] Criminal justice scholars have argued that current parole restrictions are built on the assumption that parolees are not yet prepared for responsible self-governance after release from prison. Yet, at the same time, parolees are held responsible if they exercise their autonomy to make "bad" choices.[3] The parolee is thus understood both as an individual who must take responsibility for his or her own (pro-social) change and as culpable, risky, and in need of supervision and direction.[4] The vast majority of interviewees emphasized that they experienced the conditions as mechanisms of intense control, rather than as contributing to their rehabilitation. On a practical level, parole conditions often conflicted with the demands of their everyday lives.

Like other lifers, Scott expresses that the conditions of parole inhibited his prospects for employment. Several months ago he picked up his daughter at a restaurant. On his way home he was pulled over for a broken taillight. His parole officer was notified and accused him of barhopping. As a result, he now wears an ankle bracelet. In his most recent encounter with his parole officer, he tells me, "I [was] working for my brother, he's giving me $300 cash a day [...] and they say, 'You can't work for your brother.' [...] This is what the parole guy says to me. [...] I got a job, the next day [...] I go over and tell him I have a job over [. . .] at the scrap metal yard. He says, 'Oh no, you're not working at the scrap metal yard. There's something wrong with it.'"

Similarly, Glenn shares his frustrations with me about the conditions of parole that inhibited him from obtaining work after release. While in prison he took part in music programs and is now a trained percussionist: "I applied to the Berklee School of Music to study musicology and I got in, but I was denied by parole because I wasn't allowed to go into places to perform where they serve alcohol." From the parole organization's perspective, any "slip" in abstention from alcohol or entering an establishment where alcohol is served could result in a return to crime.[5] Prohibited from continuing his studies, Glenn exclaims, "Now, how is society expecting me to function without me being able to function as a productive human being?" Glenn's account illustrates the tension between, on one hand, parole's aim to prevent parolees from returning to criminal behavior, and on the other hand, parole's goal to prepare ex-prisoners for "freedom" and enhance self-governance. When I talked to Glenn, he was re-incarcerated as a result of a "motor vehicle infraction." Several months later, I learned he has been re-paroled.

A second area of hindrance for many lifers involved the mandatory attendance of AA/NA meetings, as they typically committed their crimes while under the influence of alcohol or drugs. Even though some lifers considered the programs helpful, the majority of interviewees expressed skepticism, as Joel explains: "It didn't help me. People were there [at the AA meeting] getting high, coming in with brown bags. I mean, drug dealers came there to deal drugs. That is not helping anyone." Norman shares a similar experience: "I went because I had to go, not because I wanted to go. I mean, they got high at those meetings. They were unsupervised. How can you respect those meetings when everyone's high?" Warren was also required to attend AA meetings, even though he did not have a history of substance abuse: "Everyone was just sharing war stories, like 'Hey man, I was smoking dope and crack and all that . . .' I mean, there was nothing about change, or about fixing the problem."

A third frequently mentioned parole condition that raised concerns among the interviewees was not being allowed to associate with others who had a felony record. The vast majority of lifers found this condition to inhibit rather than encourage readjustment to society. Numerous interviewees expressed the need to relate to other ex-inmates to share experiences, find companionship, and solicit advice on reentry, such as Joel, who tells me, "Parole doesn't allow contact with other felons, but if you don't have any family those are the best people. They become your family, when you're in for like twenty to thirty years. They know what it's like in prison. Your family doesn't. These [lifers] are the people you want to talk to when things get rough." Joel stayed by himself and did not have contact with other lifers. He, and many interviewees like him, reported that support from other lifers—and particularly lifers with whom they had done time—would have been beneficial to them in "going straight." Others openly acknowledged seeking out the company of ex-lifers to discuss problems and share experiences, despite these parole conditions. For them, these lifers were companions who had been through similar processes and faced similar obstacles. Benjamin, for example, who has been out for ten years, admits, "I have a couple of friends here and there, [and] one that I'm very close with, that I know from the inside, and I hang out with him together. I know we're not supposed to."

Some interviewees, such as Leroy, attribute their re-incarceration to the absence of someone to relate to: "When I got out, what I experienced, I had the support of my family, friends, everybody you think you need. But I didn't have people I could talk to about the real things I was dealing with. I had a significant other, but she couldn't relate. [So] I had all structures in place, you know—my girlfriend, work, housing— but I did not have anyone to talk to. I'd been calling to my people here in prison, but you cannot be glued to the phone all day." He attributes his paroled revocation to the absence of someone to trust to and relate to, someone with whom to share his prison experience. When we talk, he has been re-incarcerated for six years for possessing weapons and ammunition in connection with a shooting incident. He had his last parole board hearing more than one year ago but still has not received an answer. Six months later he hears that he received a five-year setback.

Holly, who was re-incarcerated after using drugs, agrees that contact with other lifers is necessary to be able to make it on the outside: "Going out of prison, we are faced with so many questions, that we don't know until we face them. Like a bar. Like a rock of crack in front of you. We need lifer support on the outside. We've been told we cannot go have a cup of coffee with someone you know for twenty years on the inside. Lifers can help other lifers."

Still others acknowledged the need to talk to other lifers but evaded contact altogether out of fear that they could be sent back. Frank, a sixty-one-year-old parolee who was recently paroled for the third time, was one of them. He had been in and out of prison and juvenile detention since age twelve. Even though his entire social network consisted of people he knew from inside, he avoided any contact with other ex-inmates: "I have a tendency to stay away from people, because, me being under these circumstances of this intense parole, it would just take one photograph. I mean, it's called 'association,' and I'll be gone for a while. And a while for me could be a lifetime."

Similar to paroled populations described elsewhere, for many interviewees their networks of support were made up mostly or entirely of people with a history of involvement in the criminal justice system. Parole conditions that prohibited them from seeking contact with others with criminal records implied that they had to isolate themselves from people, relationships, and sources of emotional support.

Having trouble finding employment due to parole restrictions, being obliged to participate in programs, and not being allowed to associate with former prisoners contribute to what has recently been coined "the parole paradox."[6] This suggests that while parole aims to promote integration and desistance, it can actually place individuals on parole in a position that complicates efforts to attain a conventional lifestyle. It has been argued that repeated rejections by potential employers, and loss of autonomy by having to abide by numerous parole restrictions that limited their own autonomy and judgment, can make parolees hyperaware of their status as felons, and hence inhibit their progress toward identity change.[7] In this way, parole supervision accomplishes the opposite of what it is supposed to do.

Good Cop, Bad Cop

Both re-incarcerated and non-incarcerated lifers' descriptions of their current or most recent parole officer ranged from "a good guy" to "a gun-flashing girl the age of my daughter." In the 1960s the sociologist Daniel Glaser, who has published extensively in the field of criminology, developed a fourfold classification of parole officer "supervision styles," distinguishing between officers' emphases on control and assistance.[8]

The first type, the "protective agent," is high on both control and assistance, while the second, "punitive" type puts much emphasis on control and low emphasis on assistance. Glaser describes the third type as a "welfare worker," who puts great emphasis on assistance but less emphasis on control. The fourth type is the "passive agent"—these are agents who execute their jobs with the minimum required effort.[9] When I openly ask them, "How would you describe the relationship with your parole officer?" none of the lifers consider their officer a "welfare worker" or a "passive agent." This is perhaps attributable to the style of managing the lifer population. Especially in recent years, the interviewees report being supervised up close. This involved frequent home and work visits, and weekly reporting at the parole office. Both non-incarcerated and re-incarcerated lived on average nine miles from the nearest office.

There was no clear, direct relationship between parole being revoked and the interviewees' relationships with their parole officers. Russell, for example, was re-incarcerated after he had been caught drinking in a sober house. He described his parole officer as "a very good, very decent guy. He was professional but firm. He said to me, 'Just live your life, as long as it doesn't come across my desk.'" Carl, who was re-incarcerated when it came to light that his girlfriend had a criminal record, had a similarly positive experience with his parole officer: "I called him [my parole officer] every Tuesday, and he let me know when I had to come in. Sometimes, he came to my house or to work, but I was lucky. He was decent, he came during the day and at work he acted like a customer, not flashing his badge so that everyone would know I was on parole."

Wesley, who is a plumber by trade, says, "I had awesome relationships with my parole officers, as long as I communicated with them." His most recent parole officer had been on the job for twenty-five years: "She would come over to my house and she told me she'd help me get off parole. [. . .] And she invited me over to her house, asked me if I could repair her faucet." On the other end of the spectrum, Norman characterizes his parole officer as follows: "He was the worst. He was disrespectful, obnoxious. He told me one time: 'You should kiss my feet for being on parole.' What man says that to another man? He's just an arrogant ass. He suffers from a Napoleon complex. I told his supervisor that I wanted another PO [parole officer], but they never changed it." "So, given the relationship you had with this PO, how did you deal with it?" I ask. He replies, "You're at these people's mercy. As long as they are there, you have to follow the rules."

Still others, such as Cody, attribute their re-incarceration specifically to their parole officers. He describes how he was not aware of the fact that his girlfriend had been arrested before for streetwalking. When he told his parole officer about the relationship, he added as a condition of parole that he was not to see her anymore. Later on, however, she was spotted in his car. Cody says this was a coincidence: she was walking somewhere and he simply gave her a ride. About his parole officer, he says, "He is a rotten dude. I haven't lied to him. [. . .] He has sentenced me to death as far as I'm concerned. I didn't do nothing." In a transcript of the parole board hearing several months later, I read that Cody's re-parole has been denied, partly because "he is unable to maintain appropriate and positive relations with women."

One Foot Out, One Foot In

Offenders on parole are back in society, but they are not free: they can be sent back any minute, any day. Parole is, thus, a transitional state between freedom and re-incarceration.[10] This transitional state, or "liminal phase," is a period of ambiguity.[11] The prison researcher Yvonne Jewkes compared those receiving an indeterminate life sentence to individuals who are diagnosed as terminally ill. She held that both groups may experience a permanent liminality in that they are not moving between established boundaries.[12] In the case of the terminally ill patient, this involves life and death. For the lifer with an indeterminate sentence, liminality involves the phase between freedom and captivity. I would argue that this liminality is not only applicable to the life sentence, but extends to the period of time these individuals are on parole: under parole conditions, lifers move between two worlds. Interviewees expressed this as being out of prison with one foot, while the other is still in. Tonya, who had been re-incarcerated multiple times following parole violations, illustrates this dynamic as follows: "It can be taken away, I can walk out of this door and when parole wants to violate me they could just snatch me up and that's it, and they don't answer to anyone but the governor, and he is not thinking about me." The extreme form of powerlessness expressed by Tonya illustrates the combined burden of a criminal record, being black, being poor, and being subject to the whim of her parole officer.

Virtually all interviewees who were on parole at the time I interviewed them were conscious of the fact that they could be sent back to prison at any time. Giuseppe, a seventy-five-year-old parolee with Mediterranean roots, is one of them. I talk to him on a summer afternoon in the garden of a local reentry organization. He tells me that he gets angry at his fellow parolees when he feels they are not aware of their special status: "Sometimes they come out and they want everything, everything! I do not live for everything, I am an inmate, I am a lifer. Some of the guys do not want to hear that, they say, 'Giuseppe, you are out, you are not a prisoner no more.'" But, he argues, a life sentence does not end at release: "We were prisoners, now we are outside. Like [. . .] wake up! We are in prison for life!" Similarly, Hakim feels that even in his own house, in the relationship with his wife, he is never completely free from the parole control mechanism: "So the overall stress of at any moment someone knocking on the door, and even though I am not doing anything against the law, a technicality could bring be back in prison. If my wife gets mad at me, she [could] just call my [parole] officer and say, 'I get sick and tired of him, I have all these bills and he ain't helping in the household.' And then they will handcuff me and take me back to prison."

Even though the interviewees experienced the in-between status of parole in several ways, they each had in common an intense fear of being sent back to prison. For all interviewees, the ambiguity of parole was hardest to handle. Some, such as Joel, prefer not dealing with parole at all: "To this day I'd rather have done the death penalty. I had my head screwed off and on so many times. [. . .] Life sentence is a torture." Currently, Joel has been re-incarcerated in a minimum-security prison for two and a half years. He received a five-year setback at his most recent parole hearing. The constant distress these lifers experienced mainly stems from the observation that the revocation decisions for technical violations are, to a large extent, unpredictable.

Return to Prison

Return to prison is ultimately an agency or court decision. It may or may not be related to criminal activity. In practice, the reasons for revocation fall into two groups: commission of a new offense, or violation of the conditions of parole. As elsewhere in the United States, the decision to send a parolee back to prison is typically not made by a judge, but by the parole board. Criminologists have coined this term "back-end sentencing," to describe how the parole revocation process centers on board practices. Not only are back-end sentences determined by correctional officials instead of judges, the standard of evidence used is much lower than is required in a court of law (beyond a reasonable doubt).[13] In line with previously cited studies on lifers specifically, very few (two out of sixty-eight) of the interviewees committed another crime, as defined as being charged and found guilty in court (see table 9.1). The vast majority of re-incarcerated lifers I interviewed returned to prison as a result of technical violations, mostly involving drugs (16%), alcohol (24%), and domestic disputes (21%). The overall low prevalence of new criminal offenses does not imply, however, that many were not charged with new crimes: Most interviewees who were re-incarcerated following "domestic strife" were initially charged with domestic assault (verbal and/or physical) following problems with their intimate partners, but in all cases these charges were either dropped or the interviewees were found not guilty in court. Their re-incarceration, however, remained.

Table 9.1 reflects the major reasons and circumstances surrounding the interviewees' re-incarceration: more than two-thirds were re-incarcerated at least once following their initial release. This table further indicates that the seemingly clear-cut division between the non-incarcerated and the re-incarcerated group of interviewees is somewhat arbitrary: numerous interviewees who were not incarcerated at the time of the interview were incarcerated in the past for parole violations (33%). The type of parole violations did not drastically differ between the two groups of interviewees. The vast majority of the total sample was sent back to prison for technical violations, including the possession or use of substances (34%) or domestic conflict (12%).

Condemned to Fail

In other words, the relatively high rate of re-incarceration among this sample does not seem to be attributable to new crimes, but rather to parole violations, including the use of alcohol or drugs, or conflicts

TABLE 9.1. Main reasons for re-incarceration, number of re-incarcerations, and time on parole after most recent release among interviewed lifers (N=68)

	Non-incarcerated interviewees (N=30)		Re-incarcerated interviewees (N=38)		Total (N=68)	
	N	%	N	%	N	%
Re-incarcerations after release[1]						
Never re-incarcerated	20	67	0	0	20	29
Criminal violation	1	3	1	3	2	3
Technical violation	9	30	37	97	46	67
Main reason for most recent re-incarceration[2]						
Alcohol	3	10	6	16	9	13
Drugs	3	10	9	24	12	18
Alcohol & drugs	-	-	3	8	3	4
Domestic strife	-	-	8	21	8	12
Associating with others having a criminal record	-	-	1	3	1	1
Associating with intimate partner having a criminal record	-	-	4	11	4	6
Possession of weapon	-	-	2	5	2	3
Other	4	7	5	13	9	13
Times re-incarcerated after initial release						
0	20	67	0	0	20	29
1	5	17	15	39	20	29
≥ 2	5	17	23	61	28	41
Time on parole since most recent release						
< 1 year	3	10	7	18	10	15
1 year–3 years	5	17	10	26	15	22
3–5 years	5	17	8	21	13	19
> 5 years	17	57	13	34	30	44
Average time out since life sentence						
	9.3 ± 7.6		5.5 ± 5.8		7.2 ± 6.8	

1. These figures were compiled based on interview data, cross-referenced with available parole board documentation.
2. Most commonly, there are multiple reasons for re-incarcerations. Here, the most severe technical violation is given, coded according to the following hierarchy: possession of a weapon, domestic strife, alcohol and drugs, association, and, finally, the category "other," which includes traffic violations, failure to report to the parole office, and criminal violations (N=2).

with intimate partners. In that regard, the high rate of recidivism—as defined as re-incarceration for a new crime or parole violation—is in line with other studies on homicide offender recidivism.[14] This finding at the same time challenges our traditional notion of "desistance." What really seems to occur is that virtually all these lifers desisted in that they abstained from future criminal behavior. In other words, what we should be questioning is not so much how these lifers are actively "going straight," but rather how they manage their parole conditions and, similarly, how the parole system manages its parolees.

When I asked these lifers why they felt that they, and other lifers, returned to custody, answers could be grouped around four themes: re-incarcerating lifers as a political trend; "catching up" too quickly; falling back to old habits; and prison as a safe place to which they can return.

"IT'S POLITICS"

In response to the question "Why do you think you or others like you returned to prison?" Glenn replies, "Politics." Like him, many others pointed to the "prison industrial complex," which has been described as "propelling the mushrooming of the carceral population through an unholy alliance among prison-industry profiteers, custodial bureaucrats, and politicians who reinforce one another's interests by fueling public fear of offenders, advocating tough-on-crime policies, and constructing and filling penal facilities."[15]

One of the reasons for a high degree of re-incarceration among parolees, Michelle Alexander has pointed out, are the plentiful opportunities for arrest: parolees are governed by additional rules that do not apply to everyone else, such as mandatory drug testing.[16] In these cases, parolees appear to be presumed guilty until their innocence is proven. Tonya is an example of this dynamic. Her parole officer comes to her house every week and can show up unannounced at work. She has to give a urine sample every week. Several years ago, she tells me:

> I went to parole, [. . .] they pulled me for urine, the guy [. . .] cuffed me to the chair and said, "You are going to jail, it was dirty." I said, "My urine is not dirty." You know, and that was it. I lost my apartment, and my daughter had to go to Chicago, you know, just everything, my life was

gone [. . .] you know, they call me into the parole office, I always become afraid, because who is to say? You know, your life is in somebody else's hands. Suppose they mix up your urine, suppose anything, you know, right, it's just scary to have to live like that.

Tonya was sent back to jail, awaiting the laboratory results from the preliminary test:

He took me back to jail [. . .] and [I] lost everything, I had to start all over again. And then I was in jail for a month. And [one day] the [corrections] officer said:, "I have something here that you might find interesting." So the urine that he said was dirty, when they sent it out from the jail, you know they have to send it to a lab once they say that its dirty, it was clean. Because I was a lifer, I had to see the full board, and then you have to wait months for their decision, they never give you that decision right there, you have to wait for it [. . .], so . . .

It wasn't until several months later that she was released, during which time she lost her apartment, her job, and custody of her daughter.

In addition to parole conditions, parolees are subject to regular surveillance and monitoring by the police and may be stopped and searched, for any reason at all.[17] As a result, they are far more likely to be arrested than are individuals whose behavior is not subject to constant scrutiny by law enforcement. In contrast to the general population, their fingerprints are in the system.[18] For Sergio, who is of Latino descent, this resulted in being arrested for a property crime, as his fingerprints were linked to the crime scene. He claims he was a victim of racial profiling, as eyewitnesses reported seeing a "dark-skinned man." In court he was cleared of all charges but was held in custody for a parole violation, as he did not inform his parole officer of his arrest. He cries out, "But I couldn't call [my officer]—I was in jail." His case does not seem to be unique. Research has shown that recently released prisoners, when compared to the general population, are much more likely to end up being arrested.[19] This is particularly associated with the intensity of parole supervision: more intensive supervision increases the risk of all violations, regardless of the parolees' personal characteristics, offense background, and neighborhood conditions.[20] Several interviewees told me they were pulled over for a triviality, which then resulted in a background screening, which in turn led to an arrest or a notification of their parole officer. Ever since the Cinelli case happened, Hakim says:

> I have this target on my back. Any reason, or no reason, they can come in here and send me back. Figure out some technicality [. . .] see, [the parole board says] "We cannot afford having this lifer out, because if he messes up, and we have another incident, that's our political career." So the reality is that I was constantly living with the fact that they could come in just any minute and out of some small technicality, I got two parking tickets, [and my officer could say,] "We are going to violate you!" And if they violate me they are not going to let me out, you see? So [this is] my reality that I live in.

In short, what the majority of interviewees had in common was a constant fear of being sent back. They were, as Ruben summarized, "on eggshells [. . .] because there's always new rules and new changes with parole and probation, so whenever something like that [the Cinelli case] happens you have a new regime. [. . .] So I am making sure that, any point in time, my PO knows where I am. I don't want them to have anything to put me behind the wall."

CATCHING UP TOO QUICKLY

As illustrated in the previous chapters, upon release the majority of lifers had missed traditional turning points in the life course. They were either single, or involved in problematic, rather than supportive and pro-social, intimate partner relationships. They had lost contact with their children during their decades-long incarceration, or never had children. Many were struggling to secure or maintain employment. These lifers are not unique in this experience. In the 1980s the sociologist Neal Shover already pointed to this tendency in his study on fifty aging criminals: "The time spent in prison interferes with—if too many years are spent there, it nearly destroys—one's abilities to meet prevailing socially constructed timetables for most conventional careers, such as work and family. The despairing are fully aware of this fact. They realize that the years devoted to crime, and in prison, have thrown them out of synchronization with the normal timetables for achieving success."[21]

Similarly, Erving Goffman earlier on pointed out that "although some roles can be re-established by the inmate if and when he returns to the world, it is plain that other losses are irrevocable and may be painfully experienced as such. It may not be possible to make up, at a later phase of the life cycle, the time not now spent in educational or job advancement, in courting, or in rearing one's children."[22]

In short, for these interviewees, a life sentence has caused a disruption of their life course: expectations are put on hold, anticipated life-course transitions are altered, and ceremonies traditionally and conventionally used to mark rites of passage, which help the individual to mentally adjust to their new identity, are denied.[23] Because they missed these rites of passage, lifers had a sense of living in the "wrong" time and being of a different generation from their peers. Norman, who was incarcerated as a teenager for the homicide he committed, says, "I feel that life stopped when I came to prison. I still see life as a nineteen-year-old. Like, sometimes, my sense of humor is still like a nineteen-year old. I fall back into being that kid."

Many others shared this sense of de-synchronicity. Some men, for example, mentioned that in their minds they were still twenty years old, and that upon release they felt attracted to twenty-year-old women rather than age-appropriate fifty-year-old women. This sense of existing in the "wrong" time and being of a different generation from their peers is most pronounced when they leave prison.[24] Upon release, lifers had high hopes and set high standards. John Irwin has coined this "the catch-up ethic": obtaining, as soon as possible, what the ex-prisoner has missed, including an intimate relationship, children, and work.[25] Thirty-seven-year-old Dwayne is one of the youngest lifers I interviewed. He is bald and looks buff in his green prison jumpsuit. He started his life sentence at age eighteen and came out when he was thirty-four years old. Now he has been back in prison for one month following an incident of domestic strife. His wife withdrew the complaint and admits to having lied to the police and his parole officer about him hitting her. As a result he expects to be released soon. Some time after our interview, I read in the transcript of the parole board hearing that his wish was granted. As a special condition, he needs to go to "counseling for dependency on women" and is not allowed to have contact with his former spouse. He tells me, "Patience is absolutely necessary [to be successful on the outside] and taking it one step at a time, because there's this idea of catching up on the time lost. [. . .] Like, what I thought I had to have according to my age." For most men like Dwayne, the idea of "catching up" was materialized in quickly becoming involved in an intimate relationship. Their years in prison typically made them uncritical toward new potential mates. With few exceptions, many interviewees reported having met their wives and girlfriends in AA/NA meetings, sober houses, or drug rehabilitation programs. Dwayne is no exception, he says: "I was trying to find security in the institution of marriage. Maybe I was caught up in this idea of marriage as a fairytale—of having a normal life post-incarceration."

Wesley married his wife when he was in prison. After release, he tells me, "Me and my wife, we sold drugs, we robbed, I mean we stole stuff together." He was out for three months before he came back on a domestic charge that she later withdrew: "My wife told them that I'd choke her [. . .] she called 911, thinking that I messed around with another woman." Like Wesley, many lifers who were re-incarcerated following a domestic strife attributed their parole violation to their intimate partners. Walter had been together with his girlfriend for twenty-seven years and is the only interviewee whose girlfriend stood by him throughout his incarceration. Together they have an adult son. Wesley was re-incarcerated following a fight with his girlfriend, which he summarizes as follows: "Me and her got into a nasty argument [. . .] and then I came back to prison. [. . .] She called the cops and said that I hit her. In court, it was dismissed but parole held me for three and a half years."

Others attributed their re-incarceration indirectly to their female companions, such as Alan, who turned to illegitimate means to give his girlfriend a lifestyle he couldn't afford legitimately: "I think I tried to play catch-up. My girlfriend, you see, she was a stripper. And she earned a lotta cash for just working a couple of nights. Now, when she became pregnant I tried to keep on living her lifestyle, the lifestyle we had with her salary, but we couldn't. [. . .] So, the other side kicked in, that criminal side of me, when it wasn't supposed to." He was arrested and re-incarcerated for credit card fraud.

A few non-incarcerated lifers made explicit that they did not get involved in an intimate relationship in order to avoid becoming vulnerable. Thanh, for example, had been out for over six years at the time I interviewed him. When people ask him why he did not have a girlfriend, he says, "It's not the right time." He explains:

> I tell them [those who would like to have a girlfriend], "Are you getting a girlfriend just to get laid, or to love?" If you find a girlfriend, somebody to love, to find the right person who understands my situation, and who financially has to have the money, too [. . .] Some of them get together with a girl they know from prison, but they don't have any money, they get into an argument, and an argument like that, they may get mad and hit the girlfriend, something like that. And I say, I am not ready for that."

OLD HABITS DIE HARD

"If it's the lifestyle that's still there, it's easy to come back," sixty-nine-year-old Bernard asserts. "Most of my friends were all dead, because of the lifestyle they lived." They were either killed or died of the activities associated with chronic drug and/or alcohol use. He mentions that it is "probably a good thing" that his friends passed away: "There's no one left for me." "What if [your friends] were still alive?" I ask him. "Then I wouldn't have lasted out there," he plainly says. Even without his friends, he could not avoid being sent back to prison. At the time he violated the conditions of parole due to a verbal fight with his neighbors during which he was drinking, he lived in a remote village in rural Massachusetts and—despite his age and ill health—worked in construction. He attributes his alcohol use to his work: "I mean, construction is always associated with a lot of drinking." His parents and siblings passed away a long time ago. While on parole, he admits, "I was involved with others, but not with lifers, just with bank robbers and stuff."

Others, such as Hakim, were much younger when they were first released. He was convicted of murder in a so-called joint venture when he was fifteen years old and was released several years later.[26] He went to college and started working as a child psychologist. He recalls:

> For me, what had happened in this particular period, was that the children that I was working with, the parents became aware that I was an ex-inmate and they did not feel comfortable, knowing that I was an ex-inmate working with their children. The agency fired me, and that trig-

gered off all that negativity because I could not understand or rationalize. I'm not in the criminal world, I am married, I am a taxpayer and you are going to penalize me for me having a record? And I did not quite rationalize that out right now. I am twenty-two now. In my mind, it did connect, and my resolve broke down and I went back into that mode where, "OK, you hurt me, I hurt you." Meaning, in my mind, I am saying, "I am trying to go straight and this is what I'm getting? So, let me do what I what I know," and I went back into the street mentality. I started robbing, but this time, banks.

He committed a second homicide several months later in a bank robbery and served another thirty-six years before being paroled. Irwin has previously observed this failure to reach the level of "doing good."[27] When this disappointment is recognized, and consciously accepted, Irwin argues, the ex-convict is reaching a critical turning point. He recognizes his thinking about the future and alters his plans, perhaps scaling down his aspirations, or he veers back to "the old bag." In very few cases, however, did I find a "calculated and articulated resistance to authority" as reported by Sampson and Laub in their study on the life histories of delinquent boys.[28] While many of the persistent offenders in their sample insisted on the rewards of crime itself,[29] or a willful resistance to perceived domination, among my sample of interviewed lifers re-engagement in criminal behavior was very rare. The vast majority were committed to going straight, but doing so, as much as possible, on their own terms.[30] The most pronounced "old habits" that interviewees returned to thus did not involve new criminal behavior, but technical violations, including the use of alcohol and drugs. Consider, for example, the case of Rodney.

I meet Rodney, a sixty-two-year-old, heavy-built native Bostonian, in prison. His way of speaking is characterized by "therapy talk," using terms and phrases that are typical of counseling and 12-step meetings. At age thirteen he started sniffing glue. He describes how this evolved into "smoking grass. And after that, amphetamines, barbiturates, and heroin." Over time his drug use escalated, he recalls: "It became a 24/7 thing. I became a drug addict. It progressed to the point where I was sticking a needle in my arm, and I never thought I would do that." He was shooting heroin by the time he was eighteen years old: "I have an addictive personality: Obsessive and compulsive." To support his addiction he was stealing and selling barbiturates and other drugs: "But I didn't sell heroin. It would be like a monkey selling bananas, you'd be your own best customer, you know what I mean? [. . .] Then I became a slave to it. The drug has taken over, and people are now a means to an end."

On the night of the homicide, at twenty-four years old, he was in withdrawal and in desperate need of heroin. He saw a woman walking by herself and intended to sneak up behind her and rob her. While struggling with her to take her purse, he stabbed her and fled with the money to buy drugs. He pleaded guilty to second-degree murder.

Throughout his incarceration he was able to sustain his addiction, using heroin and marijuana. When he was paroled after fifteen years and sent to a prerelease center, he says, "I started using heroin two weeks into the program." He had a sober girlfriend, with whose support he managed to stay clean briefly, but turned himself in after having been using again: "It's an obsession and compulsion thing," he adds. He was re-incarcerated for a period of four years and two months. This time, in prison, "I really started working on myself by going to AA meetings. Before that, it was just window-dressing." He continues, "I had let my girlfriend down who was waiting to marry me. I felt even worse about myself, and I was ripe for turning my life around. I began AA." He was released again, determined to stay sober: "By this time, I was four years sober and I had AA under my belt. I had more of an understanding." His time outside the walls only lasted for two weeks before he started using again. He explains, "I didn't come back to prison because I liked it, but because I knew how to live life in prison, and I didn't know how to live on the outside." He was re-incarcerated for another four years, during which time his girlfriend left him. "Running back to prison was a security thing," he concludes. "This time, I dove into AA again."

In his most recent release, he stayed out for twelve years. He married a woman he met in one of the reentry programs: "My wife used to be an alcoholic, but now she's twenty-eight years sober." In these twelve years he started a contracting business and was doing well financially. He attributes his current relapse to several coinciding events: his father and brother passing away, and work-related stress. "And I picked up again," he says. He turned himself in. At the time of the interview he was granted re-parole—he would be released to a halfway house as soon as the paperwork was done and they had an empty bed. When I asked if being re-paroled this time would be different from previous times, he answers, "I'll walk into that wall again. But what's gonna be my response, that's the question." He does not have illusions of staying drug-free: "Drugs and alcohol are symptoms of underlying issues, so I'm gonna go back to counseling."

PRISON AS A SAFE PLACE

Other than the physical pains of imprisonment, a profound effect of imprisonment as discussed in chapter 5 is the loss of self-efficacy. Inmates are subject to strict regulations, and activities such as meals, exercise, and visits are conducted around rules of time and place. Inmates are forced to work in prison jobs bearing no relation to their levels of skill, to their release dates, or to the types of jobs they will perform upon release.[31] The criminologists Stephen Farrall and Adam Calverley have critically argued that prison rules place people under an institutionalized routine that virtually suspends their power. creating a disempowered mentality that is not well suited to overcoming the structural impediments that many face upon release from prison.[32] While many non-incarcerated lifers reported that they were able to overcome the absence of choice by taking control over their lives during and after release, numerous re-incarcerated lifers felt that they were trapped in the system, unable to overcome the structural disadvantages that faced them.[33] Prison was, consciously or unconsciously, a safe place to which they could return.

Walter, for example, served twenty-seven years on his life sentence. By the time he was released, his parents and siblings had passed away. Even though the initial reason for his re-incarceration was a domestic dispute that his girlfriend later withdrew, he was not allowed to live with his girlfriend and their son. Instead, he was released to a shelter but was struggling to pay his rent, as his request for Supplemental Security Income had not come through. "I had no work, I was disabled," he explains. He blames several circumstances for his re-incarceration: "In the shelter, I came in contact with someone with tuberculosis. I became ill, very ill." Also, in that period he felt depressed: "I was going to AA/NA, [. . .] counseling, and doing the right things, but it was too hard to live by myself and do everything on my own." He was caught buying crack cocaine: "That night, I was so depressed, in so much pain, so lonely. So we purchased some drugs. Next thing I know, the police were knocking on the door. The cops saw the whole thing [the drug transaction] and arrested me." Throughout the interview he emphasizes the influence of the criminal justice system on his life. He thinks of parole as "a new plantation. Now they're putting bracelets on you." He says, "I don't have control on the street. It's just like a prison out there. Only a bigger prison." Trapped in this prison, he feels that the only way people can be successful on the outside is to have social support: "Solid support. A loved one, or like an organization that can support you when parole is giving you trouble." Asked how he would describe himself, he answers, "I think I am a passive person. [. . .] I try not to be a follower, and try to stay focused on getting out."

For others, such as fifty-eight-year old Dennis, the return to prison as a safe place was more explicit. When I meet Dennis in a maximum-security prison, he introduces himself with a cold and clammy handshake. He sits hunched forward in his chair and tells me how he has been diagnosed with latent schizophrenia, as a result of which he is heavily medicated. Men like Dennis had a long history of institutionalizations that could be traced back to childhood. When he was four years old he was placed in a foster home. He was first incarcerated at the age of seven, for shoplifting and arson: "Back then, they had this term in the law called 'stubborn child.' I was such a child." He spent his childhood in foster homes, juvenile detention, and under the supervision of the Department of Social Services. When he was eleven years old, he says, "I started drinking and using drugs. I was into everything [all types of drugs]."

He enlisted in the army but "that didn't turn out so well." He returned to Boston and worked in the "combat zone," an area downtown that attracted drug addicts, prostitutes, motorcycle gangs, and organized crime. He prostituted himself to make money to buy drugs. He killed a client in an attempted robbery and was convicted of second-degree murder. He says that many survival skills he had picked up on the street helped him survive "on the inside."

He served thirty-seven years in prison before being paroled: "I'm not sure if I was ready. I did every program they threw at me. [. . .] But I didn't know what to expect [from the outside world]. There were so many changes." He managed to find work as a manual laborer while living at a halfway house. He associated with other ex-inmates to whom he could relate. Prison was playing a role in his day-to-day life, and even in his dreams: "While I was in prison, thoughts and dreams I had were of inside the walls, thoughts of escaping. I would dream that I was on railroad tracks with nowhere to go. On the outside, I still dreamed of prison."

Throughout the three and a half years after release, he felt anxious about being outside prison. His anxiety increased when he stopped taking his medications, which he did because he felt the medication's side effects inhibited him from focusing on his job. Then, he says, "I started drinking, because I couldn't work with those meds. [. . .] And the alcohol took away the depression and anxiety." Soon thereafter he was re-incarcerated for failing a drug test. When I ask him what the future would hold in store for him, he replies, "I don't have a clue." He seems to be at peace with his current predicament: "I found my niche and I live in it."

Being Back

For some, being sent back to prison brought about hopelessness and helplessness concerning the future. The gate has closed behind them for an indefinite period; perhaps it will be a short period, though it could be years to come with unfulfilled hopes of release.[34] Some interviewees, such as Glenn, gave up the hopes for and efforts toward release: "I really don't think they are letting me go. It's a political issue." Others expressed a strong desire and willingness to "go straight" this time but were pessimistic about being re-paroled, and pointed to the reluctance of the current board to parole lifers. Their expectations for the future stand in stark contrast to research on "general offenders," or non-lifers who return to the community,[35] who expected it to be "pretty easy" or "very easy" to stay out of prison after release.

Going back to prison did not change their self-ascribed identity of a "good core self," or in their willingness to "give back" to society, as discussed in chapter 6. Miguel, who was re-incarcerated at the time of the interview, and who would face the board to make a case for his re-parole, tells me, "I hope the parole board is convinced, because I'm a good person and I can be a good contributing member of society." Doris, who was re-incarcerated after associating with a known felon, describes herself in a similar way: "I genuinely think I'm a decent person. The only people that don't are the parole board members." Fifty-seven-year-old Khalid, whom I meet in a maximum-security prison, had been re-incarcerated following a violent assault. Prior to his re-incarceration, he worked as a counselor at the Department of Youth Services. He looks at me through his glasses, which are held together with duct tape. Missing teeth on his upper and lower jaw cause a slur in his speech. He describes himself as follows: "I'm good. I'm capable. I'm eligible." Cedric, whose parole was revoked after a dirty urine, similarly says, "I am humble. Sympathetic. Open-minded. Approachable. Caring. I didn't know what caring was, before, but now I do. I'm caring. Harmless."

Presenting such a narrative based on a "good core self" can be interpreted as a "cultural script"[36] that lifers acquired during their life sentence, in partial preparation for the parole board hearing. Re-incarceration thus did not change these lifers' narratives in terms of portraying themselves as having a "good core self." They still viewed their former offending self as a false identity, denying that it was their "real self." They considered their re-incarceration, particularly if it was related to drugs, as falling back in old mistakes. In other words, going back was not so much a result of their "criminal self"; they saw themselves as having changed. In addition, they still expressed the desire to give back, such as Cedric recounts: "If in some way, I can give back, that's very helpful. [. . .] This whole experience changed my whole outlook on life. And I try to pass that on to young guys coming in. If only I can reach one guy, you know. Especially the ones coming in who have young kids. You can break that cycle [of generational incarceration] right here." Similarly, Dwayne, who was re-incarcerated following an alleged domestic assault, holds, "I have a vision for myself. I see myself helping others. I want to use my experience helping others." In short, re-incarceration did not change these men's self-concept or their generative motivations. For the most part, they felt they were put behind bars as a result of trivialities, often due to external factors.

"I WANT TO LIVE OUT THERE, NOT DIE IN HERE"
Being back in prison was difficult for the vast majority of re-incarcerated interviewees. For those who could be classified as "elderly," coping with the prison environment was even more taxing. It should be noted that

the terms "elderly" and "geriatric" have different meanings inside prison compared to life outside prison. State correctional departments commonly use fifty years as a marker for "older" inmates, in part motivated by the fact that the typical inmate in his fifties has the physical appearance and accompanying health problems of someone at least ten years older.[37] Elderly prisoners represent a special population in terms of health-care needs, problems of family relationships, and difficulties with individual adjustment to institutional life.[38] There has been an ongoing debate about whether to house older offenders in the prison mainstream or in special needs facilities. The mere physical condition and architectural structure of the institution create significant problems for the elderly inmate with functional limitations. In the past, prison systems were designed to house primarily young, active inmates. Now, older, more frail offenders often find the environment to be unfriendly due the prison design, which may challenge inmates' mobility capabilities,[39] as well as due to the behavior of their younger counterparts.

When I talk to Mike, he explains his reasons for being in a maximum-security setting: "I could no longer double-up. I was doubling with a younger black man, and he stayed up late at night watching movies and stuff and I just couldn't sleep. The only singles they had were at the maximum." In order to avoid having to share a cell with someone else, he asked to be transferred to a maximum-security facility. Following several disciplinary reports, his wish was granted. Even though the Massachusetts Department of Correction has two facilities that provide beds for those who can no longer feed themselves, stand in line for medication, or use the bathroom on their own,[40] there are no specific facilities for elderly inmates such as Mike, who have not yet reached a nursing state but cannot keep up with the routines of the younger prison population.

Darrel is another interviewee who, at the age of sixty-two, could be classified as "older." I initially meet him when he is on parole, in a café at the bus terminal. Months later I find out he is re-incarcerated, after taking the painkiller Oxycodone following an invasive surgery. I contact him by letter, asking how he is doing. He writes back:

These past two years have been the most difficult time I have served since my sentence began [in the early 1970s]. Right now I am just trying to survive. Because I have done so much time and have already completed every program offered here, there is really nothing for me to do. Because I am disabled I am unable to get any work so my time drags by. I am also faced with physical challenges from younger guys and gang-bangers who have no respect at all for anyone or anything. However, this is really not a problem for me because I have been around for so long and have a good name and reputation. I know a lot of people, some of [whom] are extremely dangerous men, and that backs people off. It's a shame that things are like that but that's the way the system is.

Physical safety is not their only concern in coping with prison life. Mike, for example, has been re-incarcerated after violating parole by alcohol consumption. In prison he stays occupied by making a memorial for lifers who died while serving a life sentence. He also plays chess by mail: "I think it helps for dementia." His fears of suffering from dementia in prison are linked to the conditions of the medical ward: "I saw them [dementia patients] in there, neglected, with unchanged diapers. And when I told one of the nurses in there, she just said, 'Those diapers are designed to carry three bowel movements.'"

Fear of physical and mental deterioration was significant among many older lifers, and is not unique to this Massachusetts sample. In their study of sixty elderly British prisoners, the criminologists Elaine Crawley and Richard Sparks found that like their counterparts outside the prison walls, elderly prisoners suffer from a variety of age-related health problems, including poor mobility, impaired vision and hearing, and depression.[41] Like inmates in general, aging prisoners generally have not had proper access to health care on the outside. They come into the prison system with numerous chronic illnesses and consume multiple medications. Similar to findings reported elsewhere,[42] the older men and women I interviewed reported a high prevalence of hepatitis C, diabetes, and heart disease. In addition, many elderly lifers experienced trauma and suffered from depression. Mike is no exception—he had been diagnosed with depression but the medications did not work. "It only makes the thoughts worse," he says. "I am sinking. Last year I tried to kill myself. I took all my blood pressure pills."

Overall, elderly interviewees expressed painful preoccupations, the most prominent of which was a fear of dying in prison. In his letter,

Darrell wrote, "As for my re-incarceration, it has been extremely difficult on many levels. It has been very hard, and disappointing for my family, especially my kids. Because of my age and my physical situation, they are afraid that I may perish here." Cody has been back behind the walls for a year and shares Darrell's fear of a prison death given his age and the length of his parole setbacks: "They sentenced me to a death sentence. I am sixty-nine years old, they [the board] gave me a four-year set back. I could die in here." He asserts, "Guys my age, we would never reoffend. [. . .] I'm an older guy now. I try to eat the right thing. I want to live out there, not die in here."

Darrell's and Cody's fears are not unsubstantiated. Around the same time, I learned that Bernard, who was sixty-nine at the time of our interview and in very poor health, had passed away. He was granted parole at his most recent hearing, a month prior to his passing, but failed to receive the decision in time. Such painful observations were a daily reality for many re-lifers who were sent back to prison. Other lifers, at the time when I talked to them at least, were able to stay out on parole. Next, we will delve deeper into the factors they mentioned as key to staying out.

10

Staying Out

In addition to asking them why they and others return to prison, I asked lifers how they thought about their ability to stay out. In their answers three themes emerged. A small group of individuals pointed to their old age and the lifestyle associated with their age. A second theme that was particularly pronounced by non-incarcerated interviewees was the role of self-efficacy. Non-incarcerated interviewees saw themselves as successful not only because they were changed individuals, but also because they felt in control over their lives. Finally, interviewees attributed their ability to stay out to having "a healthy fear" of violating their parole conditions and the associated consequences.

Aging Out

A small group—three out of the thirty-eight non-incarcerated interviewees—could be classified as what the criminologist Donald West termed "passive inadequate" offenders based on his research on persistent petty criminals.[1] They simply stopped offending without much cognitive transformation, social support, or programming, but simply due to age or lack of interest. Giuseppe is one of them. Opposed to most interviewees, he denies having been "transformed" over the years. The fact that he was incarcerated at age fifty-five could provide an explanation for this. When I ask him what he feels the success factors of him staying out on parole are, he answers, "I am seventy-five. [. . .] I do not drive anymore. [. . .] My life has six points. This is number one," and he points to the house of a good friend on a piece of paper. "From this [point], it is fifteen minutes to my church, and fifteen minutes from my church, I am home." He continues to draw a line between the six points: "Then from my apartment it's fifteen minutes, and I'm at CVS, at the shops, laundry, and things like that." His life in a small community in rural Massachusetts is devoid of factors conducive to crime.

Furthermore, at seventy-five years of age, Giuseppe is old and not interested in drugs, excitement, or "catching up" on time lost.

It has been well established that antisocial and criminal activity increases during adolescence, peaks around age seventeen, and declines as individuals enter adulthood.[2] As discussed in chapter 2, numerous theoretical accounts identify changes that are associated with declines in crime, ranging from desistance because of "real or imagined infirmities of age,"[3] to co-occurring changes in sociological variables such as marriage, parenthood, and employment. As we have seen in the prior chapter, however, these traditional sociological variables explaining desistance do not seem to provide a satisfactory explanation for lifers staying out on parole. They do not go through some of the most significant changes in the everyday life domain, such as completing formal education, launching a career, forming sustainable romantic relationships, and becoming a parent. In the case of Giuseppe, older age is rather associated with a different set of routine activities in which he and others like him are less likely to be surrounded by crime-inducing factors.[4] The vast majority of non-incarcerated lifers, however, attributed their achievements in "going straight" to their individual efficaciousness.

Self-Efficacy

Though attracting increasing interest within desistance research, different authors use the concepts "self-efficacy," "agency," and "choice" in varying ways.[5] Here, I refer to "self-efficacy" as an internal locus of control expressed in a sense of mastery and competence, the self-perceived capacity to use good judgment and exercise agency.

Non-incarcerated interviewees, as opposed to re-incarcerated individuals, reflected a strong sense of agency in their narrative. In answer to my question about what they considered the reason for them staying out successfully, two-third of the non-incarcerated lifers answered that they took control over their lives after release. They attributed their success by having a clear goal that they strived to meet. Forty-year-old Vincent, for example, emphasized that a clear vision for the future made him the man he is today: recently married, a child on the way, and in charge of a local job agency. He tells me:

First thing I did after being released from prison was go around the corner and I got a double quarter pounder. I went to McDonald's. So then I went to parole, I had to come back, I said, "Well let's go get my permit." They're like, "What?" I said, "Let's go get my permit," 'cause I made sure I had all of my stuff so I could get my driver's license; I did all this before I got out. [. . .] In four hours I got my learner's permit to drive. I hear that nobody's ever done that before either. I believe that's not true, I think people have they just don't tell people how to do it—I share the information with people. So I got my learner's permit and I drove back to parole. And I went into parole and I showed 'em my learner's permit, they laughed, they were like, "You got your learner's permit already?" I was like, "Yeah, I had to wait to see you, so I went over and got my learner's permit." Five days later I have my license and I had my own car. And I told everybody before I left prison, I said that within two to three years, I will own my own home, and I'll make it. [And they said,] "Right." Watch me. [. . .] And if you think about it, I started here [two years ago], so if you think about it, I started this job making about thirty-five grand a year, six months after I got out. Then, two years to the day of my release, I got approved to buy my home.

Vincent shares this success story at public speaking events. Without a doubt, he is proud of what he has achieved in so little time. Throughout our conversation, he emphasizes that having a goal ("I will own my own home") is fundamental to being successful on the outside and to preparing for life outside while in prison ("I made sure I had all of my stuff so I could get my driver's license"). To achieve your goal, non-incarcerated interviewees point out, you have to be patient, take it one step at a time, and persevere. Consider, for example, the case of sixty-five-year-old Kenneth, who was virtually illiterate when he was sentenced for second-degree murder. In prison he obtained his GED, studied mathematics, and gained a paralegal degree shortly after his release. Now that he had a paralegal degree, he was able to successfully help others fight their sentences. He had been incarcerated for twenty-four years before being paroled. He tells me:

I felt, you know, that there was nothing that was not possible, that, I felt that, you know, it was almost like a redemption, it was, it was like if you actually sincerely try to do good and tried [. . .] there will be many as believers, many naysayers, people thinking you are running a scam, a con, or whatever, right? And you suffer setbacks, you will get punished for this and that, but *if you stick with it*, ultimately, having faith in people, you will prevail. And, so that was, that [obtaining a paralegal degree] was proof of that. (emphasis added)

Similar to Vincent, Kenneth attributed his educational and professional successes to his perseverance ("if you stick with it"). These successes, in turn, reinforced the belief that he was able to build a life for himself outside the prison walls, which strengthened his sense of control over his life and his future.

Clarence, who says that the key to him being successful on the outside is living up to his goal, shares this notion of control over his life. When I ask him what determines success post-release, he answers that those who are sent back to prison lack a clear goal in life. For him, he says:

My goal was I will never allow this to happen ever again, I will not put myself in a position where this [. . .] [can] happen. I was given the opportunity to stop it [. . .] You can't just do wrong, do wrong, do wrong, and get right, that's not how it works. So you gotta do some things you know, Jesus says, "Come and I'll give you rest." Well the operative word there is "come," not just "I'll give you rest." I'll take care of you, you have to do something, you come and I'll help you. Knock [on] the door and it will be open. You gotta do something, you know, um, so I had that goal I said I am not [let this happen again], that means not drinking, I'm not doing drugs, I'm not going in nobody's club, nobody's bar.

In my conversation with Thanh, when talking about success and failure post-release, he also highlights the importance of having a clear goal:

I think people just give up so quick. They do not have the determination, they don't have the self-judgment to say that there's too much tension, you know [they say], "The cost of living is so high, I worked minimum wage, I cannot afford transportation, and people discriminate me and they reject me." [. . .] I use self-judgment, you know, I taught myself that it is OK, not everyone can have a job when the unemployment is high.

A lot of people my age struggle to get a job, lost their house, they have a family, they lost it all because they couldn't find a job.

In prison Thanh obtained a barber's license. He became involved in a religious organization post-release, and recently became employed as a hairdresser in a nearby town. I ask him if he finds it difficult after these years in prison to regain that sense of control and to make decisions. He replies:

Yes, it is, because it's not easy, because after long-term imprisonment, you don't know anybody in the streets. You think about the future, what to do and everything. When I have a job, I do not say if, but when I have a job, what choice do I make? Do I steal? Do I do drugs? Or do I kill somebody? You have to take a moral value and say no. And, you know, I keep it simple: Do I want anyone to rob me? No. [. . .] And a lot of guys will say that is survival, like, "I want money." But I would say, "That's enough, that is not the right thing to do." When I do not have a job, I came to a shelter, asking for help [. . .] do not make a wrong choice. I constantly have to remind myself that, because the mind has one million options.

These narratives stand in stark contrast to roughly three-fourths (twenty-two out of thirty) of the narratives of re-incarcerated lifers who mostly attributed their failure to external factors. "What do you think the main reason is for you and others to return to prison?" I ask fifty-two-year-old Ray in a minimum-security prison. He has been re-paroled twice, but his time on the streets did not last longer than a couple of months each time, as he violated his conditions of parole by soliciting prostitutes and drinking. He answers, "Hanging with a bad crowd will bring you back. Hanging with a good crowd will save you. You have to stay with the right people, like AA people."

Fifty-two-year-old Calvin, a Caucasian man I interviewed in a maximum-security facility, stayed out for almost fourteen years before being re-incarcerated. Now he has been back for two months. He ascribes his re-incarceration to the larger economy: "I was making thirty-five dollars an hour, I had two vehicles, but the economy started going bad. I lost the job, my wife started to have migraines because of that,

I had surgery, and I started paying with credit cards. I couldn't find a job and I was starting to get depressed." Feeling depressed led him to drinking progressively. "My wife kicked me out of the house," he continues, because of his drinking. He lived with his mother for one week and went to the parking lot of a local detox clinic, where he drank one and half bottle of vodka. He explains, "'Cause they don't take you in unless you're drunk." Several days after having checked in the program, his parole officer pulled him out. "I completely forgot that I had a meeting with my parole office and another guy the day after I checked in to discuss my debts. I also couldn't pay the eighty-dollar fee for parole." He was re-incarcerated due to technical violations, not for failing to pay his supervision fee, but for "irresponsible conduct and no notified change of address."

Randall spent more than twenty years in prison. He stayed out for three years after his first parole, and like Calvin he attributes his re-incarceration due to drug relapse to the lack of social support: "Support means everything, having someone to lean on. You have to have a sound support system with people in the community." Such external attributions to success ("someone to lean on"; "a good crowd") and external attributions to failure ("it was the economy"; "a bad crowd") were commonly mentioned as reasons for failure among those who were re-incarcerated.

Such a lack of agency goes against what we would expect based on our idea of the "redemption script," comprising elements of a good core self, generative motivations, and a sense of agency. While the large majority of both incarcerated and re-incarcerated groups expressed that they had changed, and now described themselves as "law-abiding, productive members of society" who were eager to contribute, non-incarcerated lifers overall expressed a strong sense of agency. This stands in contrast to those in the re-incarcerated group, who felt they had no, or hardly any, control over their lives. Among them, expressions such as "My fate is in the hands of my parole officer," and "They did not tell me I had to do such-and-such," are common. Self-efficacy, I thus wish to argue, was not a requirement for individuals to consider themselves as "transformed" and create a narrative of change, as suggested elsewhere, but rather is an important element of the redemption narrative of being able to stay out on parole.

From a critical point of view, the lack of self-efficacy among re-incarcerated lifers could be a reflection of their current state of incarceration. It has been well documented that in contemporary prison, inmates are systematically casted as unworthy.[6] While constructing their narratives, re-incarcerated interviewees may downplay the ability to exert control over the structural disadvantages facing them and emphasize the influence of other factors, whereas non-incarcerated interviewees may do the opposite. Consider the case of Walter, who said he was trying to do "the right thing" when he was out on parole. When I talk to him, he has been back in prison for two years. "I was obeying the law and society. But they [his parole officers] didn't allow me to see my people [his girlfriend and former associates]. They blocked all other options." He was re-incarcerated for using drugs. He gave up on making plans about the future. "I don't have big plans. Because nothing goes as planned," he sighs. Like the stories of many other re-incarcerated lifers, Walter's narrative—including his future perspective—is characterized by a profound sense of helplessness. Alan, a forty-two-year-old lifer, was re-incarcerated following several parole violations, including fraud and drug use. We sit down to talk in the interview room of a medium-security facility. When I ask him to what extent he feels he is in control over his life, Alan answers, "Having a goal," and blames his re-incarceration on not having a goal: "The last two times I was paroled, I didn't have a goal." "Do you have a goal now?" I ask. He replies evasively, "Well, first I have to have a plan, then I have a goal."

Similarly, it may be argued that self-efficacy flourishes in a context characterized by some of the social factors present in the case of non-incarcerated interviewees and absent in the case of incarcerated interviewees. Previous studies on desisting offenders supports this idea, showing that desisters more often attribute positive events to broad, long-lasting personal qualities.[7] However, as we saw previously, both groups of lifers seemed to be "off-time" in terms of traditional turning points in the life course. They were either single, or involved in problematic, rather than supportive, intimate partner relationships. Over time, visits diminished, and in both groups of interviewees were typically limited to visits from parents. Prisoners had lost contact with their children during their decades-long incarceration, or never had children. Also, the groups did not differ in their access to social support networks, such as religious institutions or substance-related programs. With the notable exception of "professional exes," interviewees in both groups were struggling to secure and maintain employment.

Based on these findings, one may therefore argue that self-efficacy, or a lack thereof, may be a determining factor in explaining why some lifers are able to stay out post-release, while others return to prison. According to the view presented here, the process of staying out is thus not the result of a change in male coming-of-age societal forces (e.g., parenthood, marriage, employment),[8] as emphasized by life-course theorists.[9] Nor does it seem to be the result of an individual's resolution to change. As we have seen in chapter 6, the vast majority of interviewees said that they underwent a transformation leading to a better version of themselves. Even though it is increasingly recognized that a combination of these factors is necessarily implicated in change,[10] previous research has still downplayed the role of individual self-efficacy, while overestimating the power of social environment to instill law-abiding behavior. The lifers I talked to, however, tend to blame failure post-release to external factors, while attributing successes post-release to individual willpower. Those who were able to stay out demonstrated a strong sense of self-efficacy, while those who were re-incarcerated lacked such a sense of voluntary action.

In interpreting these narratives, we should not neglect the societal circumstances that affect the lives of these men and women. As outlined earlier, the reasons for being re-incarcerated were often of a trivial nature, a product of harsh parole guidelines and, in some cases, misguided justice—an observation also encountered elsewhere.[11] Hence, I do not intend to minimize the structural inequalities ex-offenders face and the possible implications for a lack of (masculine) status that is compensated by criminal behavior.[12] Rather, those who were able to stay out reflected a sense that they have at least some choice and some amount of power that enables them to make a difference in their lives. Both groups of lifers faced numerous constraints within their immediate social contexts, and it is how the individual responds to these constraints that is central to the argument I present here. Generally speaking, social actors make choices based on the structures that surround them,[13] and agentic individuals, in turn, have the ability to shape their lives within these structures. In short, we are dealing here with an interplay between structure and agency. Individual agency, or self-efficacy, can thus be applied to navigate an individual's structural social context, or to create structural factors around oneself that in turn enhance a sense of individual control.[14]

Finally, it should be reiterated that those who violated the conditions of their parole seemed to have done so out of a *lack* of self-efficacy, giving way to impulsivity and a lack of awareness of future consequences, rather than a choice for a criminal lifestyle because of the rewards of crime itself.[15] The vast majority was desisting, in terms of not committing new crimes. They were mostly brought back behind the walls as a result of not observing the conditions of their parole.

Outliers

The dichotomous division of agentic (non-incarcerated) versus non-agentic (re-incarcerated) lifers is not complete without considering cases that did not neatly fit this division. Out of the thirty-eight re-incarcerated interviewees, ten individuals reflected a strong sense of self-efficacy in their narratives but were nevertheless considered "unsuccessful" due to their re-incarcerated status. Consider, for example, Arthur, who was sent back to prison for a technical violation: when his parole officer showed up at his house, he was at his brother's house without notification. He describes that, in his seventeen-year-long sentence, "I decided to change, and it wasn't handed to me on a silver platter. I had to do the work." Throughout the interview, he emphasizes that "there is always a choice." Even now that he has been back in prison for two years, he says, "I can choose not to eat. I can choose not to wear this monkey suit [pointing to his jumpsuit]. They can say what they want, but I have a choice. I don't have to listen to him [pointing to the correctional officer in the adjacent office]. You will be sent to the hole [solitary confinement] for that, but it's a choice. I won't let them take away my freedom, my choice, my individuality, even if I'm wearing this suit like a monkey, I'm still who I am." His vocabulary of self-control apparently convinced the members of the parole board, too, who welcomed Arthur's request to "step down" through lower security, as he held that it would "better prepare me to enter society." Several months after our interview he was granted parole, provided he spent six months in lower security, followed by one-on-one counseling and monitoring through an ankle bracelet.

Dwayne represents another outlier. He was incarcerated when he was eighteen years old for killing the man who killed his father: "My son was born two weeks after I went in, so automatically my mind was like—I had to be a different person than when I went in." He reflects how "I knew [the street life] wasn't for me; I knew that there was more out there, that I could do more." In prison, a fellow inmate introduced him to the Nation of Islam. In the period that followed, he moved away from "the criminal life" through Islam: "Islam played a major role in guiding it." He joined study groups focusing on Islam, change, and self-improvement. "I started to use incarceration as a tool, rather than something working against me." He was released after fifteen years. He tells me, "I always kept in my mind that prison was not a natural environment, that it was something that I moved through." Throughout his incarceration, he says, "Personal choice is taken away." Hence, when you get out, he adds, "You have to relearn what you like. I've heard some folks going to a restaurant and not knowing what they want [to eat], they'd be like, 'What's good?' They have to learn to choose again." In order to regain that sense of choice, he asked friends to send him catalogs of clothes: "So I could see what I wanted to look like on the outside."

Conversely, there were eight outliers involving non-incarcerated lifers, who presented few elements of personal change and a low degree of self-efficacy. Opposed to other lifers on parole, including "professional exes," these eight individuals were either unemployed or working in manual jobs. Consider forty-two-year-old Sean, for example, who admits to using and selling drugs on a regular basis ever since he was paroled two years ago, but downplays its significance: "I wasn't [doing anything else] but selling some drugs, and even when I did, and I sold drugs since I've been home, but I'd sell to five people [instead of many more]." When I asked him how he was successful in staying out on parole, he simply said, "I don't wanna go back to prison." He does not consider himself now at age forty-two as any different than he was at age twenty-five, describing himself as "I'm still who I am."

These outliers challenge the idea of "super-agents" or "super-dupes."[16] In this view, "super-agents" are free to act as they choose and can directly influence the outcome of their lives through their decision-making, while the lives of "super-dupes" are an outcome of their role as a subject to societal forces.[17] The interviewees, however, do not neatly fall into these dichotomous categories. Even though most who are able to stay out reflect a strong sense of self-efficacy in their narratives, and most who are re-incarcerated lack that sense of control, another major difference between the two groups is a healthy fear of going back.

A Healthy Fear

Parolees who were successful in staying out had in common a profound fear of the consequences of violating their parole conditions. In addition to emphasizing a changed self, a willingness to "go straight," and a sense of control over their lives, they expressed a strong awareness of their parole conditions, which in previous work has been termed "omniopticism": the sense of being watched by multiple others.[18] Fifty-two-year-old Benjamin, who had been out for ten years when I interview him, says, "I was thinking [. . .] if I wasn't on parole [. . .] I would smoke a joint, you know? But, I know I don't have that, that freedom to do that. You know what I'm saying? So, I mean, in that respect I can appreciate that I am on parole, so someone can kick me in the straight line. You know what I'm sayin', I am not, willing to get into anything and everything."

Fifty-three-year-old Daniel, who has been out for six years after having served twenty-six years behind bars, expresses a similar awareness: "I have no desire to get in trouble. I have no, I just don't have any . . . I can't even imagine myself committing a crime. Uhm . . . with the exception of driving without a license. Can't imagine it. And just the . . . maybe you're hyper-cognizant of that, you know [chuckles], to a fault almost, you know, I just, I just don't put myself . . . I don't go to barrooms, I don't go to, uhm, I don't hang out."

Several interviewees who were not successful in staying out also observed these parole conditions, but expressed complacency with regard to them. Mike, for example, illustrates how he managed to keep drinking without his parole officer finding out, thanks to a color-coded system. Each parolee was assigned a specific color, and the parole office would draw a color to determine who had to come in for drug testing the following day: "They made me call in every night, and if it was my color, I had to show up the next morning to give a urine, and so I wouldn't drink [that night]. It doesn't take a brain surgeon to figure that out." He said he started drinking every morning because he was feeling sick from chemotherapy, in addition to smoking marijuana to combat the nausea of chemo. At a certain point his wife called his parole officer and told him about Mike's drinking pattern. "She asked them to help me, but instead they put me back in, for seven years now," he tells me. "She called the authorities to help, but she knew better." When I ask Mike what he felt was needed for lifers to be successful in their reentry, he says: "Don't forget the parole conditions, they could cause you to go back without committing a crime. You go back to the life sentence for breaking a rule. [. . .] Parole is like a bungee cord between your shoulder blades. It can make you go back to the life sentence any time. [. . .] I wish lifers could keep a healthy fear."

Asking the same question to Randall, who was re-incarcerated for using drugs after having been out for four years, he answers, "Self-apprenticeship, a great deal of restrains, and patience. [. . .] People like myself will fail. But if we get brought back every time we fail, we will never succeed. [. . .] Most of these men are able to make it. They are fairly intelligent, if only they knew how to restrain themselves." What seems to be crucial for lifers in being able to re-create a life for themselves and staying out on parole is thus a combination of social support structures, having regained a sense of control, but, most important, a strong awareness of the restraints that govern their day-to-day life. The moment they let that awareness slip, by drinking, smoking, using drugs or hanging with a "bad crowd," they can be brought back behind the walls.

11

Reconsidering Lifer Reentry

Today, almost one out of every nine inmates is serving a life term.[1] My original purpose with this research was to shed light on the understudied population of lifers. I set out to examine the lives of long-term incarcerated individuals and inquire into the effects of long-term incarceration on those returning to society. In addition to potentially contributing to our understanding of crime throughout the life course, I hope that these findings provide a basis for future discussion of policy and legislature changes in the context of the goals, costs, and effects of long-term imprisonment.

Reframing Desistance among Lifers

Before actually talking to these sixty-eight lifers, I intended to assess how we could theoretically explain desistance among those who had served a life sentence. Soon, however, it became clear that the criminological use of the term "desistance"—staying crime-free—was not quite applicable to describe the process in which some lifers were successful in building a life post-release while others were re-incarcerated. Conventionally, desistance is understood as a developmental process in which one maintains a state of non-offending.[2] Although desistance is part of the reintegration process, it is still not synonymous with reintegration.[3] The majority of the interviewed lifers in a strict sense desisted from crime but still experienced great difficulty adjusting to life outside of prison. Those who were sent back to prison violated the conditions of their parole rather than having committed new crimes. "Success" thus entailed managing parole conditions, while "failure" implied the opposite. For the sake of readability, when applying existing theoretical models to explain success and failure, I will still use the term "desistance," despite the term's deceiving nature. Existing models to explain desistance, then, can roughly be split in two: on one hand, life-course theories; and on the other, theories of cognitive transformation.

On-Time, Off-Time, or Out of Time?

From a life-course perspective, stakes of conformity associated with intimate partner relationships, parenthood, and preexisting family ties are all thought to contribute to successful reentry. The life-history accounts of these sixty-eight lifers, however, suggested otherwise. Because of the length of their sentences, their life courses were disrupted and hence lacked the potential to lead these men to paths of desistance.

First, from this theoretical point of view, establishing and maintaining an intimate relationship would be expected to positively influence lifers in "going straight." The attachment to an intimate partner would give them a reluctance to engage in crime, because they might hurt or jeopardize their relationship.[4] Yet interviewees rarely indicated intimate partners as a positive influence—either consciously or unconsciously. Few of the non-incarcerated lifers were engaged in healthy, positive relationships after release, and to the extent that they were, they emphasized having experienced a cognitive shift well before committing to those relationships. Many re-incarcerated lifers, in contrast, attributed their re-incarceration to negative aspects of their intimate relationships. The women they had become involved with did not provide a stake in conformity, but rather encouraged behaviors that resulted in re-incarceration. Many of these failed relationships can be traced back to the interviewees' desire to fulfill a pro-social role. Arguably, the desire to "catch up" with what they missed for many years while incarcerated made them uncritical in their choice of intimate partner. Alternatively, in line with what the criminologist John Braithwaite[5] observed, "deviants" are often welcomed by similarly stigmatized "outcasts." One may suggest that many male lifers started relationships with women who suffered from poor physical and/or mental health, including suicidal behaviors, substance abuse, and criminal behaviors. Many interviewees experienced trouble with the conditions of their parole because they were found in the company of a woman with a criminal record, were found with her prescription drugs, or were found using again because their girlfriend used. In short, rather than these intimate partner relationships helping to build a life post-release, they constituted a potential liability.

Second, from a life-course perspective, (re)assuming a parental role is thought to positively influence these prisoner's success post-release.

The large majority of interviewees—both non-incarcerated and re-incarcerated—were significantly "off-time" in becoming a parent. Those who had children typically became fathers in their teenage years, which—due to the timing of the event—did not contribute to them staying away from crime, but rather contributed to their marginalized status. Others, on the other hand, were "out of time." When they were first released in their fifties, starting a family did not belong in that age-specific repertoire. To the extent that their intimate partners had children, they took on a role of a stepparent, although none of the interviewees described such a role as a transitional phase in their lives. In sum, for lifers, engaging in a relationship or becoming a parent are thus not the turning points we would expect from life-course research,[6] leading to a new identity with associated stakes in conformity,[7] but rather, for these interviewees, consists of a series of interactional dynamics. These lifers thus perceived "being a parent," or "being in a relationship," as a temporal state of being, rather than constituting a part of a newly acquired identity.

A third factor derived from life-course theory is the positive role of preexisting family ties on reentry. Again, these ties were virtually absent among both non-incarcerated and re-incarcerated lifers. Similar to findings reported elsewhere, the prolonged, deprived nature of contact with family members while incarcerated may explain why so many families do not survive the imprisonment of one of their members.[8] Further, reintegration into family life posed obstacles to these lifers, as they were separated from family members for extended periods. To the extent that family members were alive upon their release, and willing to engage in contact, interviewees indicated that they felt they had to prove themselves to their family members—to demonstrate that they had truly changed. Hence, rather being a source of support, existing family relations were absent or oftentimes constituted a source of concern.

One way of interpreting these empirical disjunctions from the life-course perspective would be to point to the meaning and experience of family life as being qualitatively different for men having served a life sentence from those who served much shorter sentences.[9] Due to the lack of new and preexisting relationships, the "off-time" occurrence of life events such as parenthood, or due to "playing catch-up," social relations failed to exert a deterrent effect on this group of offenders. As noted elsewhere, the notion of "time" unified these men's and women's range of reentry experiences—the irrevocable loss of time and life history, the dislocation in time and reduced future after release, and the enduring nature of the changes in close affective relationships with others.[10]

Even though the vast majority of lifers were thus both "off-time" and "out of time" in acquiring family roles, there was one factor that provided stability and meaning in their lives post-release: employment. Interviewees pointed out that the times they were doing well were related to being employed. Having a job was a contributing factor in reentry, especially when their job supplied a sense of control over their lives. Interviewees expressed that work gave meaning to their lives, particularly when their job, working as a "professional ex," such as a counselor or paralegal, allowed them to use the narrative they acquired in prison. Thus employment was a contributing factor in staying outside the prison walls, but not as strong as would be expected from previous research. This could be explained by the phenomenon that after release the effort to secure a conformist identity was undermined by the stigma of a felony conviction. The extensive use of criminal background checks challenged participants' efforts to establish a commitment to pro-social roles.

In short, these lifers seemed to miss traditional turning points in their life course and, accordingly, lacked key external sources of informal social control. Even though employment proved to be an important factor in "going straight," the interviewees attributed this to the sense of purpose employment gave them, rather than the role of "conventional others" at work. The feeling that they were behind schedule, and the extensive use of criminal background checks in the application process, made the relationship between employment and "doing well" less than straightforward. In sum, life-course theory appeared to fall short in terms of explaining desistance among this special population. Let us turn, then, to another prevalent theory used to conceptualize post-release success and failure.

"I'll Tell You What You Want to Hear"

Theories of cognitive transformation suggest that those who stay away from crime have made identifiable changes to their personal identity and produce a new, "improved" self, which no longer cognitively or emotionally coheres with their old, "criminal" self.[11] The narratives provided by both incarcerated and non-incarcerated lifers, however, suggest otherwise; individuals from both groups present a prototypical reform story. Almost all of them had consciously fashioned a "better" version of themselves.[12] The large majority expressed that they were now different from the person they were at the time of the homicide, all subscribed to conventional moral values, and almost all emphasized that they had redeemed themselves and were now "the person they were always meant to be." Most lifers I talked to discarded their past identity in favor of an alternative, pro-social one, and used generative motivations, ranging from speaking in public, running in-prison programs, and expressing a desire to "give back." The finding that both groups of lifers present such elements of the transformation narratives may be traced back to the role of (post-)prison programming that encourages therapeutic discoveries and emotional disentanglement from ex-offenders' "old" selves.[13] Another explanation for the omnipresence of these narratives can be found in lifer groups in prison, whose members help one another prepare for parole board hearings. These programs and interactions thus aid in the creation of new identities, produced through the autobiographical work these lifers engaged in for so many years. This observation is not unique. In her study of twenty-seven violent men, the sociologist Lois Presser found that life narratives oftentimes follow subcultural forms, including recovery narratives characteristic of "12-step" rhetoric.[14] I do not argue that these stories are fictions, in the sense of being "made up," but rather that they are devices that produce certain kinds of meaning.[15] This is not to say that these interviewees are purposely lying. Rather, they have been schooled in presenting a narrative of redemption, change, and "giving back."[16]

Finding such narratives of redemption in both lifer groups blurs the line between the concepts of "primary" and "secondary" desistance. While primary desistance refers to "any lull or crime-free gap [. . .] in the course of a criminal career," secondary desistance involves "the movement from the behavior of non-offending to the assumption of a role or identity of a non-offender or 'changed person.'"[17] All interviewees described themselves as changed into better persons over the years. Despite their identity change, a large proportion returned to prison at some point during their parole due to new crimes or, in the majority of cases, parole violations. Hence, primary and secondary desistance may be inadequate terms to describe conformity versus nonconformity among this group of lifers. The conundrum can be solved by emphasizing the role of self-efficacy, rather than the mere presence of a transformation narrative: those who are successful in staying out expressed a higher degree of self-efficacy compared with those returning to prison.

Post-release success is thus not solely the result of a change in male coming-of-age societal forces (e.g., parenthood, marriage, employment, and military service),[18] as emphasized by life-course theorists,[19] nor merely the resolution of an individual to change.[20] The interviewees who succeeded in staying out of prison differed from their re-incarcerated counterparts in terms of self-efficacy. Those who were re-incarcerated exhibited a *lack* of self-efficacy, giving way to impulsivity and a lack of knowledge of future consequences.

These findings have potential far-reaching consequences for how we should deal with lifers as a special population, both during and after their time in prison.

Translating Research into Practice

A life sentence seldom means life in prison.[21] In fact, approximately one-third of all lifers nationwide will never be eligible for parole—which leaves two-thirds of lifers serving a life sentence with the possibility of parole.[22] For them, reentry is a long-term process, one that actually starts prior to release and continues well afterward.[23] The emergence of reentry as a criminal justice policy issue in the last decade has largely ignored persons serving a life sentence. Typically, reentry programs are provided to persons within six months of their release date and offer transition services in the community upon release. However, for persons serving a life sentence, their release date is not fixed and they are often overlooked as policy-makers and correctional administrators consider reentry strategies.[24] Released prisoners in general face multiple challenges when they return home, including substance abuse, (mental) health problems, legal issues, and housing difficulties.[25] For those incarcerated for decades on end, these effects are exacerbated. Long-term imprisonment constitutes an extreme on many fronts. On one hand, it entails considerable deprivations and requires substantial long-term allocations of scarce correctional resources; on the other, long-term imprisonment may cause harm to inmates, and may hence negatively affect their likelihood to do well after release.

Reentry from the Beginning: Reclaiming Self-Efficacy in Prison

There are several reasons these lifers returned to prison. In terms of policy implications, however, it may be more useful to focus on what made them succeed, rather than made them fail. While for some, aging out of a crime-ridden lifestyle determined their success, and for others it was having a "healthy fear" of re-incarceration, the majority of those able to rebuild a life after release showed a strong sense of control over their own lives, or a belief that they had the capacity to use good judgment, could act independently, and were able to make their own choices.

By its very nature, incarceration completely transforms the potency of an individual's agency.[26] Correctional educational programs have shown to be effective in providing a self-efficacy-enhancing context not only within the walls[27] but also beyond them,[28] as those with a sense of control over their lives adjust better to life on the outside. The question, then, becomes: How can we re-instill self-efficacy post-release or, better still, maintain this sense of control throughout incarceration?

Treatment programs for ex-offenders are typically deficit-based and aim to eradicate or reduce the various problems associated with criminal behavior.[29] In such programs, the story is that ex-offenders are people with multiple deficits, ranging from substance abuse and poor educational history to mental health problems.[30] To reduce crime, conventional programs focus on teaching prisoners to eliminate these deficits by education, addiction counseling, anger management, and the like. More recent initiatives hold that a redemption ritual is a necessary part of successful reentry:[31] by being rewarded for participation in programs and by reentry courts recognizing redemption,[32] offenders would feel recognized in their efforts to change. The findings reflected in this book, however, suggest that acquiring a narrative of redemption or transformation alone may not touch on the quintessential part of desistance post-release and may do little in the way of changing actual behavior. Instead, these findings suggest that the distinguishing factor between incarcerated and non-incarcerated lifers is self-efficacy, or a lack thereof, more so than other parts of the transformation narrative, such as a good core self or generative motivations.[33] Rather than learning to present such a transformation narrative, in-prison programs should focus on restoring a sense of self-efficacy to released inmates to ensure successful reentry.[34] To succeed beyond bars, it is key to develop a sense of control that in turn allows these lifers to acquire the necessary strategies that will assist them in developing their personal and social contexts. More important than holding someone responsible for something they have done in the past—what has been termed "passive responsibility"[35]—is making sure individuals feel a sense of control over their lives and take "active responsibility" for putting things right for the future. Control over the future, then, might be a valuable therapeutic tool.[36]

Decades of incarceration result in stripping away any sense of individual control and replacing it with institutional-level control.[37] Once these lifers are paroled, they are expected to, automatically, get back into the driver's seat. This seems to be an unreasonable expectation, given that these individuals have spent all their time being told when to exercise, work, see visitors, eat, or sleep. This disempowerment creates a mentality that is not well suited to overcoming the structural impediments that many face upon release from prison.[38] Thus, to undo years spent stripping away an inmate's sense of control, there ought to be intensive programs that help inmates regain control over their lives and actions. As a result, they may be more likely to make a successful reentry into the society they left many years ago.

Reclaiming Self-Efficacy through Employment

Self-efficacy as a success factor does not operate by itself. Interviewees felt more in control of their lives, and felt they were doing well, when they were employed. The relationship between self-efficacy and employment was reciprocal: those who had a preestablished sense of control over their lives were able to overcome structural limitations imposed by criminal background checks and limited access to the labor market; having a job, in turn, gave meaning to their lives and strengthened a sense of control over their actions.

When ex-prisoners do find jobs, they tend to earn less than do employees with similar background characteristics who have not been in prison.[39] Research supports a strong programmatic emphasis on increasing ex-prisoners' employability, through skills training, job readiness, and, possibly, work-release programs during incarceration and after release.[40] Previous studies showed that programs that provide training, a range of services and supports, incentives, and access to better employers work well, especially when there are strong incentives for ex-prisoners to obtain employment.[41] In the case of lifers, such incentives were not limited to only meeting the conditions of their parole, but extended to employment giving meaning to their lives.

Because of the nature of their sentence, in terms of job-preparation programs, lifers require a different type of programming than that offered to the "general" prison population. Currently, even when employment and training programs are offered, they are rarely offered to lifers early in their terms. In their study of over one hundred Canadian long-term inmates, Edward Zamble and Frank Porporino[42] found that this may partly be attributed to the pressure of numbers, which dictates that inmates have to wait their turn. Another reason is that those who are eligible for such programs are those who are returning to society within a certain period of time, and lifers typically do not fall into that category. This was the case for Doris, who was reincarcerated for "association": her girlfriend had a felony record. In the female prison where I interview her, she says she wanted to sign up for a computer class to be able to look for jobs once she was re-paroled. Yet she was told that those spots were reserved for those who would be released soon. "Now, I'm not eligible for any programs, because I'm not getting out anytime soon," she says with a sigh. Traditionally those who are eligible for programs are those who have proved themselves well behaved and motivated to participate in such programs.[43] These practices may thus have adverse effects. In many cases the individuals who are selected are not much in need of the programs, while others, such as lifers, who might have benefited earlier in their terms, appear unsuitable by the time the programs are made available. The failure to design reentry strategies for persons serving a life sentence neglects one in nine prisoners by denying them the opportunity to participate in valuable programming.[44]

Even when decent lifer-specific preparations for the job market post-release are made available through correctional facilities, they do not imply that meaningful employment is easy to find. The most important hurdle lifers have to overcome is the stigma of a felony record. Over time, employers have become increasingly likely to ask job applicants about their criminal history and substantially more likely to conduct official criminal background checks to verify applicants' reports on their prior criminal convictions.[45] Continuously applying the "felon label" inhibits released lifers from obtaining meaningful employment and rebuilding a productive life post-release.[46] These labeling consequences result in reduced opportunities for employment. Such dynamics, as a recent National Research Council report cautions, could likewise cause ex-inmates to concentrate their job search outside the formal sector of the labor market.[47] One way to improve ex-prisoners' employment opportunities is to reduce the labeling consequences of their criminal past. "Ban the Box" movements have received popular support in recent years, promoting policies that limit employers' access to criminal background information until later in the hiring process.[48] In order to give this population a fair chance of successful reentry, we should reconsider the way background checks are currently applied.

The Inside and Outside of Reentry

Aside from education and preparation for employment, effective programs should also tackle the psychological ("inside") and social ("outside") aspects of reentry. In brief, these include mental health care addressing the effects of long-term incarceration as well as the interpersonal skills needed for a successful life beyond bars. In these programs, an individualized approach is key: a first-time parolee who committed a homicide needs a different program than does a drug-using repeat parolee who committed a drug crime, for example.[49] In order for individualized initiatives to be effective, they need to be skill-oriented, focus on dynamic criminogenic factors, and treat multiple deficits simultaneously.[50] Applying these principles to practice, evidence-based programs should be designed that focus on behavioral outcomes, target high-risk offenders, use risk instruments, begin treatment in prison, and provide continuity in the community.[51] Given the long period for which lifers have been incarcerated, intensive intervention should extend well beyond several months after release.

In the absence of any strong evidence base, it becomes important to consider the theoretical basis of reintegration practice. One of the most widely known rehabilitation theories is the good lives model, a strength-based approach to assist ex-offenders achieve their goals as well as to manage their risk.[52] It emphasizes offenders' strengths by taking seriously offenders' personal preferences and values—that is, the things that matter most to them in the world—drawing on these to motivate individuals to live better lives. In addition, it seeks to provide offenders with the competencies and opportunities to implement rehabilitation plans based on these preferences and needs.[53] The model also contains elements such as a sense of agency, the importance of personal identity, and a sense of meaning in one's life—elements consistent with the role of the professional ex.[54] The model has been proven useful in the reintegration of other types of offenders,[55] and given its strength-based approach it may prove a valuable tool for lifers returning home.

Tackling the challenges of reentry proves to be difficult, if not impossible, for most. As Glenn aptly explains, "A young man of eighteen, nineteen years old has no idea. His maturity level is nonexistent. And if you put him in society twenty years later, you'd better watch out. You have to provide him tools to adjust."

The key to building a life post-release, all lifers agree, is a gradual phasing out of prison and a gradual phasing into society. Whereas several decades ago prisoners (including lifers) would be released from maximum-security facilities, fortunately this has changed into a more gradual reentry process, characterized by diminishing degrees of supervision. Theoretically, lifers should move from maximum-security settings to medium, minimum, and pre-release facilities. Programs facilitating reentry of lifers should be designed to meet this gradual transition, commencing at the very start of a life sentence and ideally progressing into "buffering agencies," which serve to mitigate the reentry impact[56] by offering transitional services. These services include photo identifications, appropriate clothes, housing, access to transportation, and, if they are eligible, signing up for public assistance. As the National Research Council emphasized in its report on parole and community integration, these kinds of immediate needs are often not addressed before release, and it falls to family and friends to help arrange them for newly released ex-offenders. In fact, most post-release programs are not available to releasees in the first few days after release.[57] For successful reentry, it is necessary to identify the challenges prior to release and develop tailored reentry plans that target appropriate services.[58] For lifers, who often lack the social support of long-gone family members, it is important to have mentors available at the moment of release to mitigate the vast impact of return to the free world. The key is that no one should leave prison without an immediately available person and plan for post-release life.[59]

THE PSYCHOLOGICAL AFTERMATH

The effects of long-term imprisonment are not limited to simply "getting adjusted" to a new environment. A large part of the interviewed lifers dealt with a specific cluster of mental health symptoms.[60] In addition to chronic PTSD, symptoms included institutionalized personality traits (distrusting others, difficulty engaging in relationships, hampered decision-making), social-sensory disorientation (spatial disorientation, difficulty in social interactions), and social and temporal alienation (the idea of "not belonging" in a social and temporal setting). These findings are particularly relevant when it comes to successful reentry.

First and foremost, it must be recognized that prison environments are themselves potentially damaging situations whose negative psychological effects must be taken seriously and should be carefully regulated. This finding, in line with reports on damaging prison effects throughout the nation, emphasizes the need for more realistic and effective legal limits to the nature and amount of prison pain that is dispensed inside these institutions.[61]

Second, prisoners suffering from mental illness do not have access to care in the same way that non-imprisoned populations do. Additionally, to the extent that mental health care is available and accessible, mental health professionals often lack the necessary know-how and skill to deal with the unique effects of long-term incarceration. This limits their ability to facilitate prisoners transitioning back into society.

Another complicating factor concerns accessibility to counseling. Lifers who were on parole at the time of the interview expressed fear that seeking help could potentially send them back to prison. Simultaneously, the suspiciousness of others that is usually adaptive in prison inhibits ex-prisoners from seeking help.[62] Without proper treatment that is focused on these specific effects of long-term incarceration, these individuals run the risk of returning to prison—untreated.

A NEW SOCIAL WORLD

As the narratives of the men and women in this book show, lifers are confronted with a unique set of challenges related to the long period of time spent behind bars. These do not only include little family and community support, and a lack of traditional social roles upon release; for released lifers, relationships with pro-social others (intimate partner, family members) either ceased to exist during incarceration, or are not rebuilt upon release.[63] In their lives, reentry and community organizations become even more important to act as an alternative network to assist them in facing a new world.

One of these challenges faced by these lifers is "catching up too quickly": acquiring social roles, most notably intimate partner relationships, at a pace too ambitious for their own good. In providing help and guidance to lifers, reentry organizations should be aware of this pitfall and advise their clients accordingly.

Another potentially useful source of support upon release is other lifers. "I would have gone to a lifer group if they had one, 'cause there are times that you want to talk to someone who's been there [life sentence], but it's not allowed," fifty-one-year Norman says. He adds, "So I stay to myself. I won't even offer a ride to people who I know have done time. You can be back in prison any second." Norman has been back in prison for several years now after a domestic strife incident with his girlfriend, a complaint Norman said she confessed was a lie. Being on parole inhibited most interviewees from seeking contact with other ex-prisoners. This rule is based on the fear that ex-prisoners would fraternize with those who are criminally active and, accordingly, reassume a criminal lifestyle. The majority of U.S. states require "no association with persons with criminal records" as a condition of parole supervision.[64] Based on the potential benefits of lifer peer groups, policy-makers should reconsider these no-contact policies. In line with findings reported elsewhere,[65] the findings described here show that involvement in such groups might facilitate reentry in at least two ways. First, lifers can help other lifers in their initial transition from prison to society by providing advice about readjustment. Second, lifers can provide a useful source of support in the months and even years after release, especially during challenging. In fact, the recent Canadian "LifeLine" program has contributed to low rates of recidivism among released lifers. The program utilizes in-reach workers (lifers who have lived crime-free in the community for at least five years and who have proven to be positive role models) to assist and support lifers. Their role is to establish and maintain contact with lifers still in prison, support them through their time in the penitentiary, and assist them in planning for release.[66]

Other lifers, more so than counselors who have not done time, can identify with these challenges, share experiences, and provide a listening ear. As these individuals have survived their own sentences of life imprisonment, they are able to share their coping strategies during and after imprisonment with the offenders with whom they work. At the same time, such professional exes should be recognized for their potential in facilitating the successful integration of some formerly incarcerated persons.[67] Employment as a professional ex has the potential to act as a management strategy to combat stigma and exclusion.[68] If helping others, as the narratives in this book show, has such adaptive consequences, then it can be argued that reciprocal support should be more widely available to both current and former prisoners. In addition, in line with suggestions from prior research, to create more professional exes, policies can be developed to reduce legal restrictions to employment for felons, and to provide monetary support to promote the completion of certification programs (e.g., substance abuse counseling, reentry counseling).[69] Taking on the role of a professional ex has been demonstrated to aid desistance. As Thomas LeBel and colleagues aptly put it, it has the potential to transform formerly incarcerated persons from being part of "the problem" into part of "the solution" to reduce crime and recidivism.[70]

When Is Enough, Enough?

Not being able to be in contact with other ex-prisoners is but one condition by which parolees have to abide. These conditions raise questions about the role of parole and its influence on reentry. Nowadays, a considerable part of the prison admission stream consists of either probation or parole violators.[71] This tendency, combined with conservative parole board decisions, has created an overall increase in length of stay per prisoner. Criminal justice scholars have argued that this has created a correctional system that feeds on itself, as the larger parole population creates more violations, which in turn feeds the prison system.[72]

There are several key reasons to rethink current policies regarding life sentences. First, in many ways, Americans support the belief in second chances, but there is a reluctance to apply this perspective to those who commit crimes, especially serious crimes such as homicides.[73] However, as the stories in this book show, many undergo a true personal transformation, feel remorseful, and are able to contribute positively to society given the chance.

Further, reform is particularly warranted given the age of recalled lifers. As the number of older prisoners increases with parole revocations and delayed parole releases, correctional systems will be even more challenged to provide adequate physical and mental health services.[74] States continue to be faced with rising health-care costs associated with caring for prisoners older and sicker than ever before. In fact, as the sociologists Jennifer Krabill and Ronald Aday caution, age will be one of the biggest issues facing the criminal justice system in the foreseeable future.[75]

In their report on the aging prison population, Human Rights Watch emphasized that the proportionality of a sentence is typically assessed based on the circumstances that existed at the time of the crime. Nevertheless, while a prison term may have been proportionate at the time imposed, increasing age and infirmity may change the calculus against continued incarceration and in favor of some form of conditional release. Based on interviews with staff and prisoners from over twenty prisons throughout the United States, they concluded that for the vast majority of elderly prisoners it is hard to see how their continued incarceration meaningfully serves any of the purposes for which their sentences were originally imposed: retribution, incapacitation, deterrence, and rehabilitation.[76] The same accounts for the elderly re-incarcerated lifers I interviewed. Retribution for their crimes has been furthered by the decades they have spent behind bars and could, following the suggestions by Human Rights Watch, be further served if they were released from prison by restrictions on their freedom within the community and parole supervision. Incapacitation to prevent future crime seems to defy its purpose, given that these frail prisoners, who are declining physically and mentally, are not likely to endanger public safety. Similarly, in terms of lengthy sentences deterring future crime by others (general deterrence), research so far fails to establish a link between length of sentencing and levels of crime.[77] Finally, prolonged incarceration is unlikely to advance the final purpose of imprisonment: rehabilitation. For prisoners who no longer pose a public safety risk because of age and deteriorating health, and who have already served a lengthy prison sentence, from a human rights perspective, continued incarceration opposes a just and proportionate punishment. In such cases, alternative forms of punishment should be considered, which may include options such as conditional release to home confinement under parole supervision.[78]

I am aware that the serious crimes of many long-term prisoners make this group unattractive in terms of public and political support for innovative policies. However, there is little evidence that so far research has had *any* role in the adoption of long-term confinement, despite calls in recent years for more evidence-based policy. Now is the time to change the tide. As the results presented in this book show, the vast majority of re-incarcerated lifers are those who have violated the terms of their parole supervision but have not been convicted of new crimes.

REFORMING PAROLE FOR LIFERS

One reform that states and the federal government can undertake to counter this trend is to restrict the extent to which technical parole violators can be re-incarcerated, as well as the length of that re-incarceration. This ties in with the notion of giving these lifers back their citizenship. As ex-felons, these lifers are no longer a part of "us,"[79] as Norman illustrates when he tells me, "To society, my life don't mean shit." He adds, "Enough is enough. When does the punishment end?" Treating parolees as third-class citizens does little for successful reentry. Rather, give these men and women back their citizenship, including the responsibilities, but also the rights, associated with it. Such a change in policy requires a coordinated, continued approach, both at the state and local levels.

Another reform concerns the nature of parole supervision. In line with findings reported elsewhere,[80] these findings do not provide conclusive evidence that supervision prevents recidivism. Equally, it cannot be demonstrated that parole supervision was vital to the reintegration of these lifers. Rather, on the contrary, the majority of interviewees expressed that parole conditions forestalled their reentry. In general, the style of supervision most helpful to the released lifer is one built on trust and dignity, within the framework of parole requirements. As suggested elsewhere,[81] this includes giving the released lifer the opportunity to strike out independently and to cast off their prison label and identity.

In short, those who were able to stay outside the prison walls were, in large part, able to manage the conditions of their parole. More generally, the fear of being sent back to prison at any moment inhibited readjustment for many interviewees. Glenn, who was re-incarcerated for irresponsibly operating a motor vehicle, describes the insecurity associated with recall as follows: "[I am] afraid. I don't know where I belong in life. I don't know if it's even worth it to ask for freedom. To put myself through it again. Sometimes I think, 'Just let me die in prison. At least I know it here. I don't know about life outside. In society.'" Several months after our interview, Glenn has been granted re-parole. At his hearing, the parole board concluded that "he committed a driving infraction for which he served his punishment." The board found no reason for additional incarceration.

Simple examples of technical violations that resulted in re-incarceration include association with other ex-prisoners, traffic violations, or women's reliance on the parole system to "do away" with their husbands. As evidenced by the sizable number of lifers in this sample coming back on dismissed domestic violence charges, sound policy should remove the return to custody as an "escape hatch"[82] for women to remove disruptive men from the home. In line with recommendations by the Massachusetts Department of Correction, expanding the availability of community-based sanctions will increase the tools at a parole officer's disposal when responding to violations.[83] On a more fundamental level, the solution to breaking the cycle of repeated incarcerations due to parole violations lies in revising the current "contract" between the parole officer and the offender. Following the renowned criminal justice scholar Joan Petersilia, the focal point of the revised contract must be a system of earned discharge, or accelerated release, whereby parolees have the ability to reduce the total length of their parole by demonstrating arrest-free behavior and self-sufficiency.[84] She argues that today's parole contract spells out clearly the negative consequences that will be applied if a parolee fails to comply with specified conditions. It is a model almost entirely based on disincentives rather than on incentives, and as such does not meet parole's aim of behavioral change. Current parole contracts, she aptly puts, fail to include positive rewards to encourage parolees to stay involved in treatment programs. Punishment-only systems as used today tend to cause people to change their behavior briefly or only long enough to avoid additional punishment, but such changes seldom continue once the threat of sanction is lifted.[85] Rather, to accomplish and sustain behavioral change, research in various fields—including several state agencies—has shown the applicability of behavioral contracting.[86] A behavioral contract for parolees would be simply a written contract that specifies the parolees' behavioral obligations in meeting the terms of the contract and the parole agents' obligations once the parolees have met theirs.

Most parolees, including the lifers interviewed for this book, are motivated to be discharged from parole. Today, lifers have little to no opportunity to reduce the length of their imposed parole term—they are simply on parole for life. Explicit lifetime parole cannot be justified on the basis of safety or concerns about crime risk. Social science research has demonstrated that older offenders, and individuals who stay arrest-free for seven years or more, simply have very little risk for future crime, and this risk is similar to that of non-offenders.[87] Further, as the criminal justice scholars Shawn Bushway and Gary Sweeten warn, the existence of lifetime parole might create a hopeless environment that can trap an ex-offender and provide little incentive to adopt a pro-social attitude.[88] The revised parole contract thus should combine both of these elements—behavioral change and accelerated parole discharge—to produce tangible benefits for public safety and resource allocation, and should be able to break the parole-back-to-prison cycle. For example, when meeting the conditions laid out in the behavioral contract, the parolee is—depending on actual risk—given the possibility to shorten the period during which he or she is under parole supervision.[89]

TAKE THE POLITICS OUT

Punishment serves various purposes: deterrence, incapacitation, retribution, and rehabilitation. First, deterrence serves to send out a general threat of punishment to deter people from engaging in crime, as well as a specific threat of punishment to deter the individual concerned. Second, incapacitation aims to debilitate the individual—he or she cannot commit crimes while incarcerated. Third, from a retribution perspective, society is entitled to inflict harm on those who have harmed society. In the status quo regarding punishment of lifers, the final aim of punishment, rehabilitation, seems to have been abandoned. From a critical point of view, today's policies of re-incarcerating lifers after technical violations does little except satisfy a need for vengeance. If we still want rehabilitation to be a part of punishment, we should be questioning to what extent we are willing to pay the price.

Staying out is not easy. Except for being sent back to prison for technical violations—driven by finding prison a safe place to return to, catching up too quickly, or not being able to shed old habits—numerous lifers returned based on what can be termed "political reasons." Recall to prison occurred after two main incidents: the Willie Horton and the Dominic Cinelli cases. Aside from bringing about a great sense of insecurity, lifers experienced such recall as unjust, as sixty-three-year-old Carl points out: "What they should stop doing is punishing everybody for the mistake of one person." If we still wish rehabilitation to be a part of punishment, we should stop putting these lifers back behind the walls for political reasons. Or as Cody, in his green jumpsuit, puts it, "When Nixon does something, they are not punishing all presidents. But when something happens to a lifer, they're doing it to all of us."

***

Contrary to public perception, the vast majority of lifers who were re-incarcerated did not commit a new (violent) crime, but were put behind bars because of a parole violation. The vast majority of lifers have a chance of living crime-free, productive lives after release. Providing them a fair chance on the job market, adequate programming taking into account the prolonged period of confinement, and a sense of certainty in terms of reasons for recall would enable these lifers to start a life beyond bars.

NOTES

PREFACE

1 Henry, 2015.

2 Mauer, King, & Young, 2004.

3 This research was funded by the Marie Curie International Outgoing Fellowship for Career Development under grant number 299875.

4 Richardson, 2012.

5 When reporting the findings, I gave all interviewees pseudonyms. Some interviewees indicated a preference for a certain name to be used; I respected this wish if it did not resemble their legal name too closely. The only exception is Lyn, who explicitly requested being referred to by her own name.

CHAPTER 1. INTRODUCTION

1 Nellis & Chung, 2013.

2 Ibid.

3 In fact, just over 29% of all lifers nationwide will never be eligible for parole.

4 Nellis & Chung, 2013.

5 Brooks et al., 2008.

6 Nellis & Chung, 2013.

7 See also Garland, 2001; Clear, 1994; Haney, 2011a.

8 Austin, 2010.

9 Henry, 2015; National Research Council, 2014.

10 Nellis & Chung, 2013.

11 National Research Council, 2014.

12 Henry, 2015.

13 National Research Council, 2014; Petersilia, 2003.

14 Nellis & Chung, 2013.

15 Throughout the book, I use the term "reentry" to include processes that begin before the individual is released from prison, experiences at the moment of release, and those during the first years in the community. In doing so, I follow previous research by LeBel & Maruna (2012).

16 Harding, 2012.

17 Austin, Irwin, & Hardyman, 2002; Stanton, 1969.

18 Bjørkly & Waage, 2005; Coker & Martin, 1985; Eronen, Hakola, & Tiihonen, 1996; Sturup & Lindqvist, 2014; Tiihonen, Hakola, Nevalainen, & Eronen, 1995.

19 Durose, Cooper, & Snyder, 2014.

20 Baaij, Liem, & Nieuwbeerta, 2012; Neuilly, Zgoba, Tita, & Lee, 2011; Roberts, Zgoba, & Shahidullah, 2007.

21 Bjørkly & Waage, 2005; Eronen, Zgoba, & Shahidullah, 1996; Gottlieb & Gabrielsen, 1990; Sturup & Lindqvist, 2014.

22 Langan & Levin, 2002; Neuilly, Zgoba, Tita, & Lee, 2011; Roberts, Zgoba, & Shahidullah, 2007; Putkonen et al., 2003.

23 Neuilly, Zgoba, Tita, & Lee, 2011.

24 Baaij, Liem, & Nieuwbeerta, 2012; Liem, Zahn & Tichavsky, 2014; Roberts, Zgoba, & Shahidullah, 2007.

25 Kazemian & Travis, 2015.

26 Loughran et al., 2009; Meade, Steiner, Makarios, & Travis, 2013; Nagin, Cullen, & Jonson, 2009.

27 For an overview, see Kazemian & Travis, 2015.

28 Nagin, 2013.

29 Henry, 2015; National Research Council, 2014.

30 Flanagan, 1995a.

31 Harshbarger, 2004.

32 Williams & Abraldes, 2007

33 Human Rights Watch, 2012.

34 Aday & Krabill, 2013.

35 Williams & Abraldes, 2007

36 Human Rights Watch, 2012.

37 Aday & Krabill, 2013.

38 Anno, Graham, Lawrence, & Shansky, 2004.

39 Nellis & Chung, 2013.

40 Flanagan, 1995b.

41 Clear, 2007.

42 Radzinowicz, 1968.

43 Cf. Cohen & Taylor 1981; p. 216.

44 LeBel & Maruna, 2012.

45 Anderson, 2012; Gawande, 2009.

46 Heinlein, 2013; Mullane, 2012; Munn & Bruckert, 2013.

47 Appleton, 2010.

48 Irwin, 2010.

49 Munn & Bruckert, 2013; p. 169.

50 Nellis & Chung, 2013.

51 Ibid.

52 Appleton, 2010; Coker & Martin, 1985.

53 Appleton, 2010.

54 Mauer, King, & Young, 2004.

55 Nellis & Chung, 2013.

56 Cullen, 1994; p. 531.

57 Tonry, 1999.
58 G. J. Duncan, B. Gustafson, R. Hauser, G. Schmaus, S. Jenkins, H. Messinger, R. Muffels, B. Nolan, J. C. Ray, W. Voges, "Poverty and Social-Assistance Dynamics in the United States, Canada and Europe," in: K. McFate, R. Lawson, R., and W. J. Wilson, eds., *Poverty, Inequality, and the Future of Social Policy: Western States in the New World Order* (New York: Russell Sage Foundation, 1995), cited in Comfort, 2009.
59 J. Cullen, *The American Dream* (Oxford: Oxford University Press, 2003), cited in Comfort, 2009.
60 Visher & O'Connell, 2012.
61 Polizzi & Maruna, 2010; p. 184.
62 See LeBel & Maruna, 2012.
63 Gadd & Farrall, 2004.
64 See Fleisher, 2013.

CHAPTER 2. UNDERSTANDING DESISTANCE

1 Farrall & Bowling, 1999.
2 King, 2013; LeBel, Burnett, Maruna, & Bushway, 2008.
3 LeBel, Burnett, Maruna, & Bushway, 2008; p. 138.
4 Berk et al., 2009; Loeber, Farrington, & Cotter, 2011; Loeber, Lacourse, & Homish, 2005.
5 Hirschi & Gottfredson, 1983; p. 552.
6 Gottfredson & Hirschi, 1990; p. 141.
7 Sweeten, Piquero, & Steinberg, 2013.
8 Gove, 1985
9 Aday, 2003.
10 Steffensmeier, Allan, Harer, & Streifel, 1989; Steffensmeier & Harer, 1987.
11 Giordano, 2013.
12 Moffitt, 1993, 1994.
13 Roberts, Zgoba, & Shahidullah, 2007.
14 Eronen, Hakola, & Tiihonen, 1996; Tiihonen, Hakola, Nevalainen, & Eronen, 1995.
15 Sweeten, Piquero, & Steinberg, 2013.
16 Baaij, Liem, & Nieuwbeerta, 2012.
17 Gottlieb & Gabrielsen, 1990; Neuilly, Zgoba, Tita, & Lee, 2011.
18 A number of studies on juvenile homicide offenders as a subgroup tend to focus on juveniles who killed their parents. Given the relatively rare nature of this type of homicide, studies typically rely on a very small number of cases for analysis (Duncan & Duncan, 1971; Heide, 1992; Post, 1982; Russell, 1984; Tanay, 1973). At first glance, results seem to indicate that juvenile parricide offenders recidivate less often (10%) (Corder et al., 1976) than do juvenile homicide offenders in general (60%) (Heide, 1999; Heide, Spencer, Thompson, & Solomon, 2001; Trulson, Caudill, Haerle, & DeLisi, 2012). A closer look at some of these studies, however, reveals that they either relied on very small sample sizes or included offenders

who were still imprisoned at the end of the follow-up period (e.g., Corder et al., 1976). What further complicates generalizations of these studies are the differential measures for recidivism: some use a revocation and return to prison as a measure (e.g., Heide, Spencer, Thompson, & Solomon, 2001), whereas others use wider measures such as rearrest of any crime after release (e.g., Duncan & Duncan, 1971). Perhaps as a consequence of these differences in measures, recidivism rates differ widely (0% to 60%).

19 Laub & Sampson, 2003; Sampson & Laub, 1993.

20 Laub & Sampson, 2001, 2003; Sampson & Laub, 1993, 1997, 2003a, 2003b, 2004, 2005a, 2005b, 2005c; Sampson, Laub, & Wimer, 2006.

21 Sampson & Laub, 1993; Shover, 1985; Uggen, Manza, & Behrens, 2004; Visher, 2011.

22 Horney, Osgood, & Marshall, 1995.

23 Giordano, Cernkovich, & Rudolph, 2002.

24 LeBel, Burnett, Maruna, & Bushway, 2008.

25 Sampson & Laub, 2004; p. 173.

26 Cullen, 1994.

27 Abbott, 1997; p. 89

28 Ibid.; p. 101.

29 Cid & Martí, 2012.

30 Cullen, 1994.

31 Horney, Osgood, & Marshall, 1995; Laub & Sampson, 2003; Uggen, 2000.

32 Shover, 1985.

33 Brooks et al., 2008.

34 Cullen, 1994.

35 Giordano, Cernkovich, & Rudolph, 2002.

36 Laub & Sampson, 2003; Maruna, 2001; Sampson & Laub, 1993; Shover, 1985; Stevens, 2012.

37 Maruna, 2001.

38 Stevens, 2012.

39 Terry & Presser, 2002.

40 Abramson, Seligman, & Teasdale, 1978.

41 Maruna, 2001; p. 87.

42 Giordano, Cernkovich, & Rudolph, 2002.

43 Vaughan, 2007.

44 Maruna, 2001.

45 LeBel, Burnett, Maruna, & Bushway, 2008.

46 Ibid.; LeBel 2012.

47 Maruna, 2001.

48 Giordano, Cernkovich, & Rudolph, 2002; Giordano, Longmore, Schroeder, & Seffrin, 2008.

49 See, for example, Aresti, Eatough, & Brooks-Gordon, 2010; Hlavka, Wheelock, & Jones, 2015.

50 Appleton, 2010.

51 Maruna, 2001.

52 Liem, Zahn, & Tichavsky, 2014.

53 Baaij, Liem, & Nieuwbeerta, 2012; Dobash et al., 2007; Gottlieb & Gabrielsen, 1990; Grann & Wedin, 2002; Roberts, Zgoba, & Shahidullah, 2007.

54 Meyers, Chan, Vo, & Lazarou, 2010.

55 Hill et al., 2008.

56 Putkonen et al., 2003.

57 Golenkov, Large, & Nielssen, 2013.

58 Eronen, Hakola, & Tiihonen, 1996; Tiihonen, Hakola, Nevalainen, & Eronen, 1995.

59 Eronen, Hakola, & Tiihonen, 1996.

60 Gottlieb & Gabrielsen, 1990.

61 Meade, Steiner, Makarios, & Travis, 2013.

62 Ibid.

63 Gendreau, Cullen, & Goggin, 1999; Sampson & Laub, 1993; Wermink et al., 2010.

64 Lerman, 2009.

65 Nieuwbeerta, Nagin, & Blokland, 2009.

66 Cale, Plecas, Cohen, & Fortier, 2010.

67 Meade, Steiner, Makarios, & Travis, 2012; Zamble & Porporino, 1988.

68 Clemmer (1958; p. 299) was the first to define "prisonization" as "the taking on in greater or less degree of the folkways, mores, customs, and general culture of the penitentiary."

69 Farrall & Calverley, 2006; Wolff, Shi, & Schumann, 2012.

70 Nagin, Cullen, & Jonson, 2009.

71 Visher & O'Connell, 2012.

72 Irwin, 1970.

73 Liebling & Maruna, 2011.

74 Irwin, 2010.

75 Irwin, 1970; p. 109.

76 Austin, 2010.

77 Gottlieb & Gabrielsen, 1990; Roberts, Zgoba, & Shahidullah, 2007.

78 Heide, 1999.

79 Hagan, 1997; Heide, Spencer, Thompson, & Solomon,, 2001; Hill et al., 2008.

80 See, for example, Hagan, 1997; Heide, 1999.

CHAPTER 3. THE CONTEXT

1 In doing so, I follow terminology used in earlier studies, such as in Brooks et al., 2008.

2 Cid & Martí, 2012; Maruna, 2001.

3 Laub & Sampson, 2003.

4 Venkatesh, 2008; 2013.

5 Presser, 2008.

6 Scott & Lyman, 1968; p. 61.

7 Ibid.; p. 62.

8 Farrall & Bowling, 1999.
9 Appleton, 2010; Giordano, Longmore, Schroeder, & Seffrin, 2008.
10 QSR International, 2012.
11 Nellis & King, 2009. A "confidence interval" means that if the same population is sampled on numerous occasions, the resulting intervals would bracket the true population parameter in approximately 95% of the cases.
12 Unkovic & Albini, 1969.
13 Massachusetts Department of Correction, 2005.
14 Brooks et al., 2005.
15 Burns, Kinkade, Leone, & Philips, 1999.
16 Petersilia, 2003.
17 Ostermann, 2013.
18 Petersilia, 2003.
19 Carson and Sobel, 2015.
20 Brooks et al., 2008.
21 National Research Council, 2007.
22 Ibid.
23 Petersilia, 2007; Steen, Opsal, Lovegrove, & McKinzey, 2013.
24 Brooks et al., 2008.
25 Ibid.
26 Rhine, 2012.
27 Other common standard parole conditions include, but are not limited to, the following: reporting to the parole agent within twenty-four hours of release; not carrying weapons; reporting changes of address and employment; not traveling more than fifty miles from home or not leaving the country for more than forty-eight hours without prior approval from the parole agent; obeying all parole agent instructions; seeking and maintaining employment or participating in education and work training; and submitting to search by the police and parole officers.
28 Ostermann, 2013.
29 Steen, Opsal, Lovegrove, & McKinzey, 2013.
30 National Research Council, 2007.
31 Maruna & LeBel, 2003.
32 Solomon, Kachnowski, & Bhati, 2005.
33 Coker & Martin, 1985.
34 National Research Council, 2007.
35 Colvin, Cullen, & Van der Ven, 2002.
36 The term "busing" refers to the practice of assigning and transporting students in order to equalize prior racial segregation of schools. In practice, this involved children being transported to schools in neighborhoods other than their own.
37 Mears, Mancini, Beaver, & Gertz, 2013.
38 Toch & Adams, 2002.
39 Liebling & Arnold, 2012.
40 Ibid.

41 Bisonette, 2008.
42 Grassian, 1983.
43 Bisonette, 2008.
44 Fleury-Steiner & Longazel, 2014.
45 Cohen & Taylor, 1981.
46 Farmer, 1988.
47 Cadambi, 2010.
48 Bisonette, 2008.
49 Halleck, 1965.
50 Slovenko, 1969.
51 Jones, 2009.
52 National Research Council, 2014.
53 Irwin & Owen, 2011.
54 Toch, 2010.
55 Ibid.
56 Massachusetts Executive Office of Public Safety and Security, 2013.
57 Ibid.
58 Flanagan, 1995b.
59 Ibid.
60 Kazemian & Travis, 2015.
61 Petersilia, 2003.
62 Marlette, 1990.
63 Mullane, 2012.
64 Fleury-Steiner & Longazel, 2014.
65 Petersilia, 2003.
66 National Research Council, 2007.
67 Fleury-Steiner & Longazel, 2014.
68 See, for example, Liptak, 2005. For criticism of the parole boards' exercise of their release discretion, see American Law Institute, 2011.
69 Solomon, Kachnowski, & Bhati, 2005.

CHAPTER 4. LIVES SPIRALING OUT OF CONTROL

1 Goffman, 1961b.
2 Scott & Lyman, 1968; p. 52.
3 This observation is not unique for this sample. In her analysis of twenty-seven stories of violent men, Lois Presser (2008) reported that these men attributed past criminal behavior to poverty, alienation from school, substance abuse, and antisocial peers.
4 These reform schools actually provided the data source for the "Glueck men" described by Sampson & Laub (1993, 2003b): they followed boys who were incarcerated in these schools throughout their lives.
5 See ibid. for a discussion on experiences at the Lyman School.
6 Masis, 2009.

7 Ibid.
8 Sampson & Laub, 1997.
9 Scott & Lyman, 1968.
10 Goffman, 1961b; p. 51.
11 Aresti, Eatough, & Brooks-Gordon, 2010; Maruna & Copes, 2005.
12 Hochstetler, Copes, & Williams, 2010; Maruna, 2004; Presser, 2008.
13 Huebner, DeJong, & Cobbina, 2009; Traylor & Richie, 2012.
14 Leigey & Reed, 2010.
15 Mauer, King, & Young, 2004.
16 Children's Law Center of Massachusetts, 2009.

CHAPTER 5. A LIFE SENTENCE

1 Owen, 1998.
2 In cases such as Leroy's, being placed in a maximum-security facility may actually reinforce violent behavior rather than discourage it. Various studies provide evidence for this relationship, finding that placement in a higher-security setting has a stronger criminogenic effect—measured in attitudes toward anger and violence—compared to placement in a lower-security setting, particularly for those with fewer prior arrests and convictions. See Lerman, 2009; Haney, 2011a.
3 Nellis & Chung, 2013.
4 Krabill & Aday, 2007.
5 MacKenzie, Robinson, & Campbell, 1989.
6 Goffman, 1961a
7 Cohen & Taylor, 1981.
8 Haney, 2011b.
9 Ibid.
10 Santos, 1995.
11 Foucault, 1995; p. 164.
12 Cohen & Taylor, 1981.
13 Fagan, 2010.
14 Sykes, 1958.
15 Ibid.; p. 286.
16 Ibid.; p. 287.
17 This resembles modern-day conditions of solitary confinement. See, for example, Metzner & Fellner, 2010.
18 Gawande, 2009.
19 Ibid.
20 Fleury-Steiner & Longazel, 2014.
21 Metzner & Fellner, 2010.
22 Grassian, 1983.
23 Sykes, 1958; p. 288.
24 Ibid.; p. 71.
25 Haney, 2011b.

26 Kupers, 2010; p. 114.

27 Fleisher and Krienert, 2009.

28 Mumola, 2000.

29 Crawley & Sparks, 2006, 2011; Krabill & Aday, 2007.

30 Fleisher & Krienert, 2009.

31 Giallombardo, 1966; Heffernan, 1972; Ward & Kassebaum, 1965.

32 Owen, 1998.

33 MacKenzie, Robinson, & Campbell, 1989, 1995.

34 Owen, 1998.

35 MacKenzie, Robinson, & Campbell, 1989.

36 Collica, 2013; Genders & Player, 1990.

37 Sykes, 1958; p. 292.

38 Harvey, 2005.

39 Irwin & Owen, 2011.

40 Ibid.

41 Schauer, 2011.

42 Irwin, 1970.

43 Ibid.

44 For similar findings, see Irwin & Owen, 2011.

45 Cowles & Sabath, 1995; Zamble, 1995; Zamble & Porporino, 1988.

46 Coker & Martin, 1985.

47 Unger & Buchanan, 1985; cf. Cowles & Sabath, 1995; Johnson & Dobrzanska, 2005.

48 Owen, 1998.

49 Cohen & Taylor, 1981.

50 Flanagan, 1995a.

51 Toch & Adams, 2002.

52 Crewe, 2011; Santos, 1995; Zamble, 1995.

53 Crewe, 2011.

54 Toch, 2010.

55 Hirschi & Gottfredson, 1983.

56 Johnson & Dobrzanska, 2005.

57 Santos, 1995; Zamble, 1995.

58 Cohen & Taylor, 1981.

59 MacKenzie & Goodstein, 1995.

60 Toch, 1995.

61 Lucas, 1836; p. 239; cited in Foucault, 1995.

62 Santos, 1995.

63 See also Toch & Adams, 2002.

CHAPTER 6. A PRODUCTIVE, LAW-ABIDING CITIZEN

1 Zamble & Porporino, 1988.

2 Giordano, Cernkovich, & Rudolph, 2002.

3 Shover, 1985.

4 Aresti, Eatough, & Brooks-Gordon, 2010.

5 Farrall & Calverley, 2006.

6 Giordano, Longmore, Schroeder, & Seffrin, 2008.

7 Maruna, Wilson, & Curran, 2006.

8 Giordano, Cernkovich, & Rudolph, 2002.

9 Ibid.

10 Aresti, Eatough, & Brooks-Gordon, 2010; Giordano, Cernkovich, & Rudolph, 2002; Laub & Sampson, 2003; Maruna, 2001; Sampson & Laub, 1993; Stevens, 2012.

11 Maruna, 2001.

12 Ibid.; p. 140.

13 Ibid.; p. 133.

14 Sykes & Matza, 1957.

15 Bandura, 1990.

16 Maruna, 2001; Maruna & Mann, 2006.

17 Paternoster & Bushway, 2009.

18 Gadd and Farrall, 2004.

19 Goffman, 1961b; cf. Presser, 2008; Fleisher, 2013.

20 Presser, 2008.

21 See also Vaughan, 2007.

22 Presser, 2004.

23 Presser, 2008.

24 Maruna, 2001.

25 Ibid.

26 Ibid.

27 Stevens, 2012.

28 Massachusetts Parole Board, 2013a.

29 Ibid.

30 Ibid.

31 Massachusetts Parole Board, 2013b.

32 For a discussion, see Maruna & Mann, 2006.

33 Massachusetts Parole Board, 2013a.

34 See, for example, Kentucky Department of Corrections, 2013.

35 Burns, Kinkade, Leone, & Philips, 1999.

36 Talarico, 1975; p. 136; cited in Burns, Kinkade, Leone, & Philips, 1999.

37 Burns, Kinkade, Leone, & Philips,1999; p. 16.

38 Caplan, 2007.

39 Burns, Kinkade, Leone, & Philips, 1999.

40 Steen, Opsal, Lovegrove, & McKinzey, 2013.

41 Coker & Martin, 1985.

CHAPTER 7. LIFE AFTER LIFE IMPRISONMENT

1 Irwin, 1970.

2 Wilson, 1987.

3 Clear, 2007.

4 In many states, though not in Massachusetts, prisoners released on parole are legally required to return to their county of last residence, thus contributing to a return to old neighborhoods (Kirk, 2012).

5 Kubrin & Stewart, 2006.

6 Clear, 2007.

7 Massachusetts Department of Correction, 2013.

8 Legal Action Center, 2004; Mauer & Chesney-Lind, 2002; Uggen, Manza, & Thompson, 2006.

9 Wacquant, 2010.

10 For more information, see http://www.mass.gov/eopss/crime-prev-personal-sfty/bkgd-check/cori/.

11 Wacquant, 2010; p. 76.

12 Legal Action Center, 2004.

13 National Research Council, 2007.

14 Alexander, 2012; p. 191

15 Nationwide, Massachusetts ranked eleventh in terms of having the least strict legal roadblocks to reentry (Legal Action Center, 2004). Following the 2004 report, Massachusetts Governor Deval Patrick issued an order to prohibit background checks of prospective or current employees before s/he is deemed otherwise qualified for employment (Legal Action Center, 2009).

16 LeBel, 2008; Winnick & Bodkin, 2008.

17 LeBel, 2008.

18 Winnick & Bodkin, 2008.

19 Aresti, Eatough, & Brooks-Gordon, 2010.

20 See also LeBel, 2008.

21 LeBel, Richie, & Maruna, 2015.

22 Legal Action Center, 2004.

23 LeBel & Maruna, 2012.

24 Alexander, 2012.

25 LeBel & Maruna, 2012.

26 Alexander, 2012.

27 Binswanger et al., 2011; Pager, 2003; Visher, Debus-Sherrill, & Yahner, 2010.

28 Berg & Huebner, 2011; Holzer, Raphael, & Stroll, 2003.

29 Cowles & Sabath, 1995.

30 Flanagan, 1995c.

31 Western, 2006.

32 Visher, Debus-Sherrill, & Yahner, 2010.

33 Travis, Western, & Redburn, 2014; Western, Kling, & Weiman, 2001; Winnick & Bodkin, 2008. As of 2010, the law prohibits Massachusetts employers from asking any criminal history questions on their initial application forms. In addition to changing their application forms to comply with the law, employers should consider alternative methods to obtain what can be important and valuable criminal

history information. The large majority of interviewed lifers, however, were seeking employment before to this legal change took effect.

34 LeBel, 2012.
35 Bushway & Sweeten, 2007.
36 Petersilia, 2003, 2011.
37 Alexander, 2012; Brooks et al., 2008.
38 LeBel & Maruna, 2012.
39 Sampson and Laub, 1993; Uggen, 2000.
40 LeBel, 2007.
41 LeBel, 2008.
42 Aresti, Eatough, & Brooks-Gordon, 2010; Maruna, 2001; LeBel, Richie, & Maruna, 2015.
43 Brown, 1991.
44 Marsh, 2011.
45 Maruna, 2001.
46 Marsh, 2011.
47 LeBel, Richie, & Maruna, 2015.
48 See, for example, LIFERS Public Safety Steering Committee of the State Correctional Institution at Graterford, Pennsylvania, 2004.
49 Farrall & Caverley, 2006; p. 181.
50 Giordano, Cernkovich, & Rudolph, 2002; Maruna, 2001; Shover, 1985.
51 Visher & O'Connell, 2012.
52 Berg & Huebner, 2011; Mears, Cochran, Siennick, & Bales, 2012.
53 Duwe & Clark, 2011; Mears, Cochran, Siennick, & Bales, 2012; Berg & Huebner, 2011.
54 Lopoo & Western, 2005.
55 Farrall, Sharpe, Hunter, & Calverley, 2011; Western, 2004.
56 U.S. Census Bureau, 2011.
57 Sampson & Laub, 1993.
58 Sampson and Laub, 2004.
59 Laub & Sampson, 2003; Sampson & Laub, 1993.
60 Shover, 1985.
61 Comfort, 2009.
62 Ibid.
63 Ibid.
64 Sampson and Laub, 1993; Shover, 1985; Uggen, Manza, & Behrens, 2004; Visher, 2011.
65 Visher & O'Connell, 2012.
66 Nock, 2007.
67 Traylor & Richie, 2012.
68 Lord, 1995.
69 Collica, 2013; Dye & Aday, 2013; MacKenzie, Robinson, & Campbell, 1989.
70 Sampson & Laub 1993, 2003b.

71 Giordano, Cernkovich, & Rudolph, 2002.

72 Cid & Martí, 2012.

73 LeBel, Burnett, Maruna, & Bushway, 2008.

74 Visher & O'Connell, 2012.

75 Becker, 2003.

CHAPTER 8. RESIDUAL EFFECTS OF IMPRISONMENT

1 Bonta & Gendreau, 1995; p. 84. They admitted that the studies in their review were of cross-sectional nature and based on small subject populations.

2 Flanagan 1995a. These studies have indicated no evidence of systematic decline in intellectual capacity, measured by standard intelligence tests, as a consequence of long-term imprisonment. Likewise, no significant deterioration was found in inmates' personalities.

3 Flanagan, 1995a.

4 Bonta & Gendreau; 1995; Flanagan, 1995a; Zamble, 1995.

5 Haney, 2011a.

6 Ibid.

7 Goff, Rose, Rose, & Purves, 2007.

8 American Psychiatric Association, 1980.

9 Goff, Rose, Rose, & Purves, 2007; Haney, 2012.

10 Jamieson & Grounds, 2011.

11 Haney, 2006.

12 Balis, 2007.

13 Leigey & Reed, 2010.

14 MacDonald, 2013.

15 Haney, 2012.

16 See also Munn, 2011.

17 Liem & Kunst, 2013.

18 Haney, 2012.

19 Haney, 2006.

20 Haney, 2012.

21 The notion of "liminality" originated in the work of the anthropologist Arnold van Gennep (1908) and was further developed by Victor Turner (1982). The term "liminality" is used to denote a stage in which a life-course transition is made, or, as Turner (1982; p. 24) explains, "A period and area of ambiguity, a sort of social limbo." In a liminal space, the individual disengages from past and future roles, before finally being incorporated into a new, relatively stable, and well-defined position in society (Jewkes, 2011). I will return to the notion of liminality in discussing parole.

22 Munn, 2011.

23 Haney, 2012

24 Binswanger et al., 2011; Haney, 2006.

25 Steen, Opsal, Lovegrove, & McKinzey, 2013.

CHAPTER 9. GOING BACK

1 As outlined in chapter 3, two individuals wrapped up their sentences and four had their cases overturned.

2 Opsal, 2015; p. 189.

3 Turnbull & Hannah Moffat, 2009.

4 Ibid.

5 Ibid.

6 Pogrebin, Stretesky, Walker, & Opsal, 2015.

7 Ibid.

8 Glaser, 1964.

9 Ibid.

10 Blumstein & Beck, 2005.

11 Turner, 1982.

12 Jewkes, 2011.

13 Grattet, Petersilia, Lin, & Beckman, 2009.

14 Neuilly, Zgoba, Tita, & Lee, 2011; Putkonen et al., 2003; Roberts, Zgoba, & Shahidullah, 2007.

15 Comfort, 2009; p. 193.

16 Alexander, 2012.

17 Ibid.

18 Ibid.

19 National Research Council, 2007.

20 Grattet, Petersilia, Lin, & Beckman, 2009.

21 Shover, 1985; p. 132.

22 Goffman, 1961a; p. 15.

23 Jewkes, 2011.

24 See also Jamieson & Grounds, 2011; Jewkes, 2011; Munn, 2011.

25 Irwin, 1970.

26 A joint venturer is someone who aids or assists in the commission of a crime. This is the person or people who help the principle perform the actual act.

27 Irwin, 1970.

28 Sampson & Laub, 2005c; p. 37.

29 Katz, 1988.

30 Werth, 2012.

31 Santos, 1995.

32 Farrall & Calverley, 2006.

33 For a detailed discussion, see Liem & Richardson, 2014.

34 Coker & Martin, 1985.

35 Visher, Kachnowski, LaVigne, & Travis, 2004.

36 Giordano, 2013.

37 Aday, 2003.

38 For a discussion, see Crawley & Sparks, 2006.

39 Aday & Krabill, 2013.
40 Schwartzapfel, 2012.
41 Crawley & Sparks, 2006, 2011.
42 Aday, 2003; Irwin & Owen, 2011.

CHAPTER 10. STAYING OUT

1 West, 1963.
2 Sweeten, Piquero, & Steinberg, 2013.
3 Shover, 1985; p. 99.
4 Giordano, 2013.
5 Bottoms et al., 2004.
6 Irwin & Owen, 2011.
7 Maruna, 2004.
8 Carlsson, 2013.
9 Bersani, Laub, & Nieuwbeerta, 2009; Cid & Martí, 2012; Ganem & Agnew, 2007; Laub & Sampson, 2003; Lopoo & Western, 2005; Sampson & Laub, 1993, 2003a; Sampson, Laub, & Wimer, 2006; Uggen, 2000.
10 King, 2013; Vaughan, 2007.
11 Hanrahan, Gibbs, & Zimmerman, 2005.
12 Carlsson, 2013.
13 See also Farrall, Sharpe, Hunter, & Calverley, 2011; Mouzeli, 2008.
14 Giordano, 2013.
15 Katz, 1988. This observation differs from some of the men studied by Sampson & Laub (2004), who reported making a conscious choice for continuing a criminal lifestyle.
16 Farrall & Bowling, 1999.
17 See, for example, Appleton, 2010; Maruna, 2001.
18 Munn, 2011.

CHAPTER 11. RECONSIDERING LIFER REENTRY

1 Nellis & Chung, 2013.
2 Davis, Bahr, & Ward, 2012; Laub & Sampson, 2001, 2003; Maruna, 2001.
3 Davis, Bahr, & Ward, 2012.
4 Ganem & Agnew, 2007.
5 Braithwaite, 1989.
6 Abbott, 1997.
7 Sampson & Laub, 2004.
8 Aday & Krabill, 2013; Farrall & Calverley, 2006; Uggen, Manza, & Thompson, 2006.
9 Gadd & Farrall, 2004.
10 Jamieson & Grounds, 2011.
11 Maruna, 2001; Paternoster & Bushway, 2009; Stevens, 2012.
12 See also Liem & Richardson, 2014.
13 Stevens, 2012.

14 Presser, 2008.
15 See Haraway, 1997; cf. Lawler, 2008.
16 See, for example, California Department of Corrections, 2010; Kentucky Department of Corrections, 2013.
17 Bottoms et al., 2004; p. 371.
18 Carlsson, 2013.
19 Bersani, Laub, & Nieuwbeerta, 2009; Cid & Martí, 2012; Ganem & Agnew, 2007; Laub & Sampson, 2003; Lopoo & Western, 2005; Sampson & Laub, 1993, 2003a, 2003b; Sampson, Laub, & Wimer, 2006; Uggen, 2000.
20 Giordano, Longmore, Schroeder, & Seffrin, 2008; Maruna, 2001.
21 Kazemian & Travis, 2015.
22 Nellis, 2010.
23 Maruna, 2004.
24 Nellis & Chung, 2013.
25 Nagin, Cullen, & Jonson, 2009; Pager, 2003; Petersilia, 2003; Richards & Jones, 2004.
26 Farrall & Calverley, 2006.
27 Allred, Harrison, & O'Connell, 2013.
28 Johnson & Dobrzanska, 2005.
29 Ward & Brown, 2004.
30 Maruna, Immarigeon, & LeBel, 2004.
31 Maruna, 2001.
32 Maruna & LeBel, 2003.
33 Maruna, 2001.
34 See also Liem & Richardson, 2013, 2014; Liem & Garcin, 2014.
35 Maruna & Mann, 2006; p. 167.
36 Ward & Brown, 2004.
37 Sykes, 1958.
38 Farrall & Calverley, 2006.
39 National Research Council, 2007.
40 Ibid.
41 Ibid.
42 Zamble & Porporino, 1990
43 Ibid.
44 Nellis & Chung, 2013.
45 National Research Council, 2014.
46 Kurlychek & Bushway, 2006; Uggen, 2000.
47 National Research Council, 2014.
48 Ibid.
49 National Research Council, 2007.
50 MacKenzie, 2006; cf. LeBel & Maruna, 2012
51 LeBel & Maruna, 2012.
52 Day, Ward, & Shirley, 2011.
53 Ibid.

54 LeBel, Richie, & Maruna, 2015.

55 Ward & Gannon, 2006.

56 Irwin, 1970.

57 National Research Council, 2007.

58 Ibid.

59 Ibid.

60 See also Liem & Kunst, 2013.

61 Haney, 2011a.

62 Haney, 2012.

63 Farrall & Calverley, 2006.

64 Petersilia, 2003.

65 LeBel, 2007, 2009; LeBel, Richie, & Maruna, 2015.

66 Ruddell, Broom, & Young, 2010.

67 LeBel, Richie, & Maruna, 2015.

68 Ibid.

69 Ibid.

70 Ibid.

71 Austin, 2010.

72 Ibid.

73 Nellis & Chung, 2013.

74 Aday, 2003.

75 Aday & Krabill, 2013.

76 Human Rights Watch, 2012.

77 Nagin, 2013.

78 Human Rights Watch, 2012.

79 See also Alexander, 2012.

80 Coker & Martin, 1985; Petersilia & Turner, 1993; Solomon, Kachnowski, & Bhati, 2005; Yahner, Visher, & Solomon, 2008.

81 Coker & Martin, 1985.

82 Comfort, 2009.

83 Brooks et al., 2008.

84 Petersilia, 2007.

85 Bandura, 1990; cf. Petersilia, 2007.

86 Petersilia, 2007.

87 Bushway & Sweeten, 2007.

88 Ibid.

89 Grattet, Petersilia, Lin, & Beckman, 2009; Petersilia, 2007.

REFERENCES

Abbott, A. (1997). On the concept of turning point. *Comparative Social Research, 16,* 85–106.

Abramson, L. Y., Seligman, M. E., and Teasdale, J. D. (1978). Learned helplessness in humans: Critique and reformulation. *Journal of Abnormal Psychology, 87*(1), 49–74.

Aday, R. H. (2003). *Aging prisoners: Crisis in American corrections.* Westport, CT: Praeger.

Aday, R. H., and Krabill, J. J. (2013). Older and geriatric offenders: Critical issues for the 21st century. In L. Gideon (Ed.), *Special needs offenders in correctional institutions* (pp. 203–232). Thousand Oaks, CA: Sage.

Alexander, M. (2012). *The new Jim Crow: Mass incarceration in the age of colorblindness.* New York: New Press.

Allred, S. L., Harrison, L. D., and O'Connell, D. J. (2013). Self-efficacy: An important aspect of prison-based learning. *Prison Journal, 93*(2), 211–233.

American Law Institute (2011). *Model penal code: Sentencing, tentative draft no. 2.* Philadelphia: American Law Institute.

American Psychiatric Association (1980). *Diagnostic and statistical manual of mental disorders.* 3rd ed. Washington, DC: American Psychiatric Association.

Anderson, S. (2012). Greg Ousley is sorry for killing his parents: Is that enough? *New York Times,* July 19.

Anno, B. J., Graham, C., Lawrence, J. E., and Shansky, R. (2004). *Correctional health care: Addressing the needs of elderly, chronically ill, and terminally ill inmates.* Middletown, CT: Criminal Justice Institute.

Appleton, C. A. (2010). *Life after life imprisonment.* Oxford, UK: Oxford University Press.

Aresti, A., Eatough, V., and Brooks-Gordon, B. (2010). Doing time after time: An interpretative phenomenological analysis of reformed ex-prisoners' experiences of self-change, identity, and career opportunities. *Psychology, Crime, and Law, 16*(3), 169–190.

Austin, J. (2010). Reducing America's correctional populations: A strategic plan. *Justice Research and Policy, 12*(1), 9–40.

Austin, J., Irwin, J., and Hardyman, P. (2002). Exploring the needs and risks of the returning prisoner population. Paper prepared for the From Prison to Home Conference, January 30–31.

Baaij, P., Liem, M., and Nieuwbeerta, P. (2012). "Ex-imprisoned homicide offenders: Once bitten, twice shy?" The effect of the length of imprisonment on recidivism for homicide offenders. *Homicide Studies, 16*(3), 219–237.

Balis, A. F. (2007). Female prisoners and the case for gender-specific treatment and reentry programs. In R. B. Greifinger (Ed.), *Public health behind bars* (320–332). New York: Springer.

Bandura, A. (1990). Mechanisms of moral disengagement in terrorism. In W. Reich (Ed.), *Origins of terrorism: Psychologies, ideologies, states of mind* (pp. 161–191). Cambridge, UK: Cambridge University Press.

Becker, W. (2003). *Good Bye Lenin!* Berlin: X-Filme Creative Pool.

Berg, M. T., and Huebner, B. M. (2011). Reentry and the ties that bind: An examination of social ties, employment, and recidivism. *Justice Quarterly, 28*(2), 382–410.

Berk, R., Sherman, L., Barnes, G., Kurtz, E., and Ahlman, L. (2009). Forecasting murder within a population of probationers and parolees: A high stakes application of statistical learning. *Journal of the Royal Statistical Society: Series A (Statistics in Society), 172*(1), 191–211.

Bersani, B. E., Laub, J. H., and Nieuwbeerta, P. (2009). Marriage and desistance from crime in the Netherlands: Do gender and socio-historical context matter. *Journal of Quantitative Criminology, 25*(3), 3–24.

Binswanger, I. A., Nowels, C., Corsi, K. F., Long, J., Booth, R. E., Kutner, J., and Steiner, J. F. (2011). "From the prison door right to the sidewalk, everything went downhill": A qualitative study of the health experiences of recently released inmates. *International Journal of Law and Psychiatry, 34*(4), 249–255.

Bisonette, J. (2008). *When the prisoners ran Walpole.* Cambridge, MA: South End Press.

Bjørkly, S., and Waage, L. (2005). Killing again: A review of research on recidivistic single-victim homicide. *International Journal of Forensic Mental Health, 4*(1), 99–106.

Blumstein, A., and Beck, A. (2005). Reentry as a transient state between liberty and recommitment. In J. Travis and C. Visher (Eds.), *Prisoner reentry and crime in America* (pp. 50–80). Cambridge, UK: Cambridge University Press.

Bonta, J., and Gendreau, P. (1995). Reexamining the cruel and unusual punishment of prison life. In T. J. Flanagan (Ed.), *Long-term imprisonment: Policy, science, and correctional practice* (pp. 75–94). Thousand Oaks, CA: Sage.

Bottoms, A., Shapland, J., Costello, A., Holmes, D., and Muir, G. (2004). Towards desistance: Theoretical underpinnings for an empirical study. *Howard Journal of Criminal Justice, 43*(4), 368–389.

Braithwaite, J. (1989). *Crime, shame and reintegration.* Cambridge, UK: Cambridge University Press.

Brooks, L. E., Solomon, A. L., Keegan, S., Kohl, R., and Lahue, L. (2005). *Prisoner reentry in Massachusetts.* Washington, DC: Urban Institute Justice Policy Center.

Brooks, L. E., Solomon, A. L., Kohl, R., Osborne, J. W. L., Reid, J., McDonald, S. M., and Hoover, H. M. (2008). *Reincarcerated: The experiences of men returning to Massachusetts prisons.* Washington, DC: Urban Institute Justice Policy Center.

Brown, J. D. (1991). The professional ex. *Sociological Quarterly, 32*(2), 219–230.

Bureau of Justice Statistics. (1999). Prior abuse reported by inmates and probationers. Washington, DC: US Department of Justice.

Burns, R., Kinkade, P., Leone, M. C., and Philips, S. (1999). Perspectives on parole: The board members' viewpoint. *Federal Probation, 63*(1), 16–22.

Bushway, S. D., and Sweeten, G. (2007). Abolish lifetime bans for ex-felons. *Criminology and Public Policy, 6*(4), 697–706.

Cadambi, A. (2010) U.S. prisoners take control of Walpole Prison, 1973. Retrieved from http://nvdatabase.swarthmore.edu/content/us-prisoners-take-control-walpole-prison-1973.

Cale, J., Plecas, D., Cohen, I. M., and Fortier, S. (2010). An exploratory analysis of factors associated with repeat homicide in Canada. *Homicide Studies, 14*(2), 159–180.

Caplan, J. M. (2007). What factors affect parole? A review of empirical research. *Federal Probation, 71*(1), 16–19.

Carlsson, C. (2013). Masculinities, persistence, and desistance. *Criminology, 51*(3), 661–693.

Carson, E. A., and Sobel, W. J. (2015). *Prisoners in 2014*. Washington, DC: Bureau of Justice Statistics.

Children's Law Center of Massachusetts (2009). *Until they die a natural death: Youth sentenced to life without parole in Massachusetts.* Lynn: Children's Law Center of Massachusetts.

Cid, J., and Martí, J. (2012). Turning points and returning points: Understanding the role of family ties in the process of desistance. *European Journal of Criminology, 6*, 603–620.

Clear, T. R. (1994). *Harm in American penology: Offenders, victims, and their communities.* Albany: State University of New York Press.

Clear, T. R. (2007). *Imprisoning communities: How mass incarceration makes disadvantaged neighborhoods worse.* New York: Oxford University Press.

Clemmer, D. (1958). *The prison community*. New York: Rinehart.

Cohen, S., and Taylor, L. (1981). *Psychological survival: The experience of long-term imprisonment.* 2nd ed. New York: Penguin.

Coker, J. B., and Martin, J. P. (1985). *Licensed to live*. New York: Basil Blackwell.

Collica, K. (2013). Female offenders and the inmate subculture. In K. Collica (Ed.), *Female prisoners, AIDS, and peer programs* (pp. 25–34). New York: Springer.

Colvin, M, Cullen, F. T., and Van der Ven, T. (2002). Coercion, social support, and crime: An emerging theoretical consensus. *Criminology, 40*(1), 19–42.

Comfort, M. (2009). *Doing time together: Love and family in the shadow of the prison.* Chicago: University of Chicago Press.

Corder, B. F., Ball, B. C., Haizlip, T. M., Rollins, R., and Beaumont, R. (1976). Adolescent parricide: A comparison with other adolescent murder. *American Journal of Psychiatry, 133*(8), 957–961.

Cowles, E.L., and Sabath, M. J. (1995). Addressing the program needs of long-term inmates. In T. J. Flanagan (Ed.), *Long-term imprisonment: Policy, science, and correctional practice (pp. 210–219).* Thousand Oaks, CA: Sage.

Crawley, E., and Sparks, R. (2006). Is there life after imprisonment? How elderly men talk about imprisonment and release. *Criminology and Criminal Justice, 6*(1), 63–82.

Crawley, E., and Sparks, R. (2011). Older men in prison: Survival, coping and identity. In A. Liebling and S. Maruna (Eds.), *The effects of imprisonment (pp. 343–366).* London: Routledge.

Crewe, B. (2011). Codes and conventions: The terms and conditions of contemporary inmate values. In A. Liebling and S. Maruna (Eds.), *The effects of imprisonment* (pp. 177–208). London: Routledge.

Cullen, F. T. (1994). Social support as an organizing concept for criminology: Presidential address to the Academy of Criminal Justice Sciences. *Justice Quarterly, 11*(4), 527–559.

Davis, C., Bahr, S. J., and Ward, C. (2012). The process of offender reintegration: Perceptions of what helps prisoners reenter society. *Criminology and Criminal Justice, 13*(4), 446–469.

Day, A., Ward, T., and Shirley, L. (2011). Reintegration services for long-term dangerous offenders: A case study and discussion. *Journal of Offender Rehabilitation, 50*(2), 66–80.

Dobash, R. P., Dobash, R. E., Cavanagh, K., Smith, D., and Medina-Ariza, J. (2007). Onset of offending and life course among men convicted of murder. *Homicide Studies, 11*(4), 243–271.

Duncan, J. W., and Duncan, G. M. (1971). Murder in the family: A study of some homicidal adolescents. *American Journal of Psychiatry, 127*(11), 74–78.

Durose, M. R., Cooper, A. D., and Snyder, H. N. (2014). *Recidivism of prisoners released in 30 states in 2005: Patterns from 2005 to 2010.* Washington, DC: Bureau of Justice Statistics.

Duwe, G., and Clark, V. (2011). Blessed be the social tie that binds: The effects of prison visitation on offender recidivism. *Criminal Justice Policy Review, 24*(3), 271–296.

Dye, M. H., and Aday, R. H. (2013). "I just wanted to die": Preprison and current suicide ideation among women serving life sentences. *Criminal Justice and Behavior, 40*(8), 832–849.

Eronen, M., Hakola, P., and Tiihonen, J. (1996). Factors associated with homicide recidivism in a 13-year sample of homicide offenders in Finland. *Psychiatric Services, 47*(4), 403–406.

Fagan, J. (2010). The contradictions of juvenile crime and punishment. *Daedalus, 139*(3), 43–61.

Farmer, J. F. (1988). Case study in regaining control of a violent state prison. *Federal Probation, 52*(1), 41–47.

Farrall, S., and Bowling, B. (1999). Structuration, human development and desistance from crime. *British Journal of Criminology, 39*(2), 253–268.

Farrall, S., and Calverley, A. (2006). *Understanding desistance from crime.* New York: Open University Press.

Farrall, S., Sharpe, G., Hunter, B., and Calverley, A. (2011). Theorizing structural and individual-level processes in desistance and persistence: Outlining an integrated perspective. *Australian and New Zealand Journal of Criminology, 44*(2), 218–234.

Flanagan, T.J. (1995a). Adaptation and adjustment among long-term prisoners. In T. J. Flanagan (Ed.), *Long-term imprisonment: Policy, science, and correctional practice (pp. 109–116)*. Thousand Oaks, CA: Sage.

Flanagan, T. J. (1995b). Long-term incarceration: Issues of science, policy, and correctional practice. In T. J. Flanagan (Ed.), *Long-term imprisonment: Policy, science, and correctional practice (pp. 3–9)*. Thousand Oaks, CA: Sage.

Flanagan, T. J. (1995c). Sentence planning for long-term inmates. In T. J. Flanagan (Ed.), *Long-term imprisonment: Policy, science, and correctional practice (pp. 234–244)*. Thousand Oaks, CA: Sage.

Fleisher, M. S. (2013). "Levenslang": Schadebeperking door levenslange gevangenisstraffen. ["Lifelong": Damage control by life sentences.] *Justitiële Verkenningen, 39*, 85–95.

Fleisher, M. S., and Krienert, J. L. (2009). *The myth of prison rape: Sexual culture in American prisons*. Plymouth, UK: Rowman & Littlefield.

Fletcher, B. R., Shaver, L. D., Moon, D. G., and Billy, L. J. (1993). *Women prisoners: A forgotten population*. Westport, CT: Praeger.

Fleury-Steiner, B., and Longazel, J. G. (2014). *The pains of mass imprisonment*. Abingdon, UK: Routledge.

Foucault, M. (1995). *Discipline and punish: The birth of the prison*. New York: Vintage.

Gadd, D., and Farrall, S. (2004). Criminal careers, desistance, and subjectivity: Interpreting men's narratives of change. *Theoretical Criminology, 8*(2), 123–156.

Ganem, N. M., and Agnew, R. (2007). Parenthood and adult criminal offending: The importance of relationship quality. *Journal of Criminal Justice, 35*(6), 630–643.

Garland, D. (2001). *The culture of control: Crime and social order in contemporary society*. Chicago: University of Chicago Press.

Gawande, A. (2009). Hellhole. *New Yorker*, March 30.

Genders, E., and Player, E. (1990). Women lifers: Assessing the experience. *Prison Journal, 70*(1), 46–57.

Gendreau, P., Cullen, F. T., and Goggin, C. (1999). *The effects of prison sentences on recidivism*. Ottawa: Solicitor General Canada.

Gennep, van, A. (1908) 1960. *The rites of passage*. Trans. M. Vizedom and G. Caffee. Chicago: University of Chicago Press.

Giallombardo, R. (1966). *Society of women: A study of a women's prison*. New York: Wiley.

Giordano, P. (2013). [Personal Communication].

Giordano, P., Cernkovich, S. A., and Rudolph, J. L. (2002). Gender, crime, and desistance: Toward a theory of cognitive transformation. *American Journal of Sociology, 107*(4), 990–1064.

Giordano, P., Longmore, M. A., Schroeder, R. D., and Seffrin, P. M. (2008). A life-course perspective on spirituality and desistance from crime. *Criminology, 46*(1), 99–132.

Glaser, D. (1964). *The effectiveness of a prison and parole system*. Indianapolis: Bobbs-Merrill.

Goff, A., Rose, E., Rose, S., and Purves, D. (2007). Does PTSD occur in sentenced prison populations? A systematic literature review. *Criminal Behaviour and Mental Health, 17*(3), 152–162.

Goffman, E. (1961a). *Asylums: Essays on the social situation of mental patients and other inmates.* Garden City, NY: Doubleday.

Goffman, E. (1961b). *Encounters: Two studies in the sociology of interaction.* Oxford, UK: Bobbs-Merrill.

Golenkov, A., Large, M., and Nielssen, O. (2013). A 30-year study of homicide recidivism and schizophrenia. *Criminal Behaviour and Mental Health, 23*(5), 347–355.

Gottfredson, M, and Hirschi, T. (1990). *A general theory of crime.* Stanford, CA: Stanford University Press.

Gottlieb, P., and Gabrielsen, G. (1990). The future of homicide offenders: Results from a homicide project in Copenhagen. *International Journal of Law and Psychiatry, 13*(3), 191–205.

Gove, W. R. (1985). The effect of age and gender on deviant behavior: A biopsychosocial perspective. In A. S. Rossi (Ed.), *Gender and the life course* (pp. 115–144). New York: Aldine de Gruyter.

Grann, M., and Wedin, I. (2002). Risk factors for recidivism among spousal assault and spousal homicide offenders. *Psychology, Crime, and Law, 8*(1), 5–23.

Grassian, S. (1983). Psychological effects of solitary confinement. *American Journal of Psychiatry, 140* (11), 1450–1454.

Grattet, R., Petersilia, J., Lin, J., and Beckman, M. (2009). Parole violations and revocations in California: Analysis and suggestions for action. *Federal Probation, 73*(1), 2–11.

Hagan, M. P. (1997). An analysis of adolescent perpetrators of homicide and attempted homicide upon return to the community. *International Journal of Offender Therapy and Comparative Criminology, 41*(3), 250–259.

Halleck, S. (1965). American psychiatry and the criminal: A historical review. *American Journal of Psychiatry, 121*(9), i–xxi.

Haney, C. (2006). *Reforming punishment: Psychological limits to the pains of imprisonment.* Washington, DC: American Psychological Association.

Haney, C. (2011a). The contextual revolution in psychology and the question of prison effects. In A. Liebling and S. Maruna (Eds.), *The effects of imprisonment* (pp. 66–93). London: Routledge.

Haney, C. (2011b). The perversions of prison: On the origins of hypermasculinity and sexual violence in confinement. *American Criminal Law Review, 48*(1), 121–141.

Haney, C. (2012). Prison effects in the era of mass incarceration. *Prison Journal,* doi:10.1177/0032885512448604.

Hanrahan, K., Gibbs, J. J., and Zimmerman, S. E. (2005). Parole and revocation: Perspectives of young adult offenders. *Prison Journal, 85*(3), 251–269.

Haraway, D. (1997). *Modest_Witness@Second_Millennium.FemaleMan©Meets_Onco-Mouse™: Feminism and technoscience.* New York: Routledge.

Harding, R. (2012). Regulating prison conditions: Some international comparisons. In J. Petersilia and K. R. Reitz (Eds.), *The Oxford handbook of sentencing and corrections*. Oxford, UK: Oxford University Press.

Harshbarger, S. (2004). *Strengthening public safety, increasing accountability, and instituting fiscal responsibility in the Department of Correction.* Boston: Governor's Commission on Corrections Reform.

Harvey, J. (2005). Crossing the boundary: The transition of young adults into prison. In A. Liebling and S. Maruna (Eds.), *The effects of imprisonment (pp. 232–254).* Portland, OR: Willan.

Heffernan, E. (1972). *Making it in prison: The square, the cool, and the life.* New York: Wiley InterScience.

Heide, K. M. (1992). *Why kids kill parents: Child abuse and adolescent homicide.* Columbus: Ohio State University Press.

Heide, K. M. (1999). *Young killers: The challenge of juvenile homicide.* Thousand Oaks, CA: Sage.

Heide, K. M., Spencer, E., Thompson, A., and Solomon, E. P. (2001). Who's in, who's out, and who's back: Follow-up data on 59 juveniles incarcerated in adult prison for murder or attempted murder in the early 1980s. *Behavioral Sciences and the Law, 19*(1), 97–108.

Heinlein, S. (2013). *Among murderers: Life after prison.* Berkeley: University of California Press.

Henry, J. S. (2015). Reducing severe sentences. *Criminology and Public Policy, 14*(2), 397–405.

Hill, A., Haberman, N., Klusmann, D., Berner, W., and Briken, P. (2008). Criminal recidivism in sexual homicide perpetrators. *International Journal of Offender Therapy and Comparative Criminology, 52*(1), 5–20.

Hirschi, T., and Gottfredson, M. (1983). Age and the explanation of crime. *American Journal of Sociology, 89*(3), 552–584.

Hlavka, H., Wheelock, D., and Jones, R. (2015). Exoffender accounts of successful reentry from prison. *Journal of Offender Rehabilitation, 54*(6), 406–428.

Hochstetler, A., Copes, H., and Williams, J. P. (2010). "That's not who I am": How offenders commit violent acts and reject authentically violent selves. *Justice Quarterly, 27*(4), 492–516.

Holzer, H. J., Raphael, S., and Stoll, M. A. (2003). Employment barriers facing ex-offenders. *Center for the Study of Urban Poverty Working Paper Series.*

Horney, J., Osgood, D. W., and Marshall, I. H. (1995). Criminal careers in the short-term: Intra-individual variability in crime and its relation to local life circumstances. *American Sociological Review, 60*(5), 655–673.

Huebner, B.M., DeJong, C., and Cobbina, J. (2009). Women coming home: Long-term patterns of recidivism. *Justice Quarterly, 27*(2), 225–254.

Human Rights Watch (2012). *Old behind bars: The aging prison population in the United States.* New York: Human Rights Watch.

Irwin, J. (1970). *The felon*. Englewood Cliffs, NJ: Prentice Hall.

Irwin, J. (2010). *Lifers: Seeking redemption in prison*. London: Routledge.

Irwin, J., and Owen, B. A. (2011). Harm and the contemporary prison. In A. Liebling and S. Maruna (Eds.), *The effects of imprisonment* (pp. 94–117). London: Routledge.

Jamieson, R., and Grounds, A. (2011). Release and adjustment: perspectives from studies of wrongfully convicted and politically motivated prisoners. In A. Liebling and S. Maruna (Eds.), *The effects of imprisonment* (pp. 94–117). London: Routledge.

Jewkes, Y. (2011). Loss, liminality and the life sentence: Managing identity through a disrupted lifecourse. In A. Liebling and S. Maruna (Eds.), *The effects of imprisonment* (pp. 366–388). London: Routledge.

Johnson, R., and Dobrzanska, A. (2005). Mature coping among life-sentenced inmates: An exploratory study of adjustment dynamics. *Corrections Compendium, 30*(6), 8–9.

Jones, T. (2009). *Titicut Follies* by Frederick Wiseman: Annotation. Retrieved from http://medhum.med.nyu.edu/view/13015.

Katz, J. (1988). *Seductions of crime: The sensual and moral attractions of doing evil*. New York: Basic Books.

Kazemian, L., and Travis, J. (2015). Imperative for inclusion of long termers and lifers in research and policy. *Criminology and Public Policy, 14*(2), 1–30.

Kentucky Department of Corrections. (2013). Inmate programs. Retrieved from http://corrections.ky.gov/depts/AI/KCIW/Pages/InmatePrograms.aspx.

King, S. (2013). Transformative agency and desistance from crime. *Criminology and Criminal Justice, 13*(3), 317–335.

Kirk, D. S. (2012). Residential change as a turning point in the life course of crime: Desistance or temporary cessation? *Criminology, 50*(2), 329–358.

Krabill, J. J., and Aday, R. H. (2007). Exploring the social world of aging female prisoners. *Women and Criminal Justice, 17*(1), 27–53.

Kubrin, C. E., and Stewart, E. A. (2006). Predicting who reoffends: The neglected role of neighborhood context in recidivism studies. *Criminology, 44*(1), 165–197.

Kupers, T. A. (2010). Role of misogyny and homophobia in prison sexual abuse. *UCLA Women's Law Journal, 18*(1), 107–130.

Kurlychek, M. C., and Bushway, S. D. (2006). Scarlet letters and recidivism: Does an old criminal record predict future offending? *Criminology and Public Policy, 5*(3), 483–504.

Langan, P. A., and Levin, D. J. (2002). Recidivism of prisoners released in 1994. Washington, DC: U.S. Department of Justice.

Laub, J. H., and Sampson, R. J. (2001). Understanding desistance from crime. *Crime and Justice, 28*, 1–69.

Laub, J. H., and Sampson, R. J. (2003). *Shared beginnings, divergent lives: Delinquent boys to age 70*. Cambridge, MA: Harvard University Press.

Lawler, S. (2008). *Identity: Sociological perspectives*. Cambridge, UK: Polity Press.

LeBel, T. P. (2007). An examination of the impact of formerly incarcerated persons helping others. *Journal of Offender Rehabilitation, 46*(1–2), 1–24.

LeBel, T. P. (2008). Perceptions of and responses to stigma. *Sociology Compass, 2*(2), 409–432.

LeBel, T. P. (2009). Formerly incarcerated persons' use of advocacy/activism as a coping orientation in the reintegration process. In B. Veysey, J. Christian, and D. Martinez (Eds.), *How offenders transform their lives* (pp. 165–187). Portland, OR: Willan.

LeBel, T. P. (2012). Invisible stripes? Formerly incarcerated persons' perceptions of stigma. *Deviant Behavior, 33*(2), 89–107.

LeBel, T. P., Burnett, R., Maruna, S., and Bushway, S. (2008). "The chicken and egg" of subjective and social factors in desistance from crime. *European Journal of Criminology, 5*(2), 131–159.

LeBel, T. P., and Maruna, S. (2012). Life on the outside: Transitioning from prison to the community. In J. Petersilia and K. R. Reitz (Eds.), *The Oxford handbook of sentencing and corrections* (pp. 657–683). New York: Oxford University Press.

LeBel, T. P., Richie, M., and Maruna, S. (2015). Helping others as a response to reconcile a criminal past: The role of the wounded healer in prisoner reentry programs. *Criminal Justice and Behavior, 42*(1), 108–120.

Legal Action Center (2004). *After prison: Roadblocks to reentry.* New York: Legal Action Center.

Legal Action Center (2009). *After prison: Roadblocks to reentry, 2009 Update.* New York: Legal Action Center.

Leigey, M. E., and Reed, K. L. (2010). A woman's life before serving life: Examining the negative pre-incarceration life events of female life-sentenced inmates. *Women and Criminal Justice, 20*(4), 302–322.

Lerman, A. E. (2009). The people prisons make: Effects of incarceration on criminal psychology. In S. Raphael and M. A. Stoll (Eds.), *Do prisons make us safer? The benefits and costs of the prison boom* (pp. 151–176). New York: Russell Sage Foundation.

Liebling, A., and Arnold, H. (2012). Social relationships between prisoners in a maximum security prison: Violence, faith, and the declining nature of trust. *Journal of Criminal Justice, 40*(5), 413–424.

Liebling, A., and Maruna, S. (2011). Introduction: The effects of imprisonment revisited. In A. Liebling and S. Maruna (Eds.), *The effects of imprisonment* (pp. 1–29). London: Routledge.

Liem, M., and Garcin, J. (2014). Post-release success among paroled lifers. *Laws, 3*(4), 798–823.

Liem, M., and Kunst, M. J. J. (2013). Is there a recognizable post-incarceration syndrome among released "lifers"? *International Journal of Law and Psychiatry, 36*(3–4), 333–337.

Liem, M., and Richardson, N. (2013). The role of transformation narratives in desistance among released lifers. Paper presented at the American Sociological Association, New York.

Liem, M., and Richardson, N. (2014). The role of transformation narratives in desistance among released lifers. *Criminal Justice and Behavior, 41*(6), 692–712.

Liem, M., and Sturman, J. (2013). The role of efficacy in desistance among released lifers. Paper presented at the American Sociological Association, New York.

Liem, M., Zahn, M., and Tichavsky, L. (2014). Criminal recidivism among homicide offenders. *Journal of Interpersonal Violence, 29*(14), 2630–2651

LIFERS Public Safety Steering Committee of the State Correctional Institution at Graterford, Pennsylvania (2004). Ending the culture of street crime. *Prison Journal, 84*(4), 48S–68S.

Liptak, A. (2005). To more inmates, life term means dying behind bars. *New York Times*, October 2.

Loeber, R., Farrington, D. P., and Cotter, R. B. (2011). *Young homicide offenders and victims: Risk factors, prediction, and prevention from childhood.* New York: Springer.

Loeber, R., Lacourse, E., and Homish, D. L. (2005). Homicide, violence, and developmental trajectories. In R. E. Tremblay, W. W. Hartup, and J. Archer (Eds.), *Developmental origins of aggression* (pp. 202–219). New York: Guilford Press.

Lopoo, L. M., and Western, B. (2005). Incarceration and the formation and stability of marital unions. *Journal of Marriage and Family, 67*(3), 721–734.

Lord, E. (1995). A prison superintendent's perspective on women in prison. *Prison Journal, 75*(2), 257–269.

Loughran, T. A., Mulvey, E. P., Schubert, C. A., Fagan, J., Piquero, A. R., and Losoya, S. H. (2009). Estimating a dose-response relationship between length of stay and future recidivism in serious juvenile offenders. *Criminology, 47*(3), 699–740.

Lucas, C. (1836). *De la réforme des prisons ou de la Théorie de l'emprisonnement, de ses principes, de ses moyens, et de ses conditions pratiques.* [The reform of prisons or the theory of imprisonment, its principles, its capabilities, and its practical conditions.] Paris: E. LeGrand & J. Bergounioux.

MacDonald, M. (2013). Women prisoners, mental health, violence and abuse. *International Journal of Law and Psychiatry, 36*(3–4), 293–303.

MacKenzie, D. L. (2006). *What works in corrections: Reducing the criminal activities of offenders and delinquents.* Cambridge, UK: Cambridge University Press.

MacKenzie, D. L., and Goodstein, L. (1995). Long-term incarceration impacts and characteristics of long-term offenders. In T. J. Flanagan (Ed.), *Long-term imprisonment: Policy, science, and correctional practice* (pp. 64–73). Thousand Oaks, CA: Sage.

MacKenzie, D. L., Robinson, J. W., and Campbell, C. S. (1989). Long-term incarceration of female offenders prison adjustment and coping. *Criminal Justice and Behavior, 16*(2), 223–238.

MacKenzie, D. L., Robinson, J. W., and Campbell, C. S. (1995). Long-term incarceration of female offenders. In T. J. Flanagan (Ed.), *Long-term imprisonment: Policy, science, and correctional practice (pp. 128–137).* Thousand Oaks, CA: Sage.

Marlette, M. (1990). Furloughs tightened: Success rates high. *Corrections Compendium, 14*(1), 1–21.

Marsh, B. (2011). Narrating desistance: Identity change and the 12-step script. *Irish Probation Journal, 8*, 49–68.

Maruna, S. (2001). *Making good: How ex-convicts reform and rebuild their lives.* Washington, DC: American Psychological Association.

Maruna, S. (2004). Desistance from crime and explanatory style: A new direction in the psychology of reform. *Journal of Contemporary Criminal Justice, 20*(2), 184–200.

Maruna, S., and Copes, H. (2005). What have we learned from five decades of neutralization research? *Crime and Justice, 32*, 221–320.

Maruna, S., Immarigeon, R., and LeBel, T. P. (2004). Ex-offender reintegration: Theory and practice. In S. Maruna and R. Immarigeon (Eds.), *After crime and punishment* (pp. 3–26). Cullompton, UK: Willan.

Maruna, S., and LeBel, T. P. (2003). Welcome home? Examining the reentry court concept from a strengths-based perspective. *Western Criminology Review, 4*(2), 91–107.

Maruna, S., and Mann, R. E. (2006). A fundamental attribution error? Rethinking cognitive distortions. *Legal and Criminological Psychology, 11*(2), 155–177.

Maruna, S., Wilson, L., and Curran, K. (2006). Why God is often found behind bars: Prison conversions and the crisis of self-narrative. *Research in Human Development, 3*(2–3), 161–184.

Masis, J. (2009). Good, bad of reform school recalled. *Boston Globe*, July 19.

Massachusetts Department of Correction (2005). *Block brief: Offenders with life sentences*. Milford: Massachusetts Department of Correction, Research and Planning Division.

Massachusetts Department of Correction (2013). Department of Correction reentry continuum. Retrieved from http://www.mass.gov/eopss/docs/doc/reentry-continuum.pdf.

Massachusetts Executive Office of Public Safety and Security (2013). Departmental programs. Retrieved in 2015 from http://www.mass.gov/eopss/law-enforce-and-cj/prisons/offender-progs/departmental-programs.html.

Massachusetts Executive Office of Public Safety and Security (2016). Criminal Offender Record Information (CORI). Retrieved from http://www.mass.gov/eopss/crime-prev-personal-sfty/bkgd-check/cori/.

Massachusetts Parole Board. (2013a). Guidelines for life sentence decisions. Retrieved from http://www.mass.gov/eopss/agencies/parole-board/guidelines-for-life-sentence-decisions.html.

Massachusetts Parole Board. (2013b). *Parole hearing process overview: For offenders serving second-degree life sentences*. Natick: Massachusetts Parole Board.

Mauer, M., and Chesney-Lind, M., (2002). *Invisible punishment*. New York: New Press.

Mauer, M., King, R. S., and Young, M. C. (2004). *The meaning of "life": Long prison sentences in context*. Washington, DC: Sentencing Project.

Meade, B., Steiner, B., Makarios, M., and Travis, L. (2013). Estimating a dose-response relationship between time served in prison and recidivism. *Journal of Research in Crime and Delinquency, 50*(4), 525–550.

Mears, D. P., Cochran, J. C., Siennick, S. E., and Bales, W. D. (2012). Prison visitation and recidivism. *Justice Quarterly, 29*(6), 888–918.

Mears, D. P., Mancini, C., Beaver, K. M., and Gertz, M. (2013). Housing for the "worst of the worst" inmates: Public support for supermax prisons. *Crime and Delinquency, 59*(4), 587–615.

Metzner, J. L., and Fellner, J. (2010). Solitary confinement and mental illness in U.S. prisons: A challenge for medical ethics. *Journal of the American Academy of Psychiatry and the Law Online, 38*(1), 104–108.

Meyers, W. C., Chan, H. C., Vo, E. J., and Lazarou, E. (2010). Sexual sadism, psychopathy, and recidivism in juvenile sexual murderers. *Journal of Investigative Psychology and Offender Profiling, 7*(1), 49–58.

Moffitt, T. E. (1993). Adolescence-limited and life-course-persistent antisocial behavior: A developmental taxonomy. *Psychological Review, 100*(4), 674–701.

Moffitt, T. E. (1994). Natural histories of delinquency. In E. G. M. Weitekamp and H.-J. Kerner (Eds.), *Cross-national longitudinal research on human development and criminal behavior* (pp. 3–61). Alphen aan den Rijn, NL: Kluwer.

Mullane, N. (2012). *Life after murder.* New York: Public Affairs.

Mumola, C. J. (2000). *Incarcerated parents and their children.* Washington, DC: U.S. Department of Justice, Bureau of Justice Statistics.

Munn, M. (2011). Living in the aftermath: The impact of lengthy incarceration on post-carceral success. *Howard Journal of Criminal Justice, 50*(3), 233–246.

Munn, M., and Bruckert, C. (2013). *On the outside: From lengthy imprisonment to lasting freedom.* Vancouver: University of British Columbia Press.

Nagin, D. S. (2013). Deterrence: A review of the evidence by a criminologist for economists. *Annual Review of Economics 5*(1), 83–105.

Nagin, D. S., Cullen, F. T., and Jonson, C. L. (2009). Imprisonment and reoffending. *Crime and Justice, 38*(1), 115–200.

National Research Council (2007). *Parole, desistance from crime, and community integration.* Washington, DC: National Academies Press.

National Research Council (2014). *The growth of incarceration in the United States: Exploring causes and consequences.* Washington, DC: National Academies Press.

Nellis, A. (2010). Throwing away the key: The expansion of life without parole sentences in the United States. *Federal Sentencing Reporter, 23*(1), 27–32.

Nellis, A., and Chung, J. (2013). *Life goes on: The historic rise in life sentences in America.* Washington, DC: Sentencing Project.

Nellis, A., and King, R. S. (2009). *No exit: The expanding use of life sentences in America.* Washington, DC: Sentencing Project.

Neuilly, M. A., Zgoba, K. M., Tita, G. E., and Lee, S. S. (2011). Predicting recidivism in homicide offenders using classification tree analysis. *Homicide Studies, 15*(2), 154–176.

Nieuwbeerta, P., Nagin, D. S., and Blokland, A. A. J. (2009). Assessing the impact of first-time imprisonment on offenders' subsequent criminal career development: A matched samples comparison. *Journal of Quantitative Criminology, 25*(3), 227–257.

Nock, S. L. (2007). Marital and unmarried births to men. *ASPE Research Brief.* Washington, DC: U.S. Department of Health and Human Services.

Opsal, T. (2015). "It's their world, so you've just got to get through": Women's experiences of parole governance. *Feminist Criminology, 10*(2), 188–207.

Ostermann, M. (2013). Active supervision and its impact upon parolee recidivism rates. *Crime and Delinquency, 59*(4), 487–509.

Owen, B. A. (1998). *"In the mix": Struggle and survival in a women's prison.* Albany: State University of New York Press.

Pager, D. (2003). The mark of a criminal record. *American Journal of Sociology, 108*(5), 937–975.

Paternoster, R., and Bushway, S. (2009). Desistance and the "feared self": Toward an identity theory of criminal desistance. *Journal of Criminal Law and Criminology, 99*(4), 1103–1156.

Petersilia, J. (2003). *When prisoners come home: Parole and prisoner reentry.* Oxford, UK: Oxford University Press.

Petersilia, J. (2007). Employ behavioral contracting for "earned discharge" parole. *Criminology and Public Policy, 6*(4), 807–814.

Petersilia, J. (2011). Beyond the prison bubble. *Federal Probation, 75,* 2–4.

Petersilia, J., and Turner, S. (1993). Intensive probation and parole. *Crime and Justice, 17,* 281–335.

Pogrebin, M. R., Stretesky, P. B., Walker, A., and Opsal, T. (2015). Rejection, humiliation, and parole: A study of parolees' perspectives. *Symbolic Interaction, 38(3), 413–430.*

Polizzi, D., and Maruna, S. (2010). In search of the human in the shadows of correctional practice. *Journal of Theoretical and Philosophical Criminology, 2*(2), 158–197.

Post, S. (1982). Adolescent parricide in abuse families. *Child Welfare, 61*(7), 445–455.

Presser, L. (2004). Violent offenders, moral selves: Constructing identities and accounts in the research interview. *Social Problems, 51*(1), 82–101.

Presser, L. (2008). *Been a heavy life: Stories of violent men.* Urbana: University of Illinois Press.

Putkonen, H., Komulainen, E., Virkkunen, M., Eronen, M., and Lonnqvist, J. (2003). Risk of repeat offending among violent female offenders with psychotic and personality disorders. *American Journal of Psychiatry, 160*(5), 947–951.

QSR International (2012). *NVivo Qualitative Data Analysis Software.* Version 10.

Radzinowicz, L. (1968). The regime for long-term prisoners in conditions of maximum security. *Report of the Advisory Council on the Penal System.* London: Her Majesty's Stationery Office.

Rhine, E. E. (2012). The present status and future prospects of parole boards and parole supervision. In J. Petersilia and K. R. Reitz (Eds.), *The Oxford handbook of sentencing and corrections* (pp. 627–656). New York: Oxford University Press.

Richards, S., and Jones, R. (2004). Beating the perpetual incarceration machine: Overcoming structural impediments to re-entry. In S. Maruna and R. Immarigeon (Eds.), *After crime and punishment: Pathways to offender reintegration* (pp. 201–231). Portland, OR: Willan.

Richardson, M. (2012). Lifers: An Exploration of coping among male life sentence prisoners. *Irish Probation Journal, 9, 141–161.*

Roberts, A. R., Zgoba, K. M., and Shahidullah, S. M. (2007). Recidivism among four types of homicide offenders: An exploratory analysis of 336 homicide offenders in New Jersey. *Aggression and Violent Behavior, 12*(5), 493–507.

Rocheleau, A. M. (2013). An empirical exploration of the "pains of imprisonment" and the level of prison misconduct and violence. *Criminal Justice Review, 38*(3), 354–374.

Ruddell, R., Broom, I., and Young, M. (2010). Creating hope for life-sentenced offenders. *Journal of Offender Rehabilitation, 49*(5), 324–341.

Russell, D. H. (1984). A study of juvenile murderers of family members. *International Journal of Offender Therapy and Comparative Criminology, 28*(3), 177–193.

Sampson, R. J., and Laub, J. H. (1993). *Crime in the making: Pathways and turning points through life.* Cambridge, MA: Harvard University Press.

Sampson, R. J., and Laub, J. H. (1997). A life-course theory of cumulative disadvantage and the stability of delinquency. *Developmental theories of crime and delinquency, 7,* 133–161.

Sampson, R. J., and Laub, J. H. (2003a). Desistance from crime over the life course. In J. T. Mortimer and M. Shanahan (Eds.), *Handbook of the life course* (pp. 295–310). New York: Kluwer Academic.

Sampson, R. J., and Laub, J. H. (2003b). Life-course desisters? Trajectories of crime among delinquent boys followed to age 70. *Criminology, 41(3),* 301–340.

Sampson, R. J., and Laub, J. H. (2004). A general age-graded theory of crime: Lessons learned and the future of life-course criminology. In D. Farrington (Ed.), *Advances in theoretical criminology: Testing integrated developmental and life course theories of offending* (vol. 14, pp. 165–182). New Brunswick, NJ: Transaction.

Sampson, R. J., and Laub, J. H. (Eds.) (2005a). Developmental criminology and its discontents: Trajectories of crime from childhood to old age. *Annals of the American Academy of Political and Social Science (Special Issue), 602..*

Sampson, R. J., and Laub, J. H. (2005b). A general age-graded theory of crime: Lessons learned and the future of life-course criminology. In D. Farrington (Ed.), *Testing integrated developmental and life course theories of offending* (vol. 13, pp. 165–181). New Brunswick, NJ: Transaction.

Sampson, R. J., and Laub, J. H. (2005c). A life-course view of the development of crime. *Annals of the American Academy of Political and Social Science, 602*(1), 12–45.

Sampson, R. J., Laub, J. H., and Wimer, C. (2006). Does marriage reduce crime? A counterfactual approach to within-individual causal effects. *Criminology, 44*(3), 465–508.

Samuels, A. (2003). In denial of murder: No parole. *Howard Journal of Criminal Justice, 42*(2), 176–180.

Santos, M. G. (1995). Facing long-term imprisonment. In T. J. Flanagan (Ed.), *Long-term imprisonment: Policy, science, and correctional practice* (pp. 36–40). Thousand Oaks, CA: Sage.

Schauer, E. J. (2011). Book review: *Life without parole: Living and dying in prison today,* by Hassine, V., and Tabriz, S. *Southwest Journal of Criminal Justice, 8,* 2.

Schwartzapfel, B. (2012). Going gray behind bars: What to do with elderly prisoners? *Boston Magazine*, May.

Scott, M. B., and Lyman, S. M. (1968). Accounts. *American Sociological Review, 33*(1), 46–62.

Shover, N. (1985). *Aging criminals*: Beverly Hills, CA: Sage.

Slovenko, R. (1969). Criminally insane unit. *American Criminal Law Quarterly, 7*, 96–100.

Solomon, A., Kachnowski, V., and Bhati, A. (2005). *Does parole work? Analyzing the impact of post-release supervision on rearrest outcomes.* Washington, DC: Urban Institute.

Stanton, J. M. (1969). Murderers on parole. *Crime and Delinquency, 15*(1), 149–155.

Steen, S., Opsal, T., Lovegrove, P., and McKinzey, S. (2013). Putting parolees back in prison: Discretion and the parole revocation process. *Criminal Justice Review, 38*(1), 70–93.

Steffensmeier, D. J., Allan, E. A., Harer, M. D., and Streifel, C. (1989). Age and the distribution of crime. *American Journal of Sociology 94*(4), 803–831.

Steffensmeier, D. J., and Harer, M. D. (1987). Is the crime rate really falling? An "aging" U.S. population and its impact on the nation's crime rate, 1980–1984. *Journal of Research in Crime and Delinquency, 24*(1), 23–48.

Stevens, A. (2012). "I am the person now I was always meant to be": Identity reconstruction and narrative reframing in therapeutic community prisons. *Criminology and Criminal Justice, 12*(5), 527–547.

Sweeten, G., Piquero, A. R., and Steinberg, L. (2013). Age and the explanation of crime, revisited. *Journal of Youth and Adolescence 42*(6), 1–18.

Sykes, C. M. (1958). *The society of captives: A study of a maximum security prison.* Princeton, NJ: Princeton University Press.

Sykes, C. M., and Matza, D. (1957). Techniques of neutralization: A theory of delinquency. *American Sociological Review, 22*(6), 664–670.

Sturup, J., and Lindqvist, P. (2014). Homicide offenders 32 years later: A Swedish population-based study on recidivism. *Criminal Behaviour and Mental Health, 24*(1), 5–17.

Tanay, E. (1973). Adolescents who kill parents: Reactive parricide. *Australian and New Zealand Journal of Psychiatry, 7*(4), 263–277.

Terry, C. M., and Presser, L. (2002). Book review: *Making good: how ex-convicts reform and rebuild their lives. Theoretical Criminology, 6*(2), 227–234.

Tiihonen, J., Hakola, P., Nevalainen, A., and Eronen, M. (1995). Risk of homicidal behaviour among persons convicted of homicide. *Forensic Science International, 72*(1), 43–48.

Toch, H. (1995). The good old days in the joint. In T. J. Flanagan (Ed.), *Long-term imprisonment: Policy, science, and correctional practice (pp. 157–163).* Thousand Oaks, CA: Sage.

Toch, H. (2010). "I am not now who i used to be then": Risk assessment and the maturation of long-term prison inmates. *Prison Journal, 90*(1), 4–11.

Toch, H., and Adams, K. (2002). *Acting out: Maladaptive behavior in confinement.* Washington, DC: American Psychological Association.

Tonry, M. (1999). Why are U.S. incarceration rates so high? *Crime and Delinquency, 45*(4), 419–437.

Travis, J., Western, B., and Redburn, F. S. (2014). *The growth of incarceration in the United States: Exploring causes and consequences.* Washington, DC: National Academies Press.

Traylor, L. L., and Richie, B. E. (2012). Female offenders and women in prison. In J. Petersilia and K. R. Reitz (Eds.), *The Oxford handbook of sentencing and corrections* (pp. 561–583). New York: Oxford University Press.

Trulson, C. R., Caudill, J. W., Haerle, D. R., and DeLisi, M. (2012). Cliqued up: The postincarceration recidivism of young gang-related homicide offenders. *Criminal Justice Review, 37*(2), 174–190.

Turnbull, S., and Hannah-Moffat, K. (2009). Under these conditions: Gender, parole and the governance of reintegration. *British Journal of Criminology, 49*(4), 532–551.

Turner, V. (1982). *Dramas, fields, and metaphors.* 2nd ed. Ithaca, NY: Cornell University Press.

Uggen, C. (2000). Work as a turning point in the life course of criminals: A duration model of age, employment, and recidivism. *American Sociological Review, 67,* 529–546.

Uggen, C., Manza, J., and Behrens, A. (2004). Less than the average citizen: Stigma, role transition, and the civic reintegration of convicted felons. In S. Maruna and R. Immarigeon (Eds.), *After crime and punishment: Pathways to offender reintegration* (pp. 258–290). Cullompton, UK: Willan.

Uggen, C., Manza, J., and Thompson, M. (2006). Citizenship, democracy, and the civic reintegration of criminal offenders. *Annals of the American Academy of Political and Social Science, 605*(1), 281–310.

Unger, C. A., and Buchanan, R. A. (1985). *Managing long-term inmates: A guide for the correctional administrator.* Washington, DC: U.S. Department of Justice, National Institute of Corrections.

Unkovic, C. M., and Albini, J. L. (1969). The lifer speaks for himself: An analysis of the assumed homogeneity of life-termers. *Crime and Delinquency, 15*(1), 156–161.

U.S. Census Bureau (2011). *Median age at first marriage.* Washington, DC: U.S. Census Bureau.

Vaughan, B. (2007). The internal narrative of desistance. *British Journal of Criminology, 47*(3), 390–404.

Venkatesh, S. A. (2008). *Gang leader for a day: A rogue sociologist takes to the streets.* New York: Penguin.

Venkatesh, S. A. (2013). The reflexive turn: The rise of first-person ethnography. *Sociological Quarterly, 54*(1), 3–8.

Visher, C. A. (2011). Incarcerated fathers: Pathways from prison to home. *Criminal Justice Policy Review, 24*(1), 9–26.

Visher, C. A., Debus-Sherrill, S. A., and Yahner, J. (2010). Employment after prison: A longitudinal study of former prisoners. *Justice Quarterly, 28*(5), 698–718.

Visher, C., Kachnowski, V., LaVigne, N., and Travis, J. (2004). *Baltimore prisoners' experiences returning home.* Washington, DC: Urban Institute.

Visher, C. A., and O'Connell, D. J. (2012). Incarceration and inmates' self perceptions about returning home. *Journal of Criminal Justice, 40*(5), 386–393.

Wacquant, L. (2010). Class, race and hyperincarceration in revanchist America. *Daedalus, 139*(3), 74–90.

Ward, T., and Brown, M. (2004). The good lives model and conceptual issues in offender rehabilitation. *Psychology, Crime & Law, 10*(3), 243–257.

Ward, D. A., and Kassebaum, G. G. (1965). *Women's prison: Sex and social structure.* Piscataway, NJ: Aldine Transaction.

Ward, T., and Gannon, T. A. (2006). Rehabilitation, etiology, and self-regulation: The comprehensive good lives model of treatment for sexual offenders. *Aggression and Violent Behavior, 11*(1), 77–94.

Wermink, H., Blokland, A., Nieuwbeerta, P., Nagin, D., and Tollenaar, N. (2010). Comparing the effects of community service and short-term imprisonment on recidivism: A matched samples approach. *Journal of Experimental Criminology, 6*(3), 325–349.

Werth, R. (2012). I do what I'm told, sort of: Reformed subjects, unruly citizens, and parole. *Theoretical Criminology, 16*(3), 329–346.

West, D. (1963). *The habitual prisoner.* London: Macmillan.

Western, B. (2004). Incarceration, marriage, and family life. *Princeton University, Department of Sociology.*

Western, B. (2006). *Punishment and inequality in America.* New York: Russell Sage Foundation.

Western, B., Kling, J. R., and Weiman, D. F. (2001). The labor market consequences of incarceration. *Crime and Delinquency, 47*(3), 410–427.

Williams, B., and Abraldes, R. (2007). Growing older: Challenges of prison and reentry for the aging population. In R. Greifinger (Ed.), *Public health behind bars: From prisons to communities* (pp. 56–72). New York: Springer.

Wilson, W. J. (1987). *The truly disadvantaged: The inner city, the underclass, and public policy.* Chicago: University of Chicago Press.

Winnick, T. A., and Bodkin, M. (2008). Anticipated stigma and stigma management among those to be labeled "ex-con." *Deviant Behavior, 29*(4), 295–333.

Wolff, N., Shi, J., and Schumann, B. E. (2012). Reentry preparedness among soon-to-be-released inmates and the role of time served. *Journal of Criminal Justice, 40*(5), 379–385.

Yahner, J., Visher, C., and Solomon, A. (2008). *Returning home on parole: Former prisoners' experiences in Illinois, Ohio, and Texas.* Washington, DC: Urban Institute.

Zamble, E. (1995). Behavior and adaptation in long-term prison inmates. In T. J. Flanagan (Ed.), *Long-term imprisonment: Policy, science, and correctional practice* (pp. 138–147). Thousand Oaks, CA: Sage.

Zamble, E., and Porporino, F. J. (1988). *Coping, behavior, and adaptation in prison inmates.* New York: Springer-Verlag.

Zamble, E., and Porporino, F.J. (1990). Coping, imprisonment, and rehabilitation: Some data and their implications. *Criminal Justice and Behavior, 17*(1), 53–70.

INDEX

ABOUT THE AUTHOR

Marieke Liem is Senior Researcher and Chair of the Violence Research Initiative at Leiden University and a Marie Curie Fellow at the Harvard Kennedy School. She studied Criminology at Cambridge University and completed her PhD in Forensic Psychology at Utrecht University, the Netherlands, in 2010.